ISAAC ALBÉNIZ

ROUTLEDGE MUSIC BIBLIOGRAPHIES

RECENT TITLES

COMPOSERS

Isaac Albéniz, 2nd Edition (2015),
Walter A. Clark

William Alwyn (2013),
John C. Dressler

C. P. E. Bach (2002),
Doris Bosworth Powers

Samuel Barber, 2nd Edition (2012),
Wayne C. Wentzel

Béla Bartók, 3rd Edition (2011),
Elliott Antokoletz and Paolo
Susanni

*Vincenzo Bellini, 2nd Edition
(2009),*
Stephen A. Willier

Alban Berg, 2nd Edition (2015),
Bryan R. Simms

*Leonard Bernstein, 2nd Edition
(2015),*
Paul R. Laird and Hsun Lin

*Johannes Brahms, 2nd Edition
(2011),*
Heather Platt

Benjamin Britten (1996)
Peter J. Hodgson

William Byrd, 3rd Edition (2012),
Richard Turbet

Elliott Carter (2000),
John L. Link

Carlos Chávez (1998),
Robert Parker

*Frédéric Chopin, 2nd Edition
(2015),*
William Smialek and Maja
Trochimczyk

Aaron Copland (2001),
Marta Robertson and Robin
Armstrong

*Frederick Delius, 2nd Edition
(2009),*
Mary Christison Huismann

*Gaetano Donizetti, 2nd Edition
(2009),*
James P. Cassaro

Edward Elgar, 2nd Edition (2013),
Christopher Kent

Gabriel Fauré, 2nd Edition (2011),
Edward R. Phillips

Alberto Ginastera (2011),
Deborah Schwartz-Kates

*Christoph Willibald Gluck,
2nd Edition (2003),*
Patricia Howard

Charles François Gounod (2009),
Timothy S. Flynn

G.F. Handel, 2nd Edition (2004),
Mary Ann Parker

*Paul Hindemith, 2nd Edition
(2009),*
Stephen Luttmann

Gustav Holst (2011),
Mary Christison Huismann

Charles Ives, 2nd Edition (2010),
Gayle Sherwood Magee

Quincy Jones (2014),
Clarence Bernard Henry

Scott Joplin (1998),
Nancy R. Ping-Robbins

Zoltán Kodály (1998),
Mícheál Houlahan and Philip
Tacka

Franz Liszt, 3rd Edition (2009),
Michael Saffle

Guillaume de Machaut (1995),
Lawrence Earp

Gustav and Alma Mahler (2008),
Susan M. Filler

Bohuslav Martinů (2014),
Robert Simon

*Felix Mendelssohn Bartholdy,
2nd edition (2011),*
John Michael Cooper with
Angela R. Mace

Olivier Messiaen (2008),
Vincent P. Benitez

*Giovanni Pierluigi da Palestrina
(2001),*
Clara Marvin

Giacomo Puccini (1999),
Linda B. Fairtile

Maurice Ravel (2004),
Stephen Zank

*Nikolay Andreevich Rimsky-
Korsakov, 2nd Edition (2015),*
Gerald R. Seaman

*Gioachino Rossini, 2nd Edition
(2010),*
Denise P. Gallo

Camille Saint-Saëns (2003),
Timothy S. Flynn

*Alessandro and Domenico
Scarlatti (1993),*
Carole F. Vidali

Heinrich Schenker (2003),
Benjamin Ayotte

Alexander Scriabin (2004),
Ellon D. Carpenter

Jean Sibelius (1998),
Glenda D. Goss

*Giuseppe Verdi, 2nd Edition
(2012), Gregory W. Harwood*

Tomás Luis de Victoria (1998),
Eugene Casjen Cramer

Richard Wagner, 2nd Edition (2010),
Michael Saffle

Anton Webern (2016),
Darin Hoskisson

Adrian Willaert (2004),
David Michael Kidger

GENRES

American Music Librarianship (2005),
Carol June Bradley

Blues, Funk, R&B, Soul, Hip Hop, and Rap (2010),
Eddie S. Meadows

Chamber Music, 3rd Edition (2010),
John H. Baron

Choral Music, 2nd Edition (2011),
Avery T. Sharp and James Michael Floyd

Church and Worship Music (2005),
Avery T. Sharp and James Michael Floyd

The Concerto (2006),
Stephen D. Lindeman

Ethnomusicology, 2nd Edition (2013),
Jennifer C. Post

Jazz Scholarship and Pedagogy, 3rd Edition (2005),
Eddie S. Meadows

The Madrigal (2012),
Susan Lewis Hammond

The Musical, 2nd Edition (2011),
William A. Everett

North American Fiddle Music (2011),
Drew Beisswenger

Opera, 2nd Edition (2000),
Guy A. Marco

Piano Pedagogy (2009),
Gilles Comeau

The Recorder, 3rd Edition (2012),
Richard Griscom and David Lasocki

Serial Music and Serialism (2001),
John D. Vander Weg

String Quartets, 2nd edition (2011),
Mara E. Parker

The Violin (2006),
Mark Katz

Women in Music, 2nd Edition (2011),
Karin Pendle and Melinda Boyd

Isaac Albéniz
A Research and Information Guide
Second Edition

Walter Aaron Clark

ROUTLEDGE MUSIC BIBLIOGRAPHIES

Routledge
Taylor & Francis Group

NEW YORK AND LONDON

Second edition published 2015
by Routledge
711 Third Avenue, New York, NY 10017

and by Routledge
2 Park Square, Milton Park, Abingdon, Oxon, OX14 4RN

Routledge is an imprint of the Taylor & Francis Group, an informa business

First published by Routledge 1998

Library of Congress Cataloging in Publication Data
Clark, Walter Aaron, compiler.
  Isaac Albéniz: a research and information guide/Walter Aaron Clark. -- Second edition.
    pages cm -- (Routledge music bibliographies)
  Includes bibliographical references and index.
  1. Albéniz, Isaac, 1860-1909--Bibliography. I. Title. II. Series: Routledge music bibliographies.
  ML134.A45C53 2016
  016.78092--dc23
  2014048183

ISBN: 978-0-415-84032-3 (hbk)
ISBN: 978-0-203-76854-9 (ebk)

Typeset in Minion
by Exeter Premedia Services Private Ltd., Chennai, India

Dedicated to Albéniz's granddaughter Rosina Moya Albéniz de Samsó. Rest assured, Señora, that we will never forget your magnificent abuelo.

Contents

Foreword

Among the elements that comprise Spanish music of the popular imagination, Isaac Albéniz (1860–1909) occupies a singular position, which has always been acknowledged by scholars as well as by mere aficionados. However, numerous legends and fabrications of his biography have been documented. Real knowledge and validation of his vast musical output remained incomplete. Only in recent years have the man and his music been the subject of study with the sort of seriousness and scientific rigor they merit. The nearly simultaneous publication of Walter Clark's *Portrait of a Romantic* and my *Catálogo Sistemático* represented a decisive milestone that marks the "before and after" in Albéniz studies, opening to discovery a rich and profound artistic personality and music whose aesthetic and technical virtues elevate him with irrefutable authority above his contemporaries.

The second edition of this research guide, with the most complete documentation and most current information, is an indispensable compendium for those who aspire to advance in the passionate adventure of Albéniz research.

For more than two centuries, the literature, history, and art of Spain have owed a debt of gratitude to Hispanists, scholars who from the distance of their origins and language have learned—and have taught us—to comprehend and to love Spanish culture by delving into both its light and its shadows. To this honorable legion belongs Professor Walter Clark, whose wise and detailed work have done so much for our music. He believes that these poor words of presentation honor his book, but in reality it is his dedication and work that honor those of us who feel and love Spain in its music.

Jacinto Torres Mulas

Preface

"I believe that Albeniz has still not received the justice that he deserves," wrote celebrated poet and music critic Gerardo Diego on July 11, 1950.[1] This book offers abundant evidence that though Diego's assertation may have been correct at that time, an international team of scholars, especially Spaniards, has stepped forward in the intervening 65 years to address and correct the injustice of neglect done to this remarkable composer.

Indeed, since the first edition of this research guide appeared in 1998, enormous strides have been made in the study of the life and music of Isaac Albéniz (1860–1909). This book not only recapitulates my findings from the 1990s but also incorporates the many publications and recordings of the past 17 years that have greatly advanced our knowledge of Albéniz's fascinating career. Much of this cornucopia was the result of conferences and publications commemorating the centennial of the composer's death, in 2009, and the sesquicentennial of his birth, in 2010. Notable among these was a major conference that took place in Garrucha, Spain, in southeast Andalusia near Almería, in the summer of 2008, in anticipation of the centennial of the composer's death. This was organized by Luisa Morales and yielded published proceedings of genuine importance (see no. 196). However, research in this relatively neglected area had approached a critical mass already in the late 1990s and reached an apex even before those commemorations. The reason for this is simple enough: it was becoming increasingly clear to scholars and performers alike that Albéniz was a much more substantial and prolific composer than most people had originally suspected, and that many exciting and important discoveries regarding his life and music remained to be made.

In addition to his justly celebrated and perennially popular masterworks for piano, there was also a plethora of exquisite songs that had unjustly been consigned to obscurity. Several editions and recordings of these have since shed light on this aspect of his creative work. Most surprising of all, perhaps, were Albéniz's underestimated accomplishments as a composer for the stage. It was never the case that his operas were unknown, only that his various biographers dismissed them as a waste of the composer's time and energy, which he should have continued to devote to his real forte: writing for the piano. It was easy enough to make such facile claims when the stage works in question lay in library archives as disordered manuscripts attracting more dust than serious scrutiny. Thanks in large measure to the efforts of the present author and especially Spanish musicologists and conductors such as Jacinto Torres, José de Eusebio, and Borja Mariño, the revivals of *San Antonio de la Florida*, *Pepita Jiménez*, *Henry Clifford*, *Merlin*, and even *The Magic Opal* have forced us to reconsider not only Albéniz's stature as a composer but also the state of Spanish music around 1900.

However, though major discoveries and recoveries have been made in regard to his songs and operas, there were also aspects of his piano music that required updating as well. Thus, we now have a truly scholarly and reliable edition of his *chef d'oeuvre*,

Iberia, courtesy of Torres and pianist Guillermo González. Torres has also resurrected Albéniz's works for piano and orchestra in modern editions. The complete piano works of Albéniz have been recorded by Miguel Baselga on the BIS label; in addition, we have critical editions of *La vega* and his piano-roll improvisations, thanks to the efforts of Cuban-American pianist and scholar Milton Rubén Laufer.

This book seeks to bring to the fore these and many other developments. Its three main parts consist of a biography, works list, and annotated bibliography. The biography aims at a summary of moderate length and detail. So many misconceptions and fictions have clouded our understanding of Albéniz's life that my main purpose here has been to set the record straight but without detailed citation of the sources, primary and secondary, that have led to this reappraisal (one can locate that information in nos. 102–04, Walter Aaron Clark, *Isaac Albéniz: Portrait of a Romantic*). The biography concludes with a discussion of Albéniz's musical style.

The catalog of works is complete and contains pertinent information about alternate titles, dates of composition, publication, first performance (where available), and manuscript location. It is based on the definitive *Catálogo sistemático descriptivo de las obras musicales de Isaac Albéniz* of Jacinto Torres (see no. 241) and uses T. numbers accordingly. This is followed by very selective lists of recent editions and recordings that will be of particular interest and value to any Albéniz scholar. Happily, editions of all of Albéniz's songs and most of his stage works are now available, as are modern editions of his major piano works. The discography in the initial edition of this guide was the first attempt at a comprehensive listing in more than 40 years and remains a valuable, if dated, source of information. The more recent annotated discography by Justo Romero (see no. 219) will prove essential to those interested in this aspect of Albéniz research. Discographers will also want to consult the dissertation by Mexican musicologist Alfonso Pérez Sánchez (see nos. 206–07), who has examined in depth various recordings of *Iberia*. My aim here is to highlight those efforts over the last 15 years or so that have contributed in a significant way to our comprehension of Albéniz's achievements in composition and their significance. I have made a special effort to include recordings that correspond to or were actually issued in conjunction with the editions.

The annotated bibliography consists of three parts:

A. Listing of archives and organizations devoted to Albéniz and a summary of their holdings, with an emphasis on primary sources;

B. Secondary sources (books and articles);

C. Reviews of Albéniz's concerts and works during his lifetime, as well as reviews of his operas after his death in 1909.

Primary sources are of the utmost importance in this kind of research, and some of the archives listed were not previously known by scholars to contain materials concerning Albéniz. This inventory can save one a great deal of time searching for documentation. Of course, secondary sources are the main focus of any bibliography, and I have attempted to ferret out all such materials, regardless of their inherent value. Knowing that an article or book is not particularly useful is in itself useful knowledge. Musicologist Robert Winter once remarked to me that the history of nineteenth-century music is ultimately written in the periodical literature of the time, an observation I have found to be very accurate. This final part of the chapter features extensive citation of articles and reviews providing revelatory insights into many aspects of Albéniz's career.

Editorial notes: Arabic numerals appearing in parentheses before or after the mention of a particular author, publication, or recording refer not to a page number but rather to the entry number in the bibliography itself, beginning with the list of scholarly editions in Chapter Two: Part B. All translations are my own. Though I have generally used modern Catalan spellings for persons, places, and institutions in that region, the names of Albéniz and his immediate family appear in Castilian, per the composer's own usage. Basque regions and names also receive Castilian spellings. English spellings of common Spanish place names, such as Seville, Catalonia, and Andalusia, are the rule.

It has been my great privilege to study in considerable depth the life and music of Albéniz. After nearly a quarter century of dedicated investigation, my admiration for his accomplishments and the pleasure I derive from his music have only increased. This guide will provide the indispensable foundation for a second edition of my biography, on which I will soon begin working; naturally, I hope it will prove helpful to all those engaged in championing the music of Albéniz, whether as scholars or performers. In any case, I remain immensely grateful for the unfailing assistance and encouragement I have received from so many people and institutions, in the U.S. and throughout Europe:

Brussels: The library of the Conservatoire Royal, the Bibliothèque Royale Albert Ier, and the archive of the Théâtre Royal de la Monnaie. I also wish to thank Albéniz scholar Jan de Kloe for sharing with me his highly original research on Albéniz's Brussels tenure.

Budapest: Maria Eckhardt of the Liszt Ferenc Memorial Museum and Research Centre, for her thorough investigations conducted on my behalf.

Leipzig: The library of the Hochschule für Musik "Felix Mendelssohn Bartholdy," the music library of the city of Leipzig, and the Staatsarchiv and Stadtarchiv also merit an expression of appreciation for their assistance.

London: Barbara J. Peters, former head of the Latymer Archive at the bank of Coutts & Co., and the Eighth Lord Latymer, great-grandson of Francis Money-Coutts. Thanks also go to the British Library, the Westminster City Archives, and the Greater London Record Office and History Library. Dr. Clifford Bevan, a leading English authority on Albéniz, also deserves a sincere expression of thanks for sharing with me his excellent and valuable research on Albéniz's operas and English connections.

Paris: Catherine Rochon of the Conservatoire National Superieur de Musique et de Danse de Paris; the Bibliothèque Nationale and Archives Nationales for their patient assistance; and the firm of Max Eschig, for its generosity.

Prague: The National and Municipal Libraries, and in particular Roman Lindauer, without whose timely assistance my work would have been much more difficult.

Barcelona: Ayuntamiento de Barcelona; Rosa Busquets of the library of the Museu Marítim; the Arxiu Municipal; directors Romà Escalas (former) and Jaume Ayats (current) and their cordial assistants at the Museu de la Música, in particular Judit Bombardó (former) and Imma Cusco (current); the Biblioteca de Catalunya, in particular Rosa Montalt Matas and Margarida Ullate Estanyol for their timely help and encouragement; and the Arxiu Històric de la Ciutat. I am also indebted to the late Josefina Sastre and the Biblioteca del Orfeó Català as well as to the theater museum of the Palau Güell for their help. I benefited from the assistance of the Arxiu Diocesà of the Arquebisbat de

Barcelona, the Institut Universitari de Documentació i Investigació Musicòlogica Josep Ricart i Matas, María Luisa Beltran Sabat of the Institut Municipal dels Serveis Funeraris de Barcelona, and Amparo Valera of the Teatre Romea. The musicologist Dr. Monserrat Bergadà Armengol provided invaluable research support, as did Dr. Patricia Caicedo, the brilliant soprano and musicologist who facilitated my research. Heartfelt thanks go to Rosina Moya Albéniz de Samsó, granddaughter of the composer, for her hospitality, and largesse.

Garrucha: Harpsichordist and musicologist Luisa Morales for dedicating the International Symposium on Spanish Keyboard Music "Diego Fernández" (FIMTE) to Albéniz in 2008 and for inviting me to join her in editing the subsequent proceedings.

Granada: María Isabel de Falla and the Archivo Manuel de Falla for providing me access to Albéniz manuscripts in their collection. I am also grateful to Dr. Marta Falces Sierra of the Universidad de Granada for her assistance and the inspiration of her own work.

Madrid: Rafael Campos and the Secretaría of the Real Conservatorio; the Biblioteca Nacional, Hemeroteca Nacional, Hemeroteca Municipal, Archivo Histórico de la Villa, Archivo del Palacio Real, Archivo General de la Administración, and the Dirección General de Costes de Personal y Pensiones Públicas, as well as the Registro Civil; Lola Higueras of the Museo Naval, and Antonio Gil of the Sociedad General de Autores de España (now the Sociedad General de Autores y Editores). I also wish to thank the Fundación Albéniz, especially director Álvaro Guibert, for its enduring promotion of Albéniz and for the use of photos in their archive. Thanks are also due to the conductor José de Eusebio, who has done so much to bring Albéniz's operas back to life; to the piano virtuoso Miguel Baselga for his magisterial interpretations and for inviting me to contribute liner notes to one of his CDs; and to the conductor Manuel Coves for sharing reviews of his appearances conducting Albéniz's *Pepita Jiménez*. I am most grateful to the eminent musicologist Dr. Jacinto Torres Mulas—in my opinion, the foremost authority on Albéniz—whose moral support, wise counsel, and gracious sharing of material over the past quarter century have made possible whatever I have been able to contribute to Albéniz research. I especially appreciate the foreword he graciously consented to contribute to the present volume.

Santander: Thanks go to Pureza Canelo, director of the Fundación Gerardo Diego, for prompt assistance in sending me copies of manuscripts by the famous poet, who had much of value to say about Spanish music in general and Albéniz's music in particular.

Zaragoza: Lluís Rodríguez Salvà, a member of the piano faculty at the Conservatorio Superior de Música de Aragón, is preparing an impressive edition of Albéniz's writings and correspondence. I am deeply grateful to him for sharing his research with me in advance of its publication.

United States: I am very thankful to Constance Ditzel and Denny Tek for their interest in and support of this project, and for the patient expertise of Routledge's excellent staff in helping me prepare the manuscript. Thanks go to the pianist and Albéniz scholar Dr. Pola Baytelman Dobry for her generous sharing of information and invitations to lecture. I am also grateful to the libraries at the University of California, Los Angeles, and the University of Kansas for their assistance. I especially appreciate the assistance I received from Caitlin St. John at the Music Library of the University of

California, Riverside, in acquiring various publications. My original overseas research was made possible by funding from the Del Amo Endowment (on two separate occasions) and the Program for Cultural Cooperation between Spain's Ministry of Culture and United States' Universities (also twice awarded). In addition, those initial investigations were supported by University of Kansas General Research allocation #3466. Funds for researching this second edition were provided by a Committee on Research Grant (2013) and a Research and Travel Award (2014), both from the Academic Senate of the University of California, Riverside. I wish to thank my doctoral adviser, the late Dr. Robert Murrell Stevenson, for his encouragement and the invaluable example of his own work. Finally, thanks go to my wife, Nancy, and my son, Robert, for their patience, understanding, and support.

Walter Aaron Clark
Murrieta, California
2015

NOTE

[1] "Yo creo que todavía no se le ha hecho a Albéniz la debida jusiticia." This observation is taken from an unpublihsed manuscript, now located in the archive of the Fundación Gerardo Diego in Santander.

List of Abbreviations

Ah: Albéniz house, the current residence of Rosina Moya Albéniz de Samsó (the daughter of Albéniz's daughter Laura) in the Barcelona area
Bc: Biblioteca de Catalunya, Barcelona
Bn: Biblioteca Nacional, Madrid
ICCMU: Instituto Complutense de Ciencias Musicales
L: Latymer Archive, Coutts & Co., London
Lc: Library of Congress, Washington, D.C.
LCM: *La Correspondencia Musical*
Ls: Staatsarchiv Leipzig
Mm: Museu Municipal de la Música, Barcelona
Oc: Biblioteca del Orfeó Català, Barcelona
Rcsm: Real Conservatorio Superior de Música, Madrid
Se: Sociedad General de Autores y Editores (formerly Sociedad General de Autores de España), Madrid
T: Torres number (catalog of works)
UMI: University Microfilms, Ann Arbor, Michigan

1

Isaac Albéniz: The Man and His Music (1860–1909)

Numerous accounts of Albéniz's life have been written since the first one, by Antonio Guerra y Alarcón (see no. 151), appeared in 1886. Even a cursory examination of any half a dozen of them soon reveals, however, that they are all plagued by inconsistencies and contradictions. One says he stowed away on a steamer in Cádiz and traveled to Cuba when he was but 12 years old; another says that the steamer was headed for Buenos Aires, not Havana; yet another says that it left from La Coruña, not Cádiz. One says that he studied for 9 months in Leipzig during the years 1875–76; another says 18 months; yet another, 3 years. One says that he studied with Liszt in Weimar, Rome, and Budapest; another says that he studied with him for a year in Italy, while yet another says that he played for Liszt but once, in the summer of 1880. And on and on it goes.

Untying this Gordian knot has required no small expenditure of time and effort. Like Alexander, one simply has to slice through it by confronting the fact that Albéniz was in the habit of telling friends, journalists, and biographers highly elaborated versions of the truth or even outright fabrications. This was apparently a source of amusement to him, and it served the practical purpose of enhancing his credentials before the public while he struggled up the professional ladder as a pianist and composer. Those interested in an in-depth examination of Albéniz's prevarications and the documentary evidence that exists to set the record straight should consult this author's *Isaac Albéniz: Portrait of a Romantic* (nos. 102–04). The summary below does not delve into these issues but rather presents a straightforward account of his career, which was remarkable enough without any embellishment. This is intended to be more detailed than an encyclopedia entry but still easily digested in one sitting. It concludes with an overview of Albéniz's stylistic evolution as a composer, something every bit as remarkable as any other aspect of his life.

CHILDHOOD AND EARLY CONCERT CAREER (1860–76)

Isaac Manuel Francisco Albéniz y Pascual was born on May 29, 1860, in the town of Camprodón in the Catalonian province of Girona, near the French border. He was the last of four children and the only son. His siblings were Enriqueta (1850–67), Clementina (1853–1933), and Blanca (1855–74). His mother, Dolors Pascual i Bardera (1821–1900), was a native of the city of Figueres in that province. Albéniz's father, Ángel Lucio Albéniz y Gauna, had been assigned to Camprodón in 1859 as a customs official. He hailed from Vitoria, in the Basque country, where he was born on March 2, 1817 (d. 1903). The Álava region of the Basque country was the ancestral home of the Albéniz family. Indeed, Albéniz is a Basque word that means skinny, slender, or thread-like; it can also mean short or clever, in a devious sort of way. As a noun, it refers to a thread, strand, or a lot of hay.

Ángel remained employed in Camprodón until May of 1863. A 6-month stint in Sitges, just south of Barcelona on the coast, preceded his taking up a new post at Barcelona in December of that same year, when Albéniz was three and a half years old. According to family tradition, Isaac showed an inclination toward music in his earliest years, and his sister Clementina, also a talented musician, gave him his first lessons in piano. His progress was so rapid that the two siblings made their first public appearance, at the Teatre Romea, when Isaac was but 4 years old (although it may have been later than this, the concert definitely took place before 1868). He also studied piano with Narciso Olivares, a local teacher in Barcelona about whom we know next to nothing. In November 1867, tragedy struck the family when Enriqueta died of typhus. Shortly after this, the family left the city.

In 1868 occurred one of the many political upheavals that plagued Spain in the nineteenth century. General Juan Prim led a conspiracy to overthrow the regime of Isabel II, and his forces entered Madrid in triumph on October 3. Ángel was employed in Barcelona until January of 1868, at which time he took up a position in the customs office in Almería, on the Mediterranean coast in Andalusia. This position was terminated in August of that year, around the time of the revolution. There followed a hiatus of almost a year before he was posted to Cáceres in the western province of Extremadura. Albéniz began studying at the Real Conservatorio Superior de Música[1] in Madrid during the 1868–69 school year. He enrolled in first-year solfège and studied piano with José Mendizábal. But Albéniz's academic efforts were desultory, and his failure to show up for the exam in second-year solfège in June 1874 effectively terminated his formal training in Madrid.

In the year 1869, Albéniz composed and published his first piece, the *Marcha militar*, T. 45, for piano. The cover bears the printed dedication "Al Excelentísimo Señor Vizconde del Bruch," who was General Prim's 12-year-old son. Interestingly, Ángel was appointed to his new position in Cáceres at this time, on July 29, 1869, and began his duties a month later, on August 23. This raises the likelihood that the little composition's purpose was to win the favor of Prim and that it succeeded. Or it may have been an expression of gratitude for a position already granted. We do not know.

Ángel remained in Cáceres until November 16, 1871, when his position was terminated. A couple of years after Ángel's return to his family in Madrid, Albéniz began to tour the country as a child prodigy. During the spring and summer of that year he appeared in Úbeda, Jaén, Córdoba, Granada, Lucena, Loja, Salar, and finally Málaga. He reappeared in Málaga in early November, bringing his season on the road to a close.

Ángel probably assisted his son in setting up these concerts and even accompanied him during the period he himself was unemployed. Some parental guidance would have been in order because the country was in the throes of civil war during this time, and it is clear from his concert itinerary that Albéniz performed in both federal and rebel (Carlist) areas. Clearly, these concerts would have provided welcome income. Many of them were for Masonic organizations, and though Albéniz never joined a lodge, Ángel was an active Freemason whose connections no doubt facilitated getting engagements. On March 15, 1873, Ángel assumed a new post in the federal office of General Accounts and Auditing. Once Ángel was settled in Madrid and working regularly, he expected his son to resume serious studies. But this Albéniz clearly did not want to do, and a spate of performances in the provinces ensued during the following academic year (1873–74), taking the young artist to El Escorial, Ávila, Toro, Salamanca, Peñaranda de Bracamonte, Valladolid, Palencia, León, Oviedo, Avilés, Gijón, Orense, Logroño, and Barcelona, where he played at the salon of the Bemareggi piano firm on October 18, 1874.[2]

Ángel must not have approved of this behavior, but he could not have been trying very hard to curtail it, either. In any case, we cannot yet confirm or refute the traditional stories of Albéniz's having run away from home to go on this tour. We can be reasonably certain that it came to an end as the result of his sister Blanca's suicide. An aspiring singer, she had failed in her audition for the Teatro de la Zarzuela in Madrid and killed herself in a fit of despair on October 16. Albéniz's concertizing ceased for 6 months after this tragedy.

However, several of Ángel's friends had been so impressed with young Albéniz's triumphs in Spain that they arranged a concert tour for him in the New World, which they hoped would provide money for his future education. Albéniz performed extensively in the Greater Antilles in the summer and fall of 1875. He traveled there on April 30 with his father, who had been appointed to the post of Inspector General in Havana. He gave successful concerts in San Juan, Mayagüez, and Caguas, Puerto Rico, during the spring and summer. He then made his way to Cuba and created a sensation in Santiago and Havana, where he resided with his father at least until November. Arrangements were then made for him to enroll in the Leipzig Hochschule fiir Musik "Felix Mendelssohn Bartholdy" so that he could fully realize his potential.

FORMAL STUDIES AND CONCERT CAREER (1876–89)

Albéniz began his studies at Leipzig on May 2, 1876, and terminated them a short time later, on June 24 of the same year. He studied theory and composition with Carl Piutti, piano with Louis Maas as well as Salomon Jadassohn, and voice with Henry Schradieck. He attended theory lectures by Oscar Paul and participated in a chamber ensemble (under the supervision of Schradieck). His professors were almost unanimous in stating that he attended regularly at the beginning and was diligent. Why he withdrew so soon, then, is a matter of speculation. One possibility is that he was discouraged by difficulties with the language. Another has to do with family resources. Ángel entered another hiatus in his work beginning July 9, 1876, and he did not resume his duties in Havana until February of 1877. His pay was suspended during this time, and he returned to Spain. This loss of income probably created financial hardship and necessitated call-ing Albéniz home from Leipzig.

In the summer of 1876 it was obvious that if young Isaac were to continue his formal education abroad, he would require financial assistance. Albéniz met Guillermo Morphy, secretary to King Alfonso XII, during the summer of 1876. Morphy was himself a composer and musicologist who had studied with François Fétis at Brussels. He was in a good position to judge musical talent and was impressed by Albéniz's accomplish-ments and potential. He secured a grant for the aspiring pianist so that he could study at the Conservatoire Royal in Brussels. Albéniz was admitted to the Conservatoire on October 17, 1876, and eventually became a student of Louis Brassin. In addition to piano, Albéniz studied harmony with Joseph Dupont and solfège with Michel Van Lamperen. Albéniz tied with Louvain native Arthur de Greef for first place ("with dis-tinction") in the July 1879 piano competition in Brassin's class. He terminated his stud-ies at the Conservatoire shortly thereafter, in September.[3] He returned to Barcelona a local hero and gave a concert at the Teatre Espanyol on September 12, 1879, that had the critics singing his praises.[4] He gave several more successful concerts in that city before rejoining his family in Madrid.

In the summer of 1880, Albéniz set out to realize his dream of studying with Franz Liszt. He made his way to Budapest via Prague and Vienna, but Liszt was not in Budapest at that time. Albéniz wrote in his diary that he played for him on August 18, 1880, but this was pure fabrication, and he probably never met, much less studied with, Liszt. Why Albéniz invented the encounter is uncertain, but he probably wanted to justify to his family—and perhaps to posterity, of which he was keenly aware even early in life—what turned out to be little more than a sight-seeing excursion. Albéniz threaded his way back to Madrid through Vienna and Paris. Overall, his lack of artistic success on this trip was a disappointment to him, and he even contemplated taking his own life as a result. (Despite his outward ebullience, there was a depressive streak in his personality, and one readily perceives this in much of his music.) During this year, Albéniz entered the reserves of the Spanish army.[5] His fascination with military trappings may have gotten the best of him, or perhaps the service was obligatory, but it in no way slowed down his concert career. Fortunately, in the early 1880s there was a lull in Spain's almost incessant civil war, and he was never called up.

By December 1880, Albéniz was back in Havana and Santiago giving concerts. He then made his way to Granada in July of the following year. He had performed there 9 years earlier, when he was only 12 years old; now, he was a grown man and an artist of impressive stature. Albéniz had a great love of Granada, which he expressed in some of his most popular piano pieces. He gave private performances in the homes of Granada's leading citizens, music lovers already familiar with his talents.

More appearances followed in Santander and Zaragoza that fall, followed by a December concert in Pamplona. One searches in vain in the press for a single negative assessment of his performances during this period. The audiences were ecstatic about his technique and musicianship, and the critics lavished their encomiums on him. January of 1882 found Albéniz still in the north country. He performed in Bilbao between the two acts of Joaquín Gaztambide's zarzuela *El juramento*. Shortly after this performance, Albéniz entered into a new musical arena by composing his own zarzuelas (Spanish operettas). Today nothing remains of these early works except their titles. *Cuanto más viejo*, T. 1, composed to a one-act libretto by Mariano Zapino Garibay, premiered in Bilbao at the Coliseo in February 1882. Though it was a hit, it did not remain in the repertoire, and we know practically nothing about the story or the music.

We know little more about a second zarzuela, *Catalanes de gracia*, T. 2, also in one act, with a libretto by Rafael Leopoldo Palomino de Guzmán. It premiered at the Teatro Salón Eslava in Madrid in late March 1882 and continued to draw large audiences well into April. But despite this success, by May, Albéniz was back on the concert trail, where he remained at least until November. No evidence of a putative third zarzuela, *El canto de salvación*, T. 3, has yet surfaced.

After a rousing triumph in Córdoba in May, Albéniz moved on to San Fernando, Cádiz, and Seville. On August 7, he performed on the opposite side of the country, in Valencia. Other appearances took him to Málaga, Pontevedra, and Vigo, where he performed with a sextet including his friends Enrique Fernández Arbós (violin) and Agustín Rubio (cello). Not one to rest on his laurels for very long, Albéniz continued on to Cartagena to give several concerts. His last known performance in 1882 took place in Madrid at the elegant salon of the Círculo Vasco-Navarro, where he played his well-rehearsed repertoire of Chopin, Scarlatti, Boccherini, Beethoven, Raff, and Mendelssohn.

The following year Albéniz moved to Barcelona and continued his concertizing from there. Around this time the young pianist met, briefly courted, and married Rosina Jordana Lagarriga (1863–1945), one of his students and the daughter of a prominent family in the Catalonian capital. This led him to adopt a more settled lifestyle. The nuptials took place on June 23, 1883, at the church of Mare de Deu de la Mercé, in the Gothic quarter of Barcelona near the harbor.[6] (With the intercession of Ángel, Albéniz was able to free himself of his military obligations, receiving his discharge from the reserves on June 7.) Albéniz did not, however, allow matrimony to keep him off the concert circuit. In September, he journeyed to Santander to join Arbós's sextet, which was busy giving concerts on the north coast. After a successful appearance in La Coruña, the group moved on to Vigo, Santiago de Compostela, and Orense. However, after La Coruña the tour was a failure and drew small audiences. Albéniz parted company with the group and passed through Madrid on his way back to Barcelona.

It was most likely during this Barcelona period that Albéniz made the acquaintance of Felipe Pedrell and studied composition with him. He knew that he had yet to acquire any real technique as a composer and that he would have to grapple with the complexities of form, counterpoint, and orchestration before he could aspire to anything higher than the charming little entertainments he was already capable of writing. By 1883, the Catalan Pedrell (1841–1922) had already established a solid reputation as an opera composer and musical nationalist. Albéniz himself certainly was unstinting in his praise of Pedrell as a teacher as well as a composer. In his letters to Pedrell, Albéniz addressed him as "Dear Master" and signed himself "your eternally affectionate disciple."[7]

Aside from the adulation his apprenticeship aroused, the most important point usually made about Albéniz's contact with Pedrell is that it reinforced his growing determination to use the musical folklore of his own country as the basis for composition. Pedrell was an advocate of musical nationalism who believed that folk song formed the ideal foundation for Spanish art music. To be sure, Pedrell was not a Catalan nationalist but pan-Spanish in his outlook, and it was this philosophy to which Albéniz also adhered.[8] Thus, the 1880s witnessed Albéniz's increasing output of charming and distinctive Spanish-style pieces for the piano, which met with an enthusiastic reception by the concertgoing public in Spain and elsewhere. Many of these works have found a permanent place in the piano repertoire, though they are most frequently heard in transcription for the guitar. They are so convincing that it is indeed easy to take their originality completely for granted. These works represent Albéniz's characteristic blend of indigenous and non-Spanish elements: lively rhythms, modality, elementary formal structure, and haunting melodic arabesques couched in poignant, chromatic harmonies reminiscent of Chopin. Though he continued to write light pieces in the international salon style so popular at that time, Albéniz's "Spanish" pieces represent the first flowering of his unique creative genius.

Albéniz signed a lucrative contract to entertain at the Cafe Colón in Barcelona. Here he was persuaded by acquaintances to speculate on the stock market, and he lost a considerable amount of money. But he simply gave more concerts to make good his losses. He toured southern France and northern Spain, appearing in Marseilles, Toulon, Biarritz, Cauterets, and Arcachón. Concerts in the Catalonian capital during 1883 included appearances at the Teatre Espanyol in January, at the Tívoli in February, and at the Liceu in May.[9] It was probably during one of these appearances that Rosina first heard him perform. Unfortunately, we know little about his activities in 1884 in Barcelona. Albéniz's final appearance there took place on March 22, 1885, in a benefit concert at the Liceu. On August 8, 1885, he gave a recital at the Casino Luchón, and part of the proceeds went to aid the poor.[10]

Albéniz's first child, named after his deceased sister Blanca, was born in 1884 in Barcelona. A second child was born during the summer of 1885 in Tiana, a hamlet outside Barcelona. The boy was named Alfonso, after the king who had made possible Albéniz's studies in Brussels. Soon thereafter, Albéniz moved his growing family to Madrid, where he gave concerts for the royal family and established his reputation as a popular composer as well as a virtuoso.

One of the most important concerts Albéniz ever gave took place at the elegant and fashionable Salón Romero in Madrid on Sunday, January 24, 1886, when he was 25 years old. It was in conjunction with this appearance that Guerra y Alarcón's biography of Albéniz appeared in print. Most of the information for this account was provided to the author by Albéniz himself, and critics reviewing the concert borrowed from it extensively. Word of his smashing success at the Salón Romero spread throughout the country, and Albéniz received numerous invitations from various cities in Spain to perform. But triumph soon blended with tragedy when Albéniz's 20-month-old daughter Blanca died of a fever on April 4, 1886.

In spite of this heartbreak, on July 17 and 19 he was back on stage in San Sebastián, appearing with a sextet (not Arbós's group) and in a recital for two pianos, accompanied by a local pianist. In 1886, Albéniz also performed in Zaragoza. On March 21, 1887, he again appeared at the Salón Romero performing many of his own works; several of his students also appeared in performances of his latest compositions. On September 20, 1887, he ventured across the waters of the Mediterranean to concertize in Palma de Mallorca, where the local press saluted his artistry.

During the rest of Albéniz's tenure in Madrid, until 1889, life settled into a routine of concerts, teaching, and dealing with family matters.[11] He spent many evenings at Morphy's home, in the company of composer and conductor Tomás Bretón, Arbós, and other musical notables. The piano pieces of this period represent most of the genres of salon music: mazurkas, waltzes, barcarolles, pavanes, minuets, romances, polkas, polonaises, serenades, etudes, and caprices. We know these figured prominently in his concerts during the 1880s and '90s, and nearly all of them bear dedications to students, friends, and family. The majority of these pieces were suitable for amateur use and served the dual purpose of bringing in income and spreading his name. Benito Zozaya and Antonio Romero in Madrid and Juan Ayné in Barcelona published most of them. In addition, Albéniz wrote all of his seven sonatas during this time, though only nos. 3–5 are complete. Nothing remains of 2 and 6, while only single movements of 1 and 7 (a scherzo and minuetto, respectively) are extant. Number 3 bears a dedication to the pianist Manuel Guervós, who premiered it at the concert in the Salón Romero on March 21, 1887. Number 4 is dedicated to his "beloved Maestro" Count Morphy (Alfonso XII gave him this title in 1885) and was premiered by Luisa Chevalier at this same concert.

The most enduring and popular of his compositions from this period are, however, his Spanish-style pieces. Albéniz freely adapted from Spanish folk music certain generic rhythmic and melodic elements that give the works their flavor. He felt a special attraction to flamenco, the exotic folk music of Andalusia (where he toured extensively during his youth and returned later as a tourist). This was certainly a source of inspiration for several numbers in *Recuerdos de viaje*, T. 72, and the *Suite española no. 1*, T. 61,[12] which contain some his finest pieces from this period.

However, Albéniz did not confine himself to works for piano in the 1880s, and he wrote some excellent vocal music, including *Rimas de Bécquer*, T. 33, on poems of the celebrated Sevillan poet Gustavo Adolfo Bécquer, and the *Seis baladas*, T. 36, to Italian texts of the Marquesa de Bolaños. Two choral works also flowed from his pen during the Madrid years: the oratorio *El Cristo* (lost), T. 34,[13] and *Salmo VI: del oficio de difuntos* (1885), T. 35, for SATB chorus, composed upon the death of his patron Alfonso XII.[14] A number of orchestral works were published in piano reduction as well, including the *Rapsodia española* for piano and orchestra, T. 16, and the Concerto No. 1 for Piano and Orchestra ("Concierto fantástico"), T. 17. Not only was Albéniz reviving the sonata in Spain, but he was also establishing a tradition of concerto writing that would blossom in the next century. He was also helping foster Spanish symphonic music, though the *Escenas sinfónicas catalanas*, T. 19, of 1889 remained unpublished until 2010 (see no. 6), and his most important contribution, *Catalonia*, T. 24, would not appear for another decade (see no. 7).

As a result of his many accomplishments, on March 30, 1886, the Queen Regent appointed Albéniz to the position of assistant professor of piano at the Real Conservatorio. Several months later, on November 11, 1886, the Dirección General de

Bellas Artes made Albéniz a member of the Royal Order of Isabel the Catholic, and the actual ceremony took place on the 22nd at the Royal Palace. On this occasion he received the designation of Ordinary Knight Commander. He was made a Full Knight Commander 2 years later.[15]

In the summer and fall of 1888, Albéniz made several highly successful appearances at the Exposición Universal in Barcelona, and these served as a springboard for the next phase in his career. The piano manufacturer Erard and Co. invited Albéniz to give a series of concerts in the French section of the Exposition, and he performed no fewer than 20 recitals between August 20 and October 11. He appeared in Madrid on March 7, 1889, at the Teatro de la Comedia with the orchestra of the Sociedad de Conciertos, conducted by Bretón. He then performed again in Vitoria. Oddly, though Albéniz seems to have played up his Basque heritage for all it was worth when he concertized in that region, he rarely did so elsewhere. His only pieces inspired by Basque folklore are two *zorticos* for piano, based on the popular dance in 5/8 meter.

THE LONDON YEARS (1889–93)

As a composer and soloist, Albéniz was bound to outgrow the Iberian Peninsula and seek a larger arena for his talents. Erard invited him to perform in their hall in Paris on April 25, 1889. The concert was devoted exclusively to his own works, and he was accompanied by the orchestra of Edouard Colonne in his Piano Concerto No. 1.[16] Those in attendance at the performance included Debussy, Ravel, Fauré, and Dukas. Albéniz's pianism and style of writing were a revelation to them in the way he was able to evoke from the piano the characteristic sounds of the Spanish guitar.

In Madrid on July 23, 1889, Rosina gave birth to another daughter, this one named after another of Albéniz's deceased sisters, Enriqueta. But Albéniz was concertizing in Britain at the time. He made his first known appearance in London at Prince's Hall in Piccadilly on June 13, 1889. In July, Albéniz performed at 19 Harley St., including in his program works by himself and his friends Arbós, Ruperto Chapí, and Bretón. With characteristic generosity, Albéniz had already determined to serve as a pathfinder for Spanish composers and performers in the concerts he gave and organized during his tenure in London. Other performances during this year took place at the Derby Drill Hall, at one of Edgar Haddock's Musical Evenings in Leeds, at a Royal Amateur Orchestral Society concert (with Arbós and Pablo Sarasate), at the Lyric Club, and at the Crystal Palace. He played at St. James's Hall in October, where he presented his own compositions in addition to works by Bach, Scarlatti, and Chopin. Perhaps the highlight of his concerts in London in 1889 was a December performance at a *conversazione* of the Wagner Society, held in the Institute over Prince's Hall. His renditions of Brassin's Wagner transcriptions earned him the praise of George Bernard Shaw, who reviewed the concert (see no. 370).

His reputation now well established, in early 1890 Albéniz set out on a tour of the provinces with a group of performers, serving as both soloist and accompanist. Their travels took them to many cities, including Birmingham, Bradford, Brighton, Bristol, Chatham, Glasgow, Halifax, Huddersfield, Lancaster, Leeds, Manchester, Rochester,

Sheffield, and Stourbridge. Despite these peregrinations, Albéniz was probably present when his last child, Laura, was born on April 20, 1890, in Barcelona. But June found him once again in London, now resolved to settle in the city that had received him so favorably.

Later that month, Albéniz signed a contract with a London businessman, Henry Lowenfeld, who would now serve as his manager and hold exclusive rights to the publication of his music. This arrangement also gave Albéniz a spacious house at 16 Michael's Grove, Brompton, a district traditionally populated by accomplished musicians and actors. It would provide ample room for Albéniz's wife and three children, who now moved to London to join him. Lowenfeld likely provided financial support for this pianist/composer's ensuing ambitious concert ventures. Albéniz organized two orchestral concerts at St. James's Hall in November 1890. The first program, on the 7th, attracted only a small audience due to the large venue, competition from Hans Richter's concert series there, and inclement weather. The second of Albéniz's orchestral extravaganzas took place on November 21 and was greeted by the press and public with more enthusiasm. Buoyed by this success and enjoying the financial backing of Lowenfeld, Albéniz set about to organize a series of 10 concerts in St. James's Hall the following year, from January through June. These programs featured not only Albéniz but also many of his friends, including Arbós and the Hungarian violinist Tividar Nachez.

To be sure, Albéniz did not confine his appearances to England during these years. In early February 1892, he and the Belgian violinist Eugène Ysaÿe appeared in one of the Valleria concerts at the Philharmonie in Berlin. Nearly a month later, on March 1, Albéniz presented a solo program at the Singakademie in Berlin, one to which the critics had ambivalent reactions (see nos. 429–38). In this same year, he performed with Arbós in Brussels and embarked on another tour of England with Arbós and the Czech cellist David Popper.

The year 1892 represented the apex of his career as a concert pianist, and after this time he gave himself over more and more to serious composition. He did continue to concertize over the next few years, but far less actively than had been his custom. The chief impetus for this development lay in his growing occupation with musical theater in London. His initial foray into this arena came in the form of incidental music to poems by Paul-Armand Sylvestre, read by the celebrated actress Sarah Bernhardt. Sylvestre's *Poèmes d'amour*, T. 31,[17] were arranged as a series of twelve *tableaux vivants* by Cyprien Godebski and premiered on Monday afternoon, June 20, 1892, at the Lyric Club, Barnes (London). Albéniz had begun composing the work only a week earlier, on June 14, and finished the manuscript but a day before the concert.

He next became involved in a production of the operetta *Incognita*, T. 4, an English adaptation of Charles Lecocq's *Le Coeur et la main*, which opened on October 6, 1892, and ran for 101 performances.[18] For this production the work was expanded from two acts to three, and Albéniz composed a finale for Act II, entitled "Oh! Horror! Horror!" as well as a quartet (Act III?) entitled "Since love will lend us wings to fly."

In the summer of 1892, Albéniz began work on an operetta entirely his own entitled *The Magic Opal*, T. 5, on a text by Arthur Law, a popular English librettist of the day. The work premiered on January 19, 1893, at the Lyric Theatre.[19] It initially proved so successful that a touring company was formed only 3 weeks after the premiere to perform *The*

Magic Opal in other cities, opening at the Royalty Theatre in Glasgow and continuing on to Edinburgh, Manchester, Brighton, Hull, Liverpool, Newcastle, Sheffield, and Leeds, finally closing at the Bolton Theatre Royal on May 20. In spite of all this, the London run ended ignominiously on February 27. This was due in part to the mediocre libretto,[20] but financial difficulties lay at the heart of the matter, as production expenses consistently outstripped ticket receipts.

Albéniz and company undertook a revision of the work, renamed *The Magic Ring*, which reduced the number of characters, simplified the plot, and cut some numbers and added others. It premiered at the Prince of Wales's Theatre on April 11, 1893, conducted by the composer. Unfortunately, this also failed to hold the public's attention; however, Albéniz's activities on the London stage did not end with *The Magic Ring*. He soon took an active part in the production of the two-act musical comedy *Poor Jonathan*, T. 6, an English-language adaptation of Karl Millöcker's *Der arme Jonathan*.[21] *Poor Jonathan* premiered at the Prince of Wales's Theatre on June 15, 1893. Albéniz not only conducted the work but also contributed several musical numbers in addition to those by Millöcker. Yet again, however, his efforts were not enough to make a success of the production.

Albéniz did not cease to compose for piano during his London tenure, and several of his best-loved works were written for his concerts in Britain, including the lovely *Zambra granadina*, T. 97, and *Espagne: Six Feuilles d'album* (or *España: Seis hojas de álbum*), T. 95, which contains the ever-popular "Tango." *Chants d'Espagne* (or *Cantos de España*), T. 101, includes some of the most celebrated and widely performed of his works, especially the "Prélude," a warhorse in the guitar repertoire. Although this piece was later inserted by publishers into the *Suite española no. 1* under the title "Asturias (Leyenda)," it is important to understand that this work was inspired by Andalusian flamenco and has absolutely nothing to do with folk music of the Asturias region in the north.[22]

Sometime during the year 1893, Albéniz entered into a revised agreement with Lowenfeld that now included a third party. This man was Francis Burdett Thomas Nevill Money-Coutts (1852–1923), a London lawyer, poet, librettist, and wealthy heir to the fortune of the Coutts banking family.[23] This was a collaboration in which Money-Coutts supplied Albéniz with a large income in exchange for Albéniz setting his poetry and librettos to music. Over time they became very close friends, and Money-Coutts supported Albéniz without any consideration of his operatic output.

According to the extant contract of 1893, Albéniz was obliged to confine his professional collaboration to Lowenfeld and Money-Coutts. When Lowenfeld dropped out of the deal the following year, Albéniz was committed to working only for Money-Coutts. This has prompted many biographers to characterize the arrangement as a "Faustian pact" in which Albéniz was forced to set mediocre texts that were out of sympathy with his temperament. But that is a gross exaggeration. We will see that Albéniz never felt himself constrained to work only for Money-Coutts and that he set librettos by other writers, or at least left several such projects in various stages of completion. One such project that he finished was a zarzuela for Madrid in 1894 on which he began serious work in late 1893. This coincided with his decision to leave London on a trip to Spain before moving permanently to Paris.

Exactly when he left London and how long he remained in Spain before taking up residence in Paris remain unanswered questions, but Albéniz clearly did not intend to build on the substantial foundation of success he enjoyed in London. Without the monetary assistance of Money-Coutts, Albéniz would have had great difficulty making this move, especially as he now intended to devote himself to composition and to perform much less often, thus greatly reducing what had been his principal source of income.

PARIS (1894–97)

Albéniz's first assignment from Money-Coutts was to set the libretto for an opera, eventually entitled *Henry Clifford*, T. 8 (it had many preliminary working titles),[24] whose action takes place during the Wars of the Roses in fifteenth-century England. Albéniz began work on this new opera about the time he decided to leave London, for reasons of health, in the fall of 1893. Another motivation for the change of locale was that Rosina did not care for the climate and ambience of London. She much preferred Paris, which she found more congenial to her temperament and where she could speak French, in which she was more fluent than English. He was no doubt also attracted to Paris as the artistic and intellectual capital of Europe.

Exactly when Albéniz settled in Paris is uncertain, but it was sometime before August 1894. We know he performed a great deal of chamber music in Barcelona during the fall and winter, and it bears pointing out that Albéniz was not only a brilliant soloist but also a sensitive and knowledgeable interpreter of chamber music.[25] Yet he did not remain in Barcelona more than a few months, at most. He had indicated already in London that he had no desire to resettle in Spain, and he never made a secret of his disenchantment with the state of culture and politics in his homeland (given his socialist and atheistic leanings, this is not hard to comprehend).[26]

Albéniz's successful performances in Paris in 1889 were a living memory, and now, 5 years later, many influential people welcomed him back with open arms. Among these were Ernest Chausson and his wife, Jeanne, who helped introduce him to Parisian musical society through their *soirées*, which attracted the city's brightest musical luminaries. At these functions, Albéniz often improvised at the piano, charming the guests with his distinctively Spanish style. His own home also became a mecca for Spanish writers, artists, and musicians. He participated in concerts given by the Société Nationale de Musique and eventually enrolled in the Schola Cantorum, where he studied counterpoint with Vincent d'Indy starting in October 1896. He also taught piano there from 1897 to 1900. It was at the Schola that he made the acquaintance of Erik Satie, Albert Roussel, and Déodat de Séverac.

Albéniz attended the 1894 premiere of Debussy's *Prélude à l'après-midi d'un faune*, as well as of the opera *Pelléas et Mélisande* (1902), and cultivated an admiration for that composer's music. Albéniz's rapport with Paris and French culture became second in importance only to that with his homeland. In Paris, he entered a new stage in his career as a composer, one marked by increased sophistication and technical ability.

By January of 1894, Albéniz had completed work in Barcelona on the piano–vocal score for the second act of *Henry Clifford*. Albéniz and Money-Coutts remained in frequent contact, and sometimes the Englishman would visit his Spanish friend in Paris to discuss details of the work. While progress continued on the new opera, Albéniz was busy with other projects. On September 13, he performed for the family of the Grand Duke of Wladimiro and other notables at the Miramar Palace in San Sebastián. But his chief occupation during the summer of 1894, in Paris, was finishing work on a one-act zarzuela entitled *San Antonio de la Florida*, T. 7, with a text by his friend Eusebio Sierra, for performance in Madrid that fall.

At that time, there were two basic kinds of zarzuela, the *género chico* ("small genre") and *generó grande* ("large genre"). The work by Albéniz and Sierra belongs to the former category in that it consists of a single act, divided into two scenes, and lasts an hour and forty-five minutes (though this was a bit on the long side for a light work, a departure from the norm that annoyed some critics). The drama is characteristically comic and frivolous and presents a love story set during a period of political instability under the reign of Fernando VII, in 1823. It is replete with *majos* and *majas*, streetwise bohemians of the time immortalized in the paintings and etchings of Francisco Goya (1746–1828), and the title itself refers to a church in Madrid that Goya decorated with frescoes and where he is buried. The work thus reflects a revival of interest in Goya during the 1890s in Madrid, a phenomenon known as *majismo*.[27]

The zarzuela premiered on October 26, 1894, at the Teatro de Apolo. It ran until November 11 of the same year, receiving a total of 15 performances. It was revived briefly before Christmas, receiving five more performances (December 17–21) before closing for good. All in all it was an average run; respectable, but not a big hit. The critics were unanimous in condemning the libretto, and they found Albéniz's music too sophisticated for the genre. The work would not be revived in Madrid until 1954, and then only for a short run.[28]

However, Albéniz and Sierra also hoped to achieve success with a Spanish adaptation of *The Magic Opal*, now to be called *La sortija* ("The Ring"). It is difficult to tell exactly how much the work was modified for performance in Madrid, but most of the operetta seems to have remained in its original version. Of course, the text was translated into Spanish, by Sierra. The operetta premiered on November 23, 1894, at the Teatro de la Zarzuela, but it got a cool reception from the public and elicited outright hostility from the critics, who castigated the authors for being "too foreignized." *La sortija* was a fiasco and folded after only three nights. Albéniz left for Paris, disillusioned and disheartened, before the end of its run.

Though he was embittered by the failure of the Madrid productions, Albéniz hoped his next stage work would fare better in Barcelona. He focused his efforts on finishing the score for *Henry Clifford* in time for its premiere at the Gran Teatre del Liceu in 1895, where it ran for five performances, from May 8 through May 12. The production was sung in Italian, under the title *Enrico Clifford*. The critics raved about the score but found the libretto inappropriate for Albéniz's musical personality. The opera promptly slid into obscurity and has never again been staged, though it has finally been recorded (no. 29). *San Antonio de la Florida* was performed at the Tívoli in Barcelona on November 6 of that same year at a benefit concert for the soprano Ángeles Montilla.[29] But the critical reaction was at best mixed.

Albéniz was not easily daunted. He determined to heed the counsel offered by friends and critics and set a libretto more in harmony with his nationalist inclinations. He prevailed on Money-Coutts to craft a libretto based on a Spanish work, the novel *Pepita Jiménez* (pub. 1874) by the celebrated author Juan Valera (1824–1905). At last he had a vehicle he believed would bring him the "glory and profit" some critics had predicted for him.[30]

Pepita Jiménez (1896–97)

After gaining Money-Coutts's approval of the project, Albéniz got in touch with Valera (1824–1905). However, Valera's initial response was highly negative, for he believed that the novel was unsuitable for the stage and would inevitably be misrepresented and distorted. But he did not stand in the way of the opera's progress, and Money-Coutts completed the libretto well before September of 1895, when the surviving manuscript of the score is dated.

The premiere of *Pepita Jiménez*, T. 9, took place in Barcelona on Sunday, January 5, 1896, at the Gran Teatre del Liceu. The work was performed in Italian, the custom at the Liceu, just as *Enrico Clifford* had been. The opera received two performances on the 5th, one on the 6th, two on the 8th, and one each on the 11th, 12th, and 19th of January, on which day it closed. Despite the praises many well-meaning critics heaped on the work, it found no place in the repertoire and would not be produced again in Spain during Albéniz's lifetime.[31]

So, in the spring of 1897, Albéniz travelled to the German-speaking world to promote *Pepita Jiménez*. He had established useful connections over the years with important people there, including the editors at Breitkopf und Härtel in Leipzig, who published the opera. It premiered at the Königliches Deutsches Landestheater Neues Deutsches Theater in Prague on June 22, 1897. In Albéniz's own mind, the performance was less than satisfactory, but the notices were generally positive, and he was greatly encouraged by this. Appearing as it did at the end of the regular season, *Pepita Jiménez* ran only two nights (it was performed once more on the ensuing Friday, the 25th of June). It did not find the permanent place in the theater's repertoire Albéniz had hoped for and was never produced there again. He seems, however, to have been resigned to this, and he had his sights set on new possibilities. Albéniz signed a contract with Angelo Neumann (director of the Neues Deutsches Theater) for the composition of a stage work to be based on a libretto entitled *La voglia* by José Echegaray. He signed another contract with Neumann to write a ballet on the novel *Aphrodite* of Pierre Louÿs.[32] Neither of these commitments bore the slightest fruit.

During this period of intense involvement with the theater, he also took increasing interest in music for solo voice. While in London in 1892, he composed "Il en est de l'amour," T. 42, to a text by M. Costa de Beauregard, which was followed 3 years later by the *Deux Morceaux de prose de Pierre Loti* ("Crepuscule" and "Tristesse"), T. 41. In 1896, Albéniz began collaborating with Money-Coutts on songs as well as operas. Among these are *To Nellie: Six Songs*, T. 39 (Nellie was Money-Coutts's nickname for his wife). Other Money-Coutts songs from this time include "Will You Be Mine?" T. 40B, and "Separated,"

T. 40C (the only extant numbers from a collection of six songs that were not published during his life). "The Gifts of the Gods," T. 40F, later appeared with "The Caterpillar," T. 40E, as a set of two songs.[33] One other song (also unpublished during his life) was "Art Thou Gone for Ever, Elaine?" T. 40A (composed in 1906). But Albéniz was not confined to Money-Coutts's poetry, and around this same time he composed the lovely "Chanson de Barberine," T. 37, to a text by Alfred de Musset. But, in fact, his future was more than ever bound up with that of his benefactor, and the following 4 years would absorb him in a project beyond the dimensions of anything he had previously attempted.

Merlin (1898–1904)

The next product of Albéniz's professional association with Money-Coutts was an operatic project on a truly grand scale. This was a trilogy based on *Le Morte d'Arthur* by the fifteenth-century English author Sir Thomas Malory. The constituent parts of the *King Arthur* trilogy were to be *Merlin*, *Launcelot*, and *Guenevere*, T. 12A–C. Though it is tempting to see this as a misguided effort, one could also view the project as consistent with Albéniz's ever-waxing devotion to Wagnerism, a love affair that went back perhaps as far as his days as a student of Louis Brassin in Brussels. It was also consistent with the rise of a Wagner cult in Spain, especially Barcelona. Thus, it is no wonder that he believed he could triumph on the stage in his homeland with a Wagnerian trilogy.[34] Albéniz attended performances of Wagner's operas whenever possible, and detailed annotations made by him in his personal copies of the full scores to the *Ring* cycle reveal a profound knowledge of the music.[35] Albéniz's commitment to Wagnerian principles in the trilogy is apparent in his use of leading motives and their presentation and development almost exclusively in the orchestra. It is also evident in his avoidance of simultaneous singing and his treatment of the voices, that is, in the emphasis on clarity of declamation and renunciation of *fioritura*.

When precisely the Arthurian project commenced is not known. The librettos were published in 1897 by John Lane in London. *Merlin* was finally published, in piano–vocal format, by Édition Mutuelle in 1906. Unfortunately, Albéniz completed only the piano–vocal score of the first of *Launcelot*'s three acts and some of the orchestral score for Act II. Marginalia in the libretto represent his furthest progress with the four acts of *Guenevere*. *Merlin* was never staged during Albéniz's lifetime. The Prelude to Act I, however, was well received at its premiere in Barcelona on November 14, 1898, during the third in a series of four concerts Vincent d'Indy conducted with the Asociació Filarmònica. *Merlin* finally premiered on December 18, 1950, at the Tívoli in Barcelona, performed by the Club de Fútbol Junior. However, its most durable and spectacular appearance was on stage at the Teatro Real in Madrid in 2003. It was also recorded on a CD starring Placido Domingo, Jr., and in a DVD produced by the BBC.[36] Is *Merlin* a great opera? No, but it is a very good opera and far beyond what even Albéniz's most ardent supporters might ever have expected from the composer of "Granada (Serenata)."

The year 1898 was one of severe health problems for Albéniz, which were even reported in the Barcelona press. He devoted that summer to seeking relief at a health spa in Plombières. His intestines had always been a source of discomfort, and his penchant for overeating only made matters worse. This was also a period of personal loss.

In 1899, his friends Ernest Chausson and Count Morphy both died. The following year his beloved mother passed away (his father, with whom he had a complex and trying relationship, died in 1903). Charles Bordes had appointed Albéniz to teach piano at the Schola Cantorum in 1897; however, on account of his intense involvement with composition, Albéniz was now less interested in teaching than he had been before, and ill health forced him to resign the position around 1900.

Albéniz's association with the Schola Cantorum inspired his most humorously charming work for piano, *Yvonne en visite!*, T. 104, whose two movements bear the titles "La Révérence" ("The Curtsy") and "Joyeuse Rencontre, et quelques pénibles événements!!" ("Joyous Encounter, and Some Painful Events!!"). It appeared in a collection of pieces for children "small and large" by musicians at the Schola Cantorum. Albéniz became involved with another important musical institution in Paris at this time, the Société Nationale de Musique, and his services as a performer and composer were in demand at their concerts. Albéniz's single most important work for orchestra, *Catalonia*, T. 24, premiered during a concert of the Société Nationale de Musique on May 28, 1899, at the Nouveau-Théâtre. It was initially conceived as a "Suite Populaire" of compositions inspired by his native province, but he abandoned work on the other pieces and contented himself with the first number.

Albéniz occupied three different residences during his Paris years. The first was at 49, rue d'Erlanger (building no longer standing) until about 1905, when he moved for a short time to 21, rue Franklin. The years 1906–09 were spent at 55, rue de Boulainvilliers, in a fashionable, upscale district. The building, completed in 1905, was virtually brand new in the year Albéniz moved there and still stands today. Thus, though he also had addresses elsewhere in France and Spain, Paris was his "home base," and he became a fixture in the French capital's cultural life. Although he had reservations about French modernism, Albéniz held Debussy in high regard (contrary to what some biographers have asserted) and was very close to Séverac, d'Indy, and Dukas. He became an especially intimate friend of Fauré.

In 1899, Albéniz began an extensive reorchestration of *Pepita Jiménez*, no doubt inspired by the lessons he had learned from the other orchestral works of this period and from Dukas, who mentored him on this subject. Albéniz's interest in orchestral writing during this time received further impetus from another collaboration with Money-Coutts. The Englishman wrote several letters to him about a series of poems entitled *The Alhambra* that Albéniz had evidently requested for setting to music and that were based on the composer's suggestions. Albéniz decided not to use these poems for songs and instead commenced a suite of pieces for orchestra inspired by them. At some point, Albéniz again changed his mind and chose to write the suite for piano rather than orchestra, but he completed only the first number, "La vega," T. 102A. José Vianna da Motta, the work's dedicatee, premiered it at a Société Nationale de Musique concert on January 21, 1899. This work signals a dramatic change in his nationalist style and is a clear harbinger of *Iberia* in its impressionist harmony and sophisticated formal design.[37]

However, Albéniz was by no means ready to give up on opera yet. He was convinced of the merit of his efforts in that arena, including *Merlin*, a production of which he did everything in his power to secure. His aspirations began to take material form in June 1901 when he, Enric Morera, and Enrique Granados entered into an agreement to establish a Teatre Líric Català in Barcelona.[38] The plan was to produce a series of 12 presentations of their works the following spring at the Teatre de Novetats, including *Merlin* as well as Morera's *Emporium* and Granados's *Follet*. Morera, however, soon betrayed the confidence of his friends and applied to Ruperto Chapí in Madrid to have his opera produced at the Teatro Lírico in that city. At some point, Albéniz approached the Liceu about producing *Merlin*. But he merely encountered the suspicion and hostility of the theater's management, which insisted on his submitting the score to a panel of "experts" for evaluation. Albéniz and Granados gave up in disgust, and the entire Catalan-lyric-theater project came to naught. The whole episode merely reinforced Albéniz's hostility toward Spain.

Albéniz rarely remained long in one place. In the spring of 1902, he left Barcelona and followed Morera to Madrid in hopes of gaining an audience for *Merlin* or *Pepita Jiménez*. His desire now was to settle in Madrid, not only for the sake of a possible *Merlin* premiere but because he was determined finally to make his mark as a *zarzuelero*. In 1902, he committed to composing a three-act zarzuela entitled *La real hembra* ("The Royal Woman"), T. 13, with a libretto by Cristóbal de Castro, a Madrid journalist who had signed a contract with the Círco de Parish for the work. Albéniz planned to spend the summer near Santander to make the translation of *Merlin* with the help of Sierra, as well as to work on *Launcelot* and a new operatic project, *Rinconete y Cortadillo*, based on a novel by Miguel de Cervantes (libretto by Henri Cain). In addition to the prospect of *Merlin* in the fall and the new zarzuela, he was attempting to bring *Pepita Jiménez* to the capital city. But Madrid's theaters had no real interest in this work. *Rinconete y Cortadillo* never made the journey from mind to manuscript, and Castro finished only the first act of the libretto for *La real hembra* before leaving town and losing interest in the project. Albéniz got no further than the prelude and first two scenes. Finally, Chapí did not live up to whatever assurances he had given Albéniz, and *Merlin* was never produced in Madrid. Albéniz gave up and retreated once again to the north.

The fall of 1902 was spent recuperating from his habitual malaise, this time in the beauty of the Swiss Alps with Money-Coutts and Nellie. November found Albéniz and his traveling companions in Milan searching for a publisher for *Merlin*. In the following year, Albéniz used the extremely generous allowance Money-Coutts was giving him to establish yet another residence, at the Chateau St. Laurent in Nice. So, Albéniz would now divide his remaining time on earth between Paris, Nice, and Tiana, just as his hero Liszt had spent his twilight years in Weimar, Rome, and Budapest.

Albéniz liked to discuss philosophical issues, and his correspondence with Money-Coutts reveals a lively dialogue on politics and religion. Despite his lack of formal education, Albéniz was fluent in Spanish, French, English, Italian, and Catalan, knew some German, and was well read. His library included novels of Daudet and Flaubert, the writings of Berlioz, plus the works of Voltaire, Byron, Hugo, Racine, Corneille, de Musset, Molière, Balzac, Plato, Louÿs, Maeterlinck, France, Plutarch, Shakespeare, Goethe, and Schiller (these last two in French translation). He also read works of contemporary Catalan authors, such as Santiago Rusiñol and Àngel Guimerà. He loved to collect books, and the generous income from Money-Coutts facilitated his buying. In addition, he collected fans and paintings. Though he could have built a valuable collection of French Impressionist paintings, he preferred to patronize Spanish artists. His daughter Laura become a noted artist in her own right, and her designs appeared on the first edition of *Iberia*, T. 105.

With his interest in literature, Albéniz was not oblivious to the fact that his talents would be better devoted to librettos more consonant with his love of Spain. In 1899, he began composing a one-act lyric drama entitled *La Sérénade*, T. 11 (author unknown), but he soon abandoned the project. In this same year, he commenced work on another lyric drama, *La morena* ("The Dark Woman"), T. 14, with a text by Alfred Mortier. This, too, was left incomplete. A reversal in Albéniz's operatic fortunes was on the way, but once more it would take place outside Spain. Ironically, it would prove the beautiful sunset and not the glimmering sunrise of his theatrical ambitions. Albéniz, dispirited by his inability to succeed as an opera composer, would thereafter pour his declining energies into writing once again for the piano, a decision greatly supported by friends and family alike. The result of this was, of course, his immortal masterpiece *Iberia*.

Iberia (1905–08)

In 1905, Albéniz finally succeeded in securing a production of *Pepita Jiménez* and his zarzuela *San Antonio de la Florida*[39] at the Théâtre Royal de la Monnaie in Brussels, with which he had kept up a long correspondence on this very matter. They premiered together on January 3, 1905, with additional performances on January 6, 10, 13 and February 1. The production was apparently a huge success, though its total of five performances might not suggest this. There were attempts on the part of Fauré and others to secure a production of *Pepita Jiménez* in Paris, but this would not happen until 1923, long after Albéniz's death. *Merlin* was performed privately in a concert version on February 13, 1905, in Brussels (with the composer at the piano), but Albéniz was not successful in getting it produced anywhere. Though *Merlin* would remain unfamiliar to the Belgian public, the possibility of a new stage work materialized as a result of the Brussels triumph. Ramon Cattier was a journalist with *La Gazette* in the Belgian capital, and he and Albéniz laid enthusiastic plans for an opera entitled *La loba* ("The She Wolf"). But the project never advanced beyond the planning stage.

This episode in Belgium marked both the high point and the end of Albéniz's musico-theatrical career. A combination of discouragement with the continued lack of interest in Spain in his operas and inability to get a production of *Merlin* anywhere persuaded him that his waning strength should be focused on what he did best, writing for the piano. However, his theatrical ventures had by no means been a waste of time and effort. First, they had brought forth from his pen some of his finest numbers, especially in *Pepita Jiménez*. Second, they had given him the best composition lessons he could have gotten, and he was now far beyond where he had been 15 years earlier in terms of his handling of texture, sonority, and large-scale form.

So, Albéniz now set about to compose a monumental set of works for the piano entitled *Iberia*, whose creation would occupy him during the years 1905–08. It belonged to what the composer referred to as his "second manner," of which "La vega" was a clear premonition. But whether *Iberia* should actually be called a "suite" is open to question. Albéniz's title simply refers to them as 12 *nouvelles impressions* ("new impressions") for piano. Performers usually program at most a few of them on a concert; all together they make for a long evening (total playing time is about 85 minutes). It could more justifiably be called a collection, as the pieces are quite distinct and are not laid out in a sequence of any significance. The harmonic and rhythmic richness and complexity of these pieces are quite extraordinary, especially in comparison to his piano pieces of the 1880s and '90s. They abound in hand crossings, counter-rhythms, difficult leaps, and nearly impossible chords, while the innumerable double accidentals make them difficult to read. As a result, *Iberia* requires almost superhuman technique, and Albéniz himself was hardly capable of playing it.

The twelve pieces of *Iberia* are arranged into four books of three pieces each. Every number evokes a peninsular locale, city, festival, or song and dance, largely concentrating on the south of Spain. The first book, consisting of "Evocación," "El puerto," and "Fête-Dieu à Séville" (the original title, but usually referred to as "El Corpus en Sevilla"), bears a dedication to Madame Jeanne Chausson and was composed in December 1905. In the autograph score, "Triana," which he composed less than a month after the first book was complete, appears as the first selection in Book Two (dedicated to Blanche Selva), followed by "Almería" and "Rondeña," which were composed later that year. This chronological order was reversed in the first published edition, however, so that "Rondeña" leads off Book Two followed by "Almería" and "Triana." Albéniz wasted little time in commencing work on Book Three (dedicated to Marguerite Hasselmans), completing the three numbers "El Albaicín," "El polo," and "Lavapiés" during November and December of 1906 while spending the winter in the temperate climate of Nice. The final book (dedicated to Madame Pierre Lalo) took longer to finish. "Málaga" and "Eritaña" were composed in the summer of 1907 in Paris, but the final number, "Jerez," which occupies the middle position in the book, was not completed until January 1908. The explanation for this is quite simple. Albéniz had originally planned to conclude the collection with *Navarra*, T. 106; however, he decided that its style did not fit with the other numbers, so he composed "Jerez" as a substitute.

The four books of *Iberia* were premiered at various locales in France by the French pianist Blanche Selva (1884–1942). But, in fact, the Catalan pianist Joaquim Malats (1872–1912) was Albéniz's favorite interpreter of these pieces, and they were composed for him. Though Selva was the first to present entire books in concert, Malats premiered several of the individual numbers in Spain. Albéniz laid great plans for a tour that would take Malats and *Iberia* throughout Europe. He was especially keen to have a Spaniard introduce the works. But Malats fell ill and could not realize these plans. Albéniz's letters to Malats certainly reveal the composer's uncommonly great admiration and affection for his countryman (see nos. 118 and 179).

The papers in France took scant notice of Selva's premieres, but in Spain the critics gave unqualified praise to the works. This is surprising, given the previous hostility of the Spanish press toward Albéniz's "foreignized" music and anything "Frenchified." In truth, the work's sympathetic reception in Spain was probably aided by the composer's poor health and premature death. Then again, purely instrumental music did not raise the critics' hackles the way stage works did, especially when it was played by an artist of Malats's stature. In the case of musical theater, Albéniz was running up against a long tradition and a deeply entrenched establishment. But in the sphere of piano music, he himself had defined the tradition and could do as he pleased.

It is important for us to remember that Albéniz's declining health made concertizing or holding any kind of regular job nearly impossible. The continued generous support from Money-Coutts permitted Albéniz to compose *Iberia*, and the Englishman never exerted pressure on him to finish the Arthurian trilogy. By the period of *Iberia*, then, Albéniz's association with Money-Coutts had ripened into a deep friendship and was not merely a business association. Their collaboration did produce one more work, the *Quatre Mélodies*, T. 44, for solo voice and piano of 1908, dedicated to Gabriel Fauré.

With the completion of *Iberia* and *Quatre Mélodies*, Albéniz began a precipitous decline into terminal illness resulting from chronic inflammation of the kidneys (Bright's disease). He spent the summer of 1908 in Bagnoles de l'Orne taking the waters and relaxing. Albéniz and his family then spent a trying winter on the Riviera, where they had gone in the futile hope that its mild climate would stimulate a recovery. A brief return to Paris in the spring and the ministrations of various specialists there did little to retard the deterioration of his health. A regular stream of visitors came to see him, and Dukas appeared religiously every day. Albéniz's heart was sorely taxed by excessive urea in his blood, due to the inefficiency of his kidneys. Now the family retreated once again to the south, this time to the French Basque country on the Atlantic side of the Pyrenees, in the small resort town of Cambo-les-Bains. Here, he and his wife and daughters settled into a suite in the Chateau St. Martin. Though Money-Coutts could not come to see him, there were several other visitors during this final struggle. Pau Casals paid a visit, in the company of Alfred Cortot and Jacques Thibaud. The most heartening development was a surprise visit by Albéniz's dear friend Granados, who read a letter from Debussy informing Albéniz that, upon the recommendation of himself, Fauré, Dukas, and d'Indy, the French government had awarded him the Croix de la Légion d'Honneur.

However, the intense emotion of Granados's visit may have caused Albéniz's condition to worsen, and death moved much closer to his doorstep. On May 18, 1909, he was given an injection of morphine to ease his pain, but this had the unintended consequence of causing arrhythmia and initiated the end. He closed his eyes forever at exactly eight o'clock that evening. In 11 more days, he would have reached his forty-ninth birthday. He left incomplete at his death two substantial works for solo piano: *Navarra* (completed by Déodat de Séverac) and *Azulejos* (completed by Enrique Granados), T. 107.

Albéniz's body was embalmed and interred temporarily in Cambo-les-Bains before being sent by train to Barcelona, where elaborate funeral preparations had been made by Granados and others. His cortège wended its way through the city on June 6, accompanied by the police, dignitaries, and a band, while thousands of ordinary citizens thronged the streets and showered the hearse with flowers, as a gesture of affection and respect for one of Catalonia's greatest musicians. He was then buried in the Cementiri del Sud-Oest, on the seaward side of historic Montjüic.

MUSICAL STYLE AND LEGACY

Albéniz continues to be a vital presence in the canon of Western music. Thousands of recordings of his music have been made, and no fewer than 40 publishing houses have printed his works. And he exerted a discernible influence on succeeding composers, especially in Spain. Research conducted by scholars in the United States and Europe over the past two decades has revealed a composer far more versatile and skilled than earlier commentators had generally suspected. In particular, Albéniz now takes his place among the leading Spanish composers of opera, one whose several major works are finally available in print and on disc for scholars to assay.

Though Albéniz himself broke his output down into two "manners," it makes more sense to divide it in the traditional fashion of early, middle, and late. The early works include his zarzuelas of 1881–82 (now lost), the sonatas and many salon pieces of the 1880s, and the suites of Spanish pieces composed up to 1894, including such well-known collections as *Recuerdos de viaje, España: Seis hojas de álbum*, and *Cantos de España*. The works of the middle period include all the stage works, the piano piece *La vega*, and the orchestral work *Catalonia*. These last two works are clear premonitions of Albéniz's late period, represented chiefly by *Iberia* and *Quatre Mélodies*.

Albéniz's three-phase career as a composer can be seen, then, to correspond roughly to the final three decades of his life, from 1880 through 1909. Each decade brought with it a new level of development, culminating in an undisputed masterpiece, *Iberia*. The other conspicuous feature of his career is that, aside from his beginnings as a zarzuela composer, the first decade was devoted largely to the composition of works for piano, while the second decade was given over to musical theater. The final creative period presents a return to piano composition. This seeming ABA form poses, however, an important variation in the da capo; for, Albéniz the composer of *Iberia* was light years beyond Albéniz the composer of *Recuerdos de viaje* in terms of musical sophistication and technical control, something he himself acknowledged. To be sure, some aspects of *Iberia* are observable in the early nationalist works, for example, the use of Spanish dance rhythms, modality (especially the so-called Andalusian, or E, mode), characteristic melodic and rhythmic flourishes, the descending minor tetrachord, and evocations of flamenco singing and guitar playing. But many of the chief characteristics of *Iberia* are completely absent in the early period.

In terms of formal structure, the early nationalist works are almost without exception in simple sectional forms, usually ABA. The characteristic *modus operandi* regarding thematic material is repetition, not development. Albéniz's melodies, no matter how charming, were suited to little more than transposition, a characteristic Romantic device. By contrast, 8 of the 12 pieces of *Iberia* are in freely adapted sonata form. Albéniz's juxtaposition of contrasting material and development of ideas create a richness and variety unprecedented in his early piano works. This is aided in part by melodies built from motivic cells that render them more capable of development.

The early works offered harmonies that were suited to the melodic material in their charm and poignancy but that rarely ventured beyond the conventional. *Iberia*, on the other hand, reveals the influence of contemporary French music in its chromaticism, use of whole-tone scales, and its myriad modes and modal mixtures. Dissonance is far more prominent, and the use of augmented-sixth chords for modulating to distant tonal areas is conspicuous. There is also a high concentration of added-note sonorities and the use of secundal and quartal harmonies, which do not occur in the early suites.

Although Albéniz's style was always characterized by lively rhythms, *Iberia*'s use of superimposed meters, rapidly shifting meters, and complex patterns of accentuation represents a quantum leap over his earlier practice. The textures of *Iberia* and the early works are essentially homophonic, but those of *Iberia* are much more animated and often exhibit a contrapuntal use of countermelodies, especially during development sections. Finally, the virtuosic exploitation of the resources of the piano, the sheer range of timbres and effects Albéniz elicits from that instrument in *Iberia*, finds no parallel in the compositions from the early period.

This dramatic evolution in his style sets him apart from most of his contemporaries in Spain, who composed for a domestic market that was not noted for its sophistication. His tremendous growth was largely the product of his lengthy residence in Paris and exposure to a very high level of musical culture. It also emanated from his experience as an opera composer, through which he achieved greater mastery of large-scale forms and an appreciation of the expressive possibilities of orchestral sonority. He exhibited remarkable versatility and wrote operas in several of the major styles of his day: English operetta in *The Magic Opal*; French and German operetta in the additional numbers for *Incognita* and *Poor Jonathan*; Spanish operetta (zarzuela) in *San Antonio de la Florida*; Italian grand opera in *Henry Clifford*; Spanish national opera in *Pepita Jiménez*; and Wagnerian opera in *Merlin*. This wealth of experience was crucial in propelling Albéniz to a new level of composition. Unfortunately, these works fall somewhat short of greatness because of the weakness of their librettos and because of Albéniz's penchant for investing musical interest in the orchestra and relegating the singers to delivering the text in a recitative that lacks the expressive range of Wagner or Verdi. The same could be said of the majority of his songs, which make so many demands on the pianist that the declamatory vocal line can sometimes appear almost incidental. (There are a few happy exceptions to this, however, such as "The Caterpillar" and "To Nellie." In these cases, the voice has a charming melody supported by an unobtrusive piano accompaniment.)

If we consider Manuel de Falla (1876–1946) as the central point toward and from which we measure the progress of Spanish nationalism in music, Albéniz is Falla's most important predecessor. Falla owes an obvious debt to Albéniz in such masterpieces as *La vida breve*, *Noches en los jardines de España*, and *Fantasía bética* in their blending of southern Spanish folklore and elements of French modernism. Joaquín Turina's (1882–1949) shift toward a nationalist idiom during his years in Paris was the direct result of Albéniz's influence, and in such guitar works as *Ráfaga*, *Fandanguillo*, and the Sonata reverberations of Albéniz's Franco-Hispanic style are clear. In the music of Joaquín Rodrigo (1901–99) and Federico Moreno Torroba (1891–1982), we clearly hear the echoes of Albéniz's works. It was indeed he who defined what Spanish art music of our time would sound like.

Moreover, Albéniz occupies an important position in the overall cultural history of his homeland. As he spent more time outside of Spain and consequently came under the influence of Wagner and French music, he aligned himself with the forward-looking internationalists in Spain who sought a closer incorporation of their country into European culture (as opposed to the xenophobic *españolismo* of the conservative faction). Rodrigo has said of Albéniz that what he represents is "the incorporation of Spain, or better said, the reincorporation of Spain into the European musical world."[40] This was best summed up by Albéniz himself when he declared that Spanish composers ought "to make Spanish music with a universal accent."[41] *Iberia*, then, exhibits a political and philosophical dimension we might otherwise overlook. It is more than beautiful music; in its novelty and scope it is a summing up of Albéniz's view of Spanish culture and its proper place in European civilization. His was a vision that has become a reality, which helps to explain his enduring relevance and appeal within Spain as well as abroad.

NOTES

[1] This was its original name (founded in 1830) and the one it bears today. During Albéniz's studies there, however, it was known as the Escuela Nacional de Música y Declamación.

[2] Independent confirmation of this concert is to be found in the manuscript *Concerts Celebrats á Barcelona 1797–1901 de Música Simfónica i de Camera*, located in the Institut Universitari de Documentació i Investigació Musicològica Josep Ricart i Matas in Barcelona. This is an important source of information concerning concert life in nineteenth-century Barcelona.

[3] An excellent source of information on Albéniz's activities in Brussels from this time forward is Jan de Kloe, "Albéniz in Brussels," *Soundboard* 30/4 (2004–05): 7–16.

[4] Reference to this is made in *Concerts Celebrats á Barcelona.* . . .

[5] His military papers are in the Mm, carpeta 1, but they do not provide the exact date of his enlistment.

[6] The Arxiu Diocesa of the Arquebisbat de Barcelona states that the marriage certificate was destroyed during the Spanish Civil War (1936–39).

[7] See four letters in the Bc, M964, dated April 20, 1891, November 23, 1901, January 24, 1902, and June 29 (no year, but during the London period). It is this last one that bears the affectionate signature.

[8] Pedrell's *Por nuestra música* (Barcelona: Juan Bta. Pujol, 1891) was a virtual manifesto of Spanish musical nationalism in opera and exerted considerable influence on Albéniz and his compatriots. Pedrell based his philosophy in part on Wagner, and in part on writings he attributed to the eighteenth-century music theorist Padre Antonio Eximeno (1729–1808).

[9] According to *Concerts Celebrats á Barcelona.* . . .

[10] A program of this concert is in the Bc, M987, v. 2.

[11] See no. 263, Jacinto Torres Mulas and Ester Aguado Sánchez, *Las claves madrileñas de Isaac Albéniz* (Madrid: Ayuntamiento de Madrid, 2008), for a remarkably detailed and visually stunning publication focusing on Albéniz's crucial and transformative years in Madrid, where he first emerged as a serious and important composer. According to this source (p. 43), another baby daughter, Cristina, died January 22, 1888, when she was accidentally suffocated by the wet nurse.

[12] This influence is especially apparent in "Rumores de La Caleta (Malagueña)" from *Recuerdos de viaje* and in "Sevilla (Sevillanas)" from the *Suite española No. 1*. To be sure, Albéniz also evoked songs and dances from regions other than Andalusia, such as the Aragonese jota and Cuban habanera.

[13] This oratorio was probably never completed.

[14] The king died on November 5, 1885, of tuberculosis.

[15] The two letters informing him of these honors are in the Bc, M986 ("D"). The actual notices of appointment are in the same collection, under "V" (Varia). Most other sources assert that he was also made a Knight of the Order of Carlos III, but the author has as yet found no documentation to support this.

[16] Tomás Bretón (1850–1923), composer of the celebrated zarzuela *La verbena de la paloma* (1894), was a close friend of Albéniz. He orchestrated and conducted performances of Albéniz's First Piano Concerto and his *Rapsodia española*. This latter work was also orchestrated by Albéniz, and that version has been reconstructed and published by Jacinto Torres (see no. 8) and recorded by Miguel Baselga (see no. 43).

[17] Thanks to Spanish conductor and musicologist José de Eusebio, an edition and recording of this work are now available from Tritó (see nos. 10 and 37).

[18] The original premiered in Paris at the Nouveautés on October 19, 1882.

[19] Spanish musicologist Borja Mariño published a critical edition of the work (Barcelona: Trito, 2010; see no. 3), and it was presented in a concert version at Madrid's Auditorio Nacional, February 27, 2010, with Silvia Sanz Torres conducting the Orquesta Sinfónica Chamartín (see no. 532).

[20] Published separately, London: Joseph Williams, 1893.

[21] The original work, with a text by H. Wittmann and J. Bauer, premiered on January 4, 1890, in Vienna.

[22] This work and its publication history are treated in some detail in Clark, *Portrait of a Romantic*, 136–75, and Torres, *Catálogo*, 293–94.

[23] He became the Fifth Lord Latymer in 1912. His surnames are usually, but not always, hyphenated. His publications often appear under the name Coutts (pronounced "coots"). He also adopted the pen name "Mountjoy."

[24] See Torres, *Catálogo*, 126–36, for an exploration of the work's genesis and various titles.

[25] Reference to this is made in *Concerts Celebrats á Barcelona*. . . .

[26] See Clark, *Portrait of a Romantic*, 137-38, 216-17, 264, for more on Albéniz's views on religion and politics.

[27] The exact year in which the action takes place is not given in either the score or libretto from the original production. The year 1823 is stated in the French libretto published for the 1905 staging in Brussels. See Walter Aaron Clark, *Enrique Granados: Poet of the Piano* (New York: Oxford University Press, 2006/2011), 110–15, for a fuller discussion of *majismo*, a movement reflected in many of Granados's works as well, starting in this decade. Granados attended the premiere of *San Antonio de la Florida* and was deeply impressed by it.

[28] In a revision by zarzuela composer Pablo Sorozábal. The work was revived many years later in Madrid, but not using Sorozábal's revision. See no. 108, Walter Aaron Clark, "La vida artística de Isaac Albéniz: innovación y renovación," program notes for a production of Isaac Albéniz's zarzuela *San Antonio de la Florida*, Teatro de la Zarzuela (Madrid), April 2003, 9–19.

[29] Angeles Montilla had sung the role of Lolika in the Madrid production of *La sortija* and was credited by some critics with saving the performance from being a complete disaster.

[30] In *La Renaixensa: Diari de Catalunya* (November 8, 1895), 6267 (see no. 583).

[31] In 1964, it was revived and produced in Madrid in a rather drastic revision by Pablo Sorozábal. It was revived again, almost a half century later, for productions in Buenos Aires (2012) and Madrid (2013). These were not revisions. See nos. 623–704 for reviews of this opera throughout its career, no. 5 for an edition by José de Eusebio, and no. 32 for a recording of the work (conducted by Eusebio) that hews closely to the composer's original intentions.

[32] *La voglia* ("The Wish") was actually an idea for a libretto that Neumann hoped Echegaray would consent to write. *Aphrodite* was a popular novel (pub. 1896) depicting courtesan life in ancient Alexandria.

[33] Though most catalogs list these as a group of two songs, based on the Édition Mutuelle publication of 1913, "The Caterpillar" was composed in 1903, 6 years after the "The Gifts of the Gods." Moreover, Albéniz always took his poems for groups of songs from the same collection. "The Gifts of the Gods" comes from Money-Coutts's *Poems* (1895), whereas "The Caterpillar" appeared in *Musa Verticordia* (1895). Both songs were translated into French by Henry Varley for the 1913 edition (entitled "Les Dons des dieux" and "La Chenille").

[34] For more on Barcelona's attraction to Wagner, see Clark, *Granados*, 76–79.

[35] Published Mainz: Schott, n.d. These are located in the library of La Escuela Superior de Canto in Madrid. They bear Albéniz's stamp, dated April 16, 1896. The scores were eventually bequeathed to Enrique Fernández Arbós, who then gave them to the school. I thank Prof. Jacinto Torres for bringing them to my attention.

[36] Conductor José de Eusebio was the driving force behind this revival. See his edition (no. 1), CD (no. 30), and DVD (no. 31). For reviews of its various performances, see nos. 705–13.

[37] See the critical edition of this work by Milton Laufer (no. 20).

[38] The actual contract is located in the Mm, carpeta 4, and is dated June 18, 1901. For more on this episode, see Clark, *Granados*, 80.

[39] Now entitled *L'Hermitage fleuri*, in a French translation by Lucien Solvay and Robert Sand. In marked contrast to the reception accorded to it in Spain, the Brussels critics had nothing but praise for the zarzuela's elegance, humor, and popular melody.

[41] From the program notes of a concert at the Liceu commemorating the centenary (Barcelona: Juan A. Pamias, 1960).

[42] In Víctor Ruiz Albéniz, *Isaac Albéniz* (Madrid: Comisaria General de Música, 1948), 102.

2

Part A: Catalog of Works

The following compilation is greatly indebted to the work of Jacinto Torres Mulas, in particular, his *Catálogo sistemático descriptivo de las obras musicales de Isaac Albéniz* (see no. 241). As is increasingly the practice among Albéniz scholars, therefore, this catalog makes use of Torres numbers (T.), that is, the works are organized and numbered in accordance with Torres's *Catálogo*. Readers seeking more detailed information are encouraged to consult that source. Unfortunately, Albéniz and his publishers carelessly assigned opus numbers, and these have little or no validity; hence, they only appear in brackets here, after the title.

The works are simply given first by medium and then in chronological order by composition date (as best as can be determined). Where the dates are identical, the works are listed alphabetically (unless the sequence of their composition in that year is known). This catalog includes published works, manuscripts (if extant), and works that are now lost. Any alternate titles, often from later editions, appear in brackets after the main title. Entries further include date of composition, premiere, and first publication, and they conclude with the location of any manuscripts (in brackets at the end of the entry).

STAGE

1.   *Cuanto más viejo.* Zarzuela in 1 act with a libretto by Mariano Zapino Garibay. Composed in or before 1882 and premiered Bilbao, Teatro de Bilbao, February 15, 1882. One performance only. Lost.

2. *Catalanes de gracia.* Zarzuela in 1 act with a libretto by Leopoldo Palomino de Guzmán. Composed 1882 and premiered Madrid, Teatro Salón Eslava, March 28, 1882. Ran until April 9, 1882. Lost.

3. *El canto de salvación.* Author unknown. Composed before 1886. Zarzuela in 2 acts. Lost.

4. *Incognita.* Two numbers added by Albéniz to the musical comedy originally titled *Le Coeur et la main* by Alexandre Charles Lecocq. The first is the finale to Act II, "Oh! Horror! Horror!" The second is a quartet, possibly from Act III, "Since love will lend us wings to fly." English song texts by Harry Greenbank. Composed 1892 and premiered London, Lyric Theatre, October 6, 1892. Ran until January 13, 1893, for a total of 103 performances. Vocal score for the finale published London: Hopwood & Crew, 1892. Only an ms. for the quartet survives, mixed in with the mss. for *The Magic Opal.* [Bc, sign. M985]

5. *The Magic Opal.* Lyric comedy in two acts with a libretto by Arthur Law. Composed in 1892 and premiered in London, Lyric Theatre, January 19, 1893; ran until March 4, 1893, for a total of 44 performances. Performed by touring company in other cities from February 16 to May 22, 1893. Vocal score and libretto published in London, Joseph Williams, 1893. "Star of My Life. Serenade" does not appear in the vocal score but was published separately by Williams in that same year. The Overture is identical to the orchestral work "En la aldea" from *Escenas sinfónicas* (T. 19A); the Intermezzo is identical to the *Serenata árabe* (T. 60); the Ballet music is identical to *Rapsodia cubana* (T. 46). Reconstructed and revived by Borja Mariño in a concert version, Madrid, Auditorio Nacional, February 27, 2010 [Bc, sign. M974, 975, 985; Ah]. Revised and retitled as *The Magic Ring* and premiered in London, Prince of Wales's Theatre, April 11, 1893; ran until May 19, 1893, for a total of 37 performances. Translated into Spanish by Eusebio Sierra and premiered in Madrid, Teatro de la Zarzuela, November 23, 1894, under the title *La sortija* [Mm, Caixa BM10]. Blended edition by Borja Mariño of all three works published in Barcelona, Tritó, 2011.

6. *Poor Jonathan* (original *Der arme Jonathan* by Karl Millöcker, 1890). Operetta in 2 acts to texts by H. Wittmann, J. Bauer, and Harry Greenbank. Albéniz contributed 16 additional numbers, including an Intermezzo, Ballet, Duet, and Vandergold's Song. Composed 1893 and premiered London, Prince of Wales's Theatre, June 19, 1893. Ran until June 30, 1893, for a total of 14 performances. Only the libretto was published, London: S.J. Garraway, 189? [Bc, sign. M975, M985]

7. *San Antonio de la Florida.* Zarzuela in one act with a libretto by Eusebio Sierra. Composed in 1894 and premiered in Madrid, Teatro de Apolo, October 26, 1894. Ran until November 11, 1894, for 15 performances; briefly revived December 17–21, 1894, for 5 more performances. Vocal score published in Barcelona, Juan Bautista Pujol y Cía., 1894 or 1895. Libretto published in Madrid, R. Velasco, 1894; Barcelona, Imprenta Gutenberg, 1895(?). Revised as a zarzuela

in two acts, translated into French by Lucien Solvay and Robert Sand, and produced in Brussels, Théâtre Royale de la Monnaie, January 3, 1905, under the title *L'Ermitage fleuri*; ran until February 1, 1905, for 6 performances. Libretto published in Brussels, Th. Lombaerts, 1904. No. 7 published separately as *Passacaille* for solo piano, Brussels, Breitkopf und Härtel, 1905. Reorchestrated by Pablo Sorozábal and produced in Madrid, Teatro Fuencarral, November 18, 1954. Original version reconstructed by José de Eusebio and produced in Madrid, Teatro de la Zarzuela, April 4, 2003 [Mm, sign. L.A.; Ah; Bc, sign. M975 and 985; Oc, Res. Ms./CF-III; Museo Nacional de la Música (Havana), Fondos del Teatro Tacón; Archives de la Ville de Bruxelles].

8.   *Henry Clifford.* Opera in 3 acts with a libretto by Francis Burdett Money-Coutts ("Mountjoy"). Composed 1893–95 and premiered Barcelona, Gran Teatre del Liceu, May 8, 1895, in Italian translation by Giuseppe Maria Arteaga Pereira under title *Enrico Clifford.* Ran until May 10, 1895, for a total of 2 performances. Vocal score published Barcelona: Juan Bautista Pujol y Cía., 1895. Italian libretto published Barcelona: Imprenta Gutenberg, 1895. [Bc, sign. M975, 978, 979; Mm, Lligall 4, 6; Oc, Res. Ms./CF-III]

9.   *Pepita Jiménez.* Lyric comedy in 2 acts with a libretto by Francis Burdett Money-Coutts (after the 1874 novel by Juan Valera). First version as an opera in 1 act composed 1895 and premiered Barcelona, Gran Teatre del Liceu, January 5, 1896, in Italian translation by Angelo Bignotti. Ran for a total of 7 performances. Second version as an opera in 2 acts composed 1896. Vocal and full scores published Leipzig: Breitkopf und Härtel, 1896 (in German, Italian, French, and German). Produced Prague, Neues Deutsches Landestheater, June 22, 1897, in German translation by Oskar Berggruen. Ran for a total of 3 performances. Reorchestration of 1899–1904 published Leipzig: Breitkopf und Härtel, 1904. Translated into French by Maurice Kufferath and produced Brussels, Théâtre Royal de la Monnaie, January 3, 1905. Ran for a total of 3 performances. Libretto published Leipzig: Breitkopf und Härtel, 1905. Produced Paris, Opéra-Comique, June 18, 1923, in new French translation by Joseph de Marliave. Vocal score published Paris: Max Eschig, 1923 (in French translation by Marliave and Italian translation by Carlo M. A. Galateri). Produced Barcelona, Gran Teatre del Liceu, January 14, 1926, in the Italian translation by Galateri. Translated into Spanish and revised as an opera in 3 acts by Pablo Sorozábal and premiered Madrid, Teatro de la Zarzuela, June 6, 1964. Orchestral score revised by Josep Pons and published Madrid: ICCMU, 1996 (not produced but recorded; see nos. 2 and 33). 1904 version edited by José de Eusebio and published Barcelona: Tritó, 2009 (not produced but recorded; see nos. 4 and 32). New staging Madrid, Teatros del Canal, May 19, 2013. [Bc, sign. M981, M982; Mm, sign. L.A., Lligall 6; Archivo Manuel de Falla in Granada; Se; copies of proofs of 1904 reorchestration with corrections in Albéniz's own hand were at the firm of Max Eschig in Paris]

10.   *Mar i cel (Mar y cielo).* Opera based on a play by Àngel Guimerà. Composed 1895–97. Incomplete. [Bc, sign. M984]

11. *La Sérénade.* Lyric drama with a libretto by an unknown author. Begun 1899. Incomplete. [Bc, sign. M984; Mm, Lligall 6]

12. *King Arthur.* Operatic trilogy with librettos by Francis Burdett Money-Coutts. Librettos published London: John Lane, 1897.

   A. *Merlin.* Opera in 3 acts. Composed 1898–1902 and performed in a concert version at the home of Emile Tassel in Brussels, February 13, 1905 (Prelude to Act I premiered Barcelona, 1898). Vocal score in English and French (translation by Maurice Kufferath) published Paris: Édition Mutuelle, 1906. French libretto published Brussels, 1905, for the concert version. Premiered Barcelona, Gran Teatre del Liceu, December 18, 1950, in a Spanish translation by Manuel Conde. English original performed in a concert version revived and conducted by José de Eusebio, Madrid, Auditorio Nacional, June 20, 1998; it was fully staged and conducted by Eusebio in Madrid, Teatro Real, May 23, 2003. [Bc, sign. M977; Mm, L.A., Lligall 5, 7, Fons Isaac Albéniz, Caixa BM10; Ah; BBC Music Library, Misc. 1526]
   B. *Launcelot.* Opera in 3 acts. Begun 1902. Incomplete. [Bc, sign. M983; Mm, L.A., Lligall 6]
   C. *Guenevere.* Opera in 4 acts. Never begun.

13. *La real hembra.* Zarzuela in 3 acts with a libretto by Cristóbal de Castro. Begun 1902. Incomplete. [Bc, sign. M984]

14. *La morena.* Lyric drama in 4 acts with a libretto by Alfred Mortier. Begun 1905. Incomplete. [Bc, sign. M984]

15. *The Song of Songs.* Incidental music to a text by Francis Burdett Money-Coutts. Begun 1905. Incomplete. [Mm, Fons Albéniz]

ORCHESTRA

16. *Rapsodia española* for piano and orchestra. Composed 1886. Premiered Madrid, Salón Romero, March 21, 1887. Two-piano arrangement published Madrid: Antonio Romero, 1887. Original orchestral version (reconstructed by Jacinto Torres) published Madrid: Instituto de Bibliografía Musical, 1997. [Mm, Fons Isaac Albéniz, Marmario, Lligall 8; score and parts of orchestration probably by Tomás Bretón located in the library of the Conservatorio Profesional de Música "Francisco Escudero," sign. R-Orq-0008]

17. Concerto No. 1 for piano and orchestra ("Concierto fantástico") [Op. 78]. Composed 1886–87. Premiered Madrid, Salón Romero, March 21, 1887. Two-piano arrangement published Madrid: Antonio Romero, 1887. Orchestral version published Madrid: Unión Musical Española, 1975.

18. *Suite característica.* Orchestrated ca. 1888. Lost. (Presumably arrangements of the solo-piano versions from the period 1881–83.) See also T. 29.

    A   "Scherzo" (same as "Scherzo" from Piano Sonata No. 1, T. 57).

    B. "En la Alhambra" (possibly the same as T. 72D; also known as "Serenata árabe" and "Serenata morisca").

    C. "Rapsodia cubana" (same as T. 46).

19.   *Escenas sinfónicas catalanas* [also known as *Scènes symphoniques catalanes, Scènes villageoises catalanes*]. Composed 1888–89. Premiered Madrid, Teatro de la Comedia, March 7, 1889. [Mm, Lligall 5]

    A. "En la aldea" (entitled "Fête villageoise catalane" in the ms. version; identical to the Overture to *The Magic Opal*, T. 5). Published separately Madrid: Unión Musical Española, 1973, as *La fiesta de aldea*.

    B. "Idilio" [also "Idylle"].

    C. "Serenata" [also "Sérénade"].

    D. "Finale: Baile campestre" [also "Bal Champêtre"].

20.   *L'Automne (Valse)*. Orchestrated ca. 1889. (Arrangement of the piano work of the same title, T. 96) [Oc, sign. G/16]

21.   Concerto No. 2 for piano and orchestra. Begun 1892. Incomplete. [Bc, sign. M985]

22.   *La Alhambra*. Begun 1896. Nos. 1 and 3 incomplete, others titles only. [Bc, sign. M984]

    A. "La vega." Composed 1897 (based on piano solo *La vega*, T. 102).

    B. "Lindaraja."

    C. "Generalife." Composed February 18, 1897 (same as "Prélude" from *Espagne. Souvenirs*, T. 103A).

    D. "Zambra."

    E. "Alarme!"

23.   *Petite Suite d'Orchestre*. Only one movement, composed 1898. [Oc, G/16]

    A. "Sérénade Lorraine."

24.   *Catalonia. Suite populaire pour orchestre en trois parties*. Composed 1899. Only first number completed (which bears the title of the suite, initially entitled *Rapsodia Almogávar*). Premiered at a concert of the Société Nationale de Musique, Paris, Nouveau-Théâtre, May 23, 1899.

    A. *Catalonia*, no. 1. Published Paris: A. Durand & Fils, Editeurs, 1899. [Bc, sign. M984; Mm, Fons Albéniz, Lligall 10]

    B. *Catalonia*, no. 2. Incomplete. [Bc, sign. M984]

25.   *Aventura de los molinos*. Composed ca. 1900. Incomplete. [Bc, sign. M984]

26.   *Iberia* (see T. 105). Orchestrated 1907. First number lost.

    A. "Évocation."

    B. "El puerto." [Bc, sign. M980]

CHAMBER ENSEMBLE

27.   *Serenata* for violin and piano. Composed ca. 1882. Lost.

28.   Trio No. 1 in F for piano, violin, and cello. Composed ca. 1883. Lost.

29.   Concert Suite for Sextet. Composed 1883. Lost (probably similar to the later *Suite característica*, T. 18).

    A. "Scherzo."
    B. "Serenata morisca."
    C. "Capricho cubano."

30.   *Berceuse* for piano, violin, and cello. Composed 1890. Published London: Stanley Lucas, Weber & Co., c. 1892. (Arrangement of "Berceuse" from *Rêves*, T. 99).

31.   *Poèmes d'amour* (also called *Légendes bibliques*). Incidental music for a recitation of poems by Armand Silvestre, translated from the original French into English by Justin Huntly McCarthy. Consists of 13 numbers (31A–L; 31B can be reutilized as nos. 9 and 13) for reciter and chamber ensemble of flute, oboe, F trumpet, string quartet, harmonium, and piano. Composed June 1892. Premiered Barnes (London), Lyric Club, June 20, 1892. Edited by José de Eusebio and published Barcelona: Tritó, 2005. [Bc, sign. M985; Mm, Fons Isaac Albéniz, Lligall 11]

SOLO VOICE/CHORUS

32.   *Romanzas.* Composed before 1886. Lost.

    A. *Un ramo de violetas.* Spanish text by Diego V. Tejera. Composed 1878.
    B. *Cuatro romanzas para mezzo-soprano.* French texts. Composed before 1886.
    C. *Tres romanzas catalanas.* Catalan texts. Composed before 1886.

33.   *Rimas de Bécquer* for voice and piano. Texts by Gustavo Adolfo Bécquer. Each song has two versions, for singing or reciting (c indicates singing; r indicates recitation). Composed before 1886. Published Madrid: Benito Zozaya, 1892.

    A(c). "Besa el aura."
    A(r). "Besa el aura."
    B(c). "Del salón en el ángulo oscuro."
    B(r). "Del salón en el ángulo oscuro."
    C(c). "Me ha herido recatándose en la sombra."
    C(r). "Me ha herido recatándose en la sombra."
    D(c). "Cuando sobre el pecho inclinas."
    D(r). "Cuando sobre el pecho inclinas."
    E(c). "¿De dónde vengo?"
    E(r). "¿De dónde vengo?"

34.   *El Cristo.* Oratorio for chorus and orchestra. Composed before 1886. Lost.

35.   *Salmo VI: del oficio de difuntos.* SATB chorus. Composed December 1885. Edited by Jacinto Torres and published Madrid: Instituto de Bibliografía Musical, 1994. [Rcsm]

36.   *Seis baladas* for voice and piano. Italian texts by the Marquesa de Bolaños. Composed ca. 1888. Published Madrid: Antonio Romero, 1888.

   A.   "Barcarola."
   B.   "La lontananza."
   C.   "Una rosa in dono."
   D.   "Il tuo sguardo."
   E.   "Morirò!"
   F.   "T'ho riveduta in sogno."

37.   *Chanson de Barberine* for voice and piano. Text by Alfred de Musset. Composed 1889. Published Madrid: Unión Musical Española, 1947. [Ah]

38.   *Lo Llacsó.* Symphonic poem for orchestra, chorus, soloists. Catalan text by Apel.les Mestres. Begun 1896. Incomplete. [Bc, sign. M984]

39.   *To Nellie: Six Songs* for voice and piano. English texts by Francis Burdett Money-Coutts (from his collection *Poems* published London: John Lane, 1896). Composed 1896. Published Paris: Heugel & Cie. (Au Ménestrel), 1896. [Ah]

   A.   "Home."
   B.   "Counsel."
   C.   "May-Day Song."
   D.   "To Nellie."
   E.   "A Song of Consolation."
   F.   "A Song (Love Comes to All)."

40.   *Six Songs* for voice and piano. English texts by Francis Burdett Money-Coutts. Composed 1896–1903. Published Madrid: Instituto de Bibliografía Musical, 1997.

   A.   "Art Thou Gone for Ever, Elaine?" Composed 1896. Edited by Anton Cardó and Jacinto Torres and published Barcelona: Tritó, 1998. [Ah]
   B.   "Will You Be Mine?" Edited by Jacinto Torres and published Madrid: Instituto de Bibliografía Musical, 1996. [Bc, sign. Res. Ms./CF-III]
   C.   "Separated!" Edited by Anton Cardó and Jacinto Torres and published Barcelona: Tritó, 1998. [Bc, Res. Ms./CF-III]
   D.   "A Song (Laugh at Loving As You May)." Composed 1896. Edited by Anton Cardó and Jacinto Torres and published Barcelona: Tritó, 1998. [Ah]
   E.   "The Caterpillar." Composed 1903. Published as *Two Songs* in Paris: Édition Mutuelle, 1913 (with "The Gifts of the Gods," in English and French, translated by Henry Varley, entitled "La Chenille" and "Les Dons des dieux").

F. "The Gifts of the Gods." Composed 1897. Published as *Two Songs* in Paris: Édition Mutuelle, 1913 (with "The Caterpillar," in English and French, translated by Henry Varley, entitled "Les Dons des dieux" and "La Chenille").

41. *Deux Morceaux de prose de Pierre Loti*. French texts by Pierre Loti. Composed ca. 1897. Published San Sebastián: A. Díaz y Cía., 1897.

A. "Crépuscule."
B. "Tristesse."

42. *Il en est de l'amour . . .* for voice and piano. French text by Charles Albert Costa de Beauregard. Composed 1897. Published Paris: E. Baudoux & Cie., 1897.

43. *Conseil tenu par les rats* for voice and piano. French text by Jean de la Fontaine. Begun ca. 1894/99. Incomplete. Edited by Anton Cardó and Jacinto Torres and published Barcelona: Tritó, 1998. [Bc, sign. M984]

44. *Quatre Mélodies*. English texts by Francis Burdett Money-Coutts (taken from his *Musa Verticordia* published London: John Lane, 1906). Composed 1908. Published Paris: Rouart, Lerolle et Cie., 1909 (in English and French, translated by M.D. Calvocoressi). [Ah]

A. "In Sickness and Health" ("Quand je te vois souffrir").
B. "Paradise Regained" ("Le Paradis retrouvé").
C. "The Retreat" ("Le Refuge").
D. "Amor summa injuria."

PIANO

45. *Marcha militar*. Composed 1869. Published Madrid: Calcografía de B. Eslava, 1869.

46. *Rapsodia cubana* [op. 66]. Composed before or in early 1881. Premiered Havana, Cuba, January 16, 1881. Published Madrid: Antonio Romero, 1886.

47A–F. *Seis pequeños valses* [op. 7 or 25]. Composed 1882. Published Barcelona: R. Guardia, 1884.

48. *Pavana-capricho* [*Pavane espagnole*] [op. 12]. Composed 1882. Published Barcelona: Valentín de Haas, 1884.

49. *Dos grandes estudios de concierto*. Composed 1882–83. Lost (possibly the same as *Gran estudio de concierto*, T. 51, and *Deseo*, T. 53).

50. *Estudio impromptu* [op. 16, 30, or 56]. Composed 1882–83. Published Madrid: Antonio Romero, 1886.

51. *Gran estudio de concierto* [op. 18]. Composed ca. 1882–83. Lost or unidentified.

52. *Fantasia sobre motivos de la jota*. Composed 1883. Lost (possibly an improvisation).

53. *Estudio de concierto* [*Deseo*] [op. 21]. Composed 1883. Published Madrid: Antonio Romero, 1886.

54. *Marcha nupcial.* Composed ca. 1883. Lost.

55. *Barcarola* [*Barcarolle catalane*] [op. 16 or 23]. Composed in or before 1884. Published Barcelona: Valentín de Haas, 1884.

56. *Dos caprichos* [*Dos caprichos andaluces*]. Composed ca. 1883. Lost (possibly "Andalusian caprichos" from *Suite espagnole no. 1*, "Sevilla," or "Staccato (Capricho)" from *Doce piezas características*, T. 86).

57. Sonata No. 1 [op. 28 or 37]. Composed ca. 1884. Published Barcelona: R. Guardia, 1884.

    A. Scherzo.

58. Tres mazurkas. Composed ca. 1884–85. Lost.

59. *Suite morisca* (comprised of "Marcha de la caravana," "La noche," "Danza de las esclavas," "Zambra"). Composed ca. 1884–85. Lost or unidentified (possibly somehow related to "Serenata morisca" from the *Suite de concierto*, T. 29B, and/ or the *Zambra granadina*, T. 97).

60. *Serenata árabe.* Composed ca. 1884–85. Published Madrid: Antonio Romero, 1886. (Identical to no. 13 from *The Magic Opal*, T. 5.)

61. *Suite espagnole no. 1* (*Suite española no. 1*) [op. 20, 22, or 47]. Composed between 1883 and 1889. The original suite consisted of all eight titles but only four scores, for T. 61A–C, H (61C composed ca. 1883; 61A–B, H composed in 1885 or early 1886). These were premiered Madrid, Salón Romero, January 24, 1886. They were published separately in Madrid by Benito Zozaya (T. 61A–C in 1886, 61H in 1901). The other numbers were later added to the suite by publishers and had originally appeared under the titles in parentheses.

    A. "Granada (Serenata)." Composed 1885 or early 1886. Published Madrid: B. Zozaya, 1886.
    B. "Cataluña (Curranda)." Composed 1886. Published Madrid: B. Zozaya, 1886. [Rcsm, Biblioteca, sign. B.T. Autogr.; facsimile available in no. 263, Torres/Aguado Sánchez, *Las claves madrileñas de Isaac Albéniz*]
    C. "Sevilla (Sevillanas)." Composed ca. 1883. Published Madrid: B. Zozaya, 1886.
    D. "Cádiz (subtitled variously Saeta, Canción, or Serenata)" (same as *Serenata española*, T. 98). Composed ca. 1889. Published Madrid: B. Zozaya, 1901.
    E. "Asturias (Leyenda)" (same as Prélude from *Chants d'Espagne*, T. 101A). Composed 1891. Published Madrid: B. Zozaya, 1901.
    F. "Aragón" (same as "Jota aragonesa" from *Deux Morceaux caractéristiques*, T. 94A). Composed ca. 1889. Published Madrid: B. Zozaya, 1901.
    G. "Castilla (Seguidillas)" (same as "Seguidillas" from *Chants d'Espagne*, T. 101E). Composed ca. 1894. Published Madrid: B. Zozaya, 1901.

    H. "Cuba (Capricho or Nocturno)." Composed 1886. Published Madrid: B. Zozaya, 1886. [Rcsm, Biblioteca, sign. B.T. Autogr.; facsimile available in no. 263, Torres/Aguado Sánchez, *Las claves madrileñas de Isaac Albéniz*]

62.   *Suite ancienne no. 1* [op. 54]. Composed 1885. Premiered Madrid, Círculo de la Unión Mercantil e Industrial, February 20, 1886. Published Madrid: Antonio Romero, 1886.

    A. "Gavota."
    B. "Minuetto"

63.   *Diva sin par (Mazurka-capricho)*. Composed 1886. Published Madrid: Antonio Romero, 1886 (under the pseudonym Príncipe Weisse Vogel).

64.   *Balbina valverde (Polka brillante)*. Composed 1886. Published Madrid: Antonio Romero, 1886 (under the pseudonym Príncipe Weisse Vogel).

65.   Sonata No. 2 [op. 60]. Composed ca. 1886. Lost.

66.   *Suite ancienne no. 2* [op. 62 or 64]. Composed 1886. Premiered Madrid, Salón Romero, March 20, 1887. Published Madrid: Antonio Romero, 1886.

    A. "Sarabande."
    B. "Chacone."

67A–G. *Siete estudios en los tonos naturales mayores* [op. 65]. Composed 1886. Published Madrid: Antonio Romero, 1886.

68.   *Seis mazurkas de salón* [op. 66]. Composed 1886. 68B,F premiered Madrid, Salón Romero, March 21, 1887. Published Madrid: Antonio Romero, 1886. *Two Mazurkas*, op. 140, published London: Stanley Lucas, Weber & Co., 1890, identical to T. 68B,E.

    A. "Isabel."
    B. "Casilda."
    C. "Aurora."
    D. "Sofia."
    E. "Christa."
    F. "María."

69.   Sonata No. 3 [op. 68]. Three movements, marked "Allegretto," "Andante," and "Allegro assai," respectively. Composed 1886. Premiered Madrid, Salón Romero, March 21, 1887. Published Madrid: Antonio Romero, 1886.

70.   *Angustia: Romanza sin palabras* [*Angoisse*]. Composed ca. 1886. Published Madrid: Antonio Romero, 1886.

71.   *Rapsodia española* for piano and orchestra. Five movements entitled "Introducción," "Petenera de Mariani," "Jota original," "Malagueña de Juan Breva," and "Estudiantina," respectively. Composed 1886. Premiered Madrid, Salón Romero, March 21, 1887. Two-piano arrangement published Madrid:

Antonio Romero, 1887. Original orchestral version (reconstructed by Jacinto Torres) published Madrid: Instituto de Bibliografía Musical, 1997. Solo-piano version published Madrid: Antonio Romero, 1887. [Mm, Fons Isaac Albéniz, Marmario, Lligall 8]

72. *Recuerdos de viaje* [op. 57, 58, 67, 71]. Composed 1886–87. Published Madrid: Antonio Romero, 1886–87.

   A. "En el mar (Barcarola)" [op. 57 or 58] (same as *On the Water (Barcarole)*, published London: Stanley Lucas, Weber & Co., 1891). Composed 1886. Premiered Madrid, Salón Romero, March 21, 1887. Published Madrid: Antonio Romero, 1886.
   B. "Leyenda (Barcarola)" [op. 67]. Composed 1886. Published Madrid: Antonio Romero, 1887.
   C. "Alborada" [op. 71]. Composed 1886. Published Madrid: Antonio Romero, 1886.
   D. "En la Alhambra" [*En la Alhambra (Capricho)*]. Composed 1886. Published Madrid: Antonio Romero, 1887.
   E. "Puerta de tierra (Bolero)" (same as *Andalucía (Bolero)*, published London: Joseph Williams, 1891). Composed 1887. Published Madrid: Antonio Romero, 1887.
   F. "Rumores de La Caleta (Malagueña)." Composed 1887. Published Madrid: Antonio Romero, 1887.
   G. "En la playa." Composed 1887. Published Madrid: Antonio Romero, 1887.

73. Menuet (G Minor). Composed ca. 1886. Published Paris: Vve. E. Girod, 1894.

74. Minuetto No. 3. Composed ca. 1886. Published Madrid: Antonio Romero, 1886.

75. Sonata No. 4 [op. 72]. Four movements, labeled "Allegro," "Scherzino (Allegro)," "Minuetto (Andantino)" (same as *Celebre Minuet*, published London: Chappell & Co., 1892), "Rondó (Allegro)." Composed 1886. Premiered Madrid, Salón Romero, March 21, 1887. Published Madrid: Antonio Romero, 1887.

76. *Suite ancienne no. 3.* Composed 1886. Published Madrid: Antonio Romero, 1887.

   A. "Minuetto."
   B. "Gavota."

77. Concerto No. 1 for piano and orchestra in A Minor ("Concierto fantástico") [Op. 78]. Composed 1886–87. Premiered March 21, 1887, Madrid, Salón Romero. Two-piano arrangement published Madrid: Antonio Romero, 1887. Orchestral version published Madrid: Unión Musical Española, 1975.

78A–F. *Seis danzas españolas.* Composed 1887. Published Madrid: Antonio Romero, 1887.

79. *Mallorca (Barcarolle, Barcarole,* or *Barcarola)* [op. 202]. Composed ca. 1887. Published London: Stanley Lucas, Weber & Co., 1891.

80.   *Recuerdos (Mazurka)* [op. 80]. Composed 1887. Published Barcelona: Juan Ayné, 1887.

81.   *Mazurka de salón* [op. 81]. Composed in or before 1887. Published Barcelona: Juan Ayné, 1887.

82.   *Pavana fácil para manos pequeñas* [op. 83]. Composed 1887. Published Madrid: Antonio Romero, 1887.

83.   *Cotillón. Album de danzas de salón* [*Cotillon valse*]. Only one number. Composed 1887. Published Madrid: Antonio Romero, 1887.

      A.   "Champagne (Carte Blanche) Wals."

84.   *Arbola [Az]pian* [*Zortzico*]. Composed in or before 1891. Published Paris: Édition Mutuelle, c. 1911.

85.   Sonata No. 5 [op. 82]. Contains four movements, labeled "Allegro no troppo," "Minuetto del gallo (Allegro assai)," "Reverie (Andante)," "Allegro." Composed 1888. Published Madrid: Antonio Romero, 1888.

86.   *Doce piezas características* [op. 92]. Composed ca. 1888. Published Madrid: Antonio Romero, ca. 1888 (nos. 1–11) and 1889 (no. 12).

      A.   "Gavotte."
      B.   "Minuetto a Silvia."
      C.   "Barcarola (Ciel sans nuages)."
      D.   "Plegaria."
      E.   "Conchita (Polka)."
      F.   "Pilar (Wals)."
      G.   "Zambra."
      H.   "Pavana."
      I.   "Polonesa."
      J.   "Mazurka."
      K.   "Staccato (Capricho)."
      L.   "Torre Bermeja (Serenata)."

87.   *Dos mazurkas de salón* [op. 95/96]. Composed 1888. Published Madrid: Benito Zozaya, 1892.

      A.   "Amalia."
      B.   "Ricordatti."

88.   Sonata No. 6. Composed in or before 1888(?). Lost.

89.   Sonata No. 7 [op. 111]. One movement only. Composed ca. 1888(?). Published Barcelona: Torres y Seguí, 1888.

      A.   Minuetto.

90. *Seconde Suite espagnole.* Composed 1889. Published Madrid: Antonio Romero, 1889.

   A. "Zaragoza (Caprice)."
   B. "Sevilla."

91. *Gitana Dance.* Lost (possibly the same as "Zambra" from *Doce piezas características,* T. 86G).

92. *Old Spanish Dance.* Lost (possibly "Sarabande" from the *Suite ancienne no. 2,* T. 66A).

93. *Cádiz-gaditana.* Composed ca. 1885. London: Carolo Ducci & Co. 1889.

94. *Deux Morceaux caractéristiques (Spanish National Songs)* [*Deux Danses espagnoles,* published Paris: Vve. E. Girod, 1889 or 1890] [op. 164]. Composed ca. 1889. Published London: Stanley Lucas, Weber & Co., 1889.

   A. "Jota aragonesa" (same as "Aragón" from *Suite espagnole no. 1,* T. 61F).
   B. "Tango."

95. *España: Six Album Leaves* [*Espagne: Six Feuilles d'album; España: Seis hojas de álbum*] [op. 165]. Composed 1890. Premiered London, Steinway Hall, June 7, 1890. Published London: Pitt & Hatzfeld, 1890.

   A. "Prélude."
   B. "Tango."
   C. "Malagueña."
   D. "Serenata."
   E. "Capricho catalán."
   F. "Zortzico."

96. *L'Automne (Valse)* [op. 170]. Composed ca. 1889. Published Barcelona: Juan Bautista Pujol y Cía., 1890.

97. *Zambra granadina (Danse orientale)* [op. 181, no. 2]. Composed in or before 1891. Published London: Carlo Ducci & Co., 1889.

98. *Sérénade espagnole* [*Celebre Sérénade espagnole*] [op. 181, no. 3]. Composed ca. 1889. Published Barcelona: Juan Bautista Pujol y Cía., 1890 (same as "Cádiz" from the *Suite espagnole no. 1,* T. 61D). [Oc, sign. G/16, H/4]

99. *Rêves* [*Sueños; Dreams*] [op. 210]. Composed 1890. Published London: Stanley Lucas, Weber & Co., ca. 1891; Paris: Vve. E. Girod, 1891.

   A. "Berceuse."
   B. "Scherzino."
   C. "Chant d'amour." Premiered London, January 31, 1891.

100. *Album of Miniatures* [*Les Saisons*] [op. 1]. Composed 1890–91. Published London: Chappell & Co., 1892; Paris: Vve. E. Girod, 1893.

A. "Spring" ["Le Printemps"].
B. "Summer" ["L'Eté"].
C. "Autumn" ["L'Automne"].
D. "Winter" ["L'Hiver"].

101. *Chants d'Espagne* [*Cantos de España*; *Airs of Spain*]. Composed 1891 (101A–C) and ca. 1894 (101D–E). Published Barcelona: Juan Bautista Pujol y Cía, 1892 (101A–C) and 1897 (101D–E).

A. "Prélude" (same as "Asturias (Leyenda)" from *Suite espagnole no. 1*, T. 61E).
B. "Orientale."
C. "Sous le palmier (Danse espagnole)" ["Bajo la palmera"].
D. "Córdoba."
E. "Seguidillas" (same as "Castilla (Seguidillas)" from *Suite espagnole no. 1*, T. 61G).

102. *The Alhambra: Suite pour le piano.* Originally intended to consist of 6 movements: "La vega," "Lindaraja," "Generalife," "Zambra," "¡Alarme!," and [Untitled]. Only the first movement was completed and published. Composed 1896–97. Published San Sebastián: A. Díaz y Cía., 1897. Premiered by José Vianna da Motta, Paris, Société Nationale de Musique, January 21, 1899. [Bc, sign. M980]

A. "La vega" (same as the ms. in the Mm, sign. 02.609, entitled *Fantasie espagnole pour le piano* (1898)).
B. "Generalife" (16 measures only).

103. *Espagne (Souvenirs).* Composed ca. 1897. Published Barcelona: Universo Musical, ca. 1899.

A. "Prélude."
B. "Asturies."

104. *Yvonne en visite!* Composed ca. 1905. Published Paris: Édition Mutuelle.

A. "La Révérence!"
B. "Joyeuse Rencontre, et quelques pénibles événements!!"

105. *Iberia: 12 nouvelles "impressions" en quatre cahiers.* Composed 1905–08. Published Paris: Édition Mutuelle, 1906–08.

1e Cahier. Composed 1905. Premiered by Blanche Selva, Paris, Salle Pleyel, May 9, 1906. Published Paris: Édition Mutuelle, 1906. (Facsimile of entire manuscript available in Torres/González, eds., *Isaac Albéniz's* Iberia: *Facsimile, Urtext, and Performing Editions*, vol. 1. See nos. 18 and 264.)

A. "Evocación" ["Prélude"]. [Bc, sign. M980]
B. "El puerto" ["Cadix"]. [Library of Congress, ML3i.H4a Case]
C. "Fête-Dieu à Séville" ["El Corpus en Sevilla"]. [Oc, Res. Ms./CF-III]

2e Cahier. Composed 1906. Premiered by Blanche Selva, St. Jean-de-Luz, France, September 11, 1907. Published Paris: Édition Mutuelle, 1907.

    D.   "Rondeña." [Oc, Res. Ms./CF-III]
    E.   "Almería." [Oc, Res. Ms./CF-III]
    F.   "Triana." [Oc, Res. Ms./CF-III]

3e Cahier. Composed 1906. Premiered by Blanche Selva, Paris, Salon of Mme. Armand de Polignac, January 2, 1908. Published Paris: Édition Mutuelle, 1907.

    G.   "El Albaicín." [Bc, sign. M980]
    H.   "El polo." [Oc, Res. Ms./CF-III]
    I.   "Lavapiés." [Mm, 02/FJM-1982; facsimile also available in no. 263, Torres/ Aguado Sánchez, *Las claves madrileñas de Isaac Albéniz*]

4e Cahier. Composed 1907–08. Premiered by Blanche Selva, Paris, Société Nationale de Musique, Salon d'Automne, February 9, 1909. Published Paris: Édition Mutuelle, 1908.

    J.   "Málaga." [Bc, sign. M980]
    K.   "Jerez." [Bc, sign. M980]
    L.   "Eritaña" ["Macarena"]. [Bc, sign. M980]

106.   *Navarra.* Composed 1908. Left unfinished upon the composer's death in 1909 and completed by Déodat de Séverac. Published Paris: Édition Mutuelle, 1912. [Bc, sign. M980]

107.   *Azulejos.* Composed 1909. Left unfinished upon the composer's death in that year and completed by Enrique Granados. Published Paris: Édition Mutuelle, 1911.

    A.   "Prélude." [Mm, Fons Albéniz]

MISCELLANEOUS

108.   Sonata for violin and piano. Composed 1877. Lost.

109.   Basse non chiffré. Figured-bass realization. Composed 1878. [Madrid, Archivo del Palacio Real]

110.   *Nellie.* Composed 1879. Unpublished.

111.   *Mefistófeles.* Piano arrangement of portion of Arrigo Boito's opera. Ca. 1885. Lost.

112.   *Marche funebre.* Two-piano arrangement of work by Tomás Bretón. 1886. Premiered Madrid, Salón Romero, February 21, 1886.

113.   *Pieza para ser ejecutada a primera vista* [sight-reading exercise for use at the Madrid Escuela Nacional de Música]. Composed 1886. Basically the same as "Minuetto" from *Suite ancienne no. 3*, T. 76 [facsimile available in no. 263, Torres/Aguado Sánchez, *Las claves madrileñas de Isaac Albéniz*]

114. *Peteneras.* Composed ca. 1900. Thirty-seven measures in manuscript of incomplete piece for piano. Dedicated to composer's daughter Laura. See Torres, *Catálogo,* 442, for information on the location of this ms.

115. *Improvisaciones.* Recorded on wax cylinders ca. 1903. See Torres, *Catálogo,* 444–45 for information on the location of these cylinders and the history of the recordings. See also the transcription/edition by Milton Laufer, no. 21.

      A.   *Improvisación no. 1* in F-sharp minor.
      B.   *Improvisación no. 2* in F-sharp minor.
      C.   *Improvisación no. 3* in D major.

116. *Guajira (Chant populaire cubain)* for Orchestra. Begun 1905. Incomplete. [Bc, sign. M984]

2

Part B: Scholarly Editions

This is a selective compilation of recent critical, performing, and/or Urtext editions. These are of scholarly value because of the editorial commentary they offer and/or because they represent the first or only available edition of that work. This section is organized first by medium or genre, and then alphabetically by editor. Only editions of original works appear, not transcriptions or arrangements. Any published reviews appear at the end of the listing.

STAGE

1. Eusebio, José de. *Merlin.* Opera in three acts: part one of the trilogy "King Arthur of the lyrical dramas founded on the Morte d'Arthur" by Sir Thomas Malory. Valencia: Piles, 1998. ISMN M350500237.

2. ———. *Pepita Jiménez*, comèdia lírica en dos actes i tres quadres, basada en la novel·la de Juan Valera [1904 version]. Barcelona: Tritó, 2009. ISBN 8488955960; ISMN 9790692045519. See also this editor's suite of orchestral numbers from the opera: *Fragments orquestrals*, Barcelona: Tritó, 2010. ISBN/ISMN 9790692046639.

3   Mariño, Borja, ed. *Isaac Albéniz: The Magic Opal, The Magic Ring, La Sortija. Òpera còmica en dos actos. Llibret d'Arthur Law.* Barcelona: Tritó, 2011. ISBN 9788492852079; ISMN 9790692047537.

4. ———, ed. *Pepita Jiménez: comedia lirica en dos actes i tres quadres, basada en la novel la de Juan Valera* [1896 version]. Vocal score. Barcelona: Tritó, 2012. ISBN/ISMN 9790692048176.

5. Soler, Josep, ed. *Pepita Jiménez.* Madrid: ICCMU, 1996. ISBN 8480482109.

ORCHESTRA

6.   *Escenes simfòniques catalanes.* Barcelona: Tritó, 2010. ISBN 9790692049104.

7.   Torres Mulas, Jacinto, and Arnau Farré, eds. *Catalonia: rapsòdia simfònica*, T. 24. Barcelona: Tritó, 2010. ISBN 9790692047094.

8.   Torres Mulas, Jacinto. *Rapsodia española para piano y orquesta*, T. 16. 2d rev. ed. Madrid: Instituto de Bibliografía Musical, 2009.

SOLO VOICE/CHORUS

9.   Barulich, Frances, and Mac McClure, eds. *Isaac Albéniz. Obra vocal: Obras para voz y piano.* Revisión y edición. 3 vols. Barcelona: Boileau, 2006. Reviewed by Walter Aaron Clark, *Notes of the Music Library Association* 64/4 (June 2008): 816–19.

      Volume I: Biography, introd. and crit. notes, in Sp., Eng., Cat., pp. 5–19; score, pp. 21–64. ISBN 8480207957; ISMN M350303630; Reg. B.3232. i20;

      Volume II: Facsim., p. 4; biography, introd. and crit. notes, in Sp., Eng., Cat., pp. 5–31; score, pp. 32–104. ISBN 8480207965; ISMN M350303647; Reg. B.3233. i23;

      Volume III: Selección de obras líricas para voz y piano: Nomenclature and table of tessituras, p. 5; biography, introd. and crit. notes, in Sp., Eng., Cat., pp. 7–18; score, pp. 19–116. ISBN 8480207973; ISMN M350303654; Reg. B.3234. i25.

10.   Eusebio, José de, ed. *Poèmes d'amour. Illustracions musicals dels poèmes d'amour d'Armand Silvestre: per a recitant i conjunt de cambra.* Barcelona: Tritó, 2005. ISBN 9788488955579; ISMN 9790692044161.

11.   Torres Mulas, Jacinto. *Salmo VI: del oficio de difuntos, para 4 voces mixtas*, T. 35. Madrid: Instituto de Bibliografía Musical, 1994.

12.   Torres Mulas, Jacinto, and Anton Cardó, eds. *Integral de la obra para voz y piano.* Barcelona: Tritó, 1998. ISBN 8488955413. Rev. ed. by Jacinto Torres Mulas, 2009. ISBN 8488955677.

PIANO

13.   Behr, Johannes, ed. *Mallorca*, op. 202. Urtext ed. Munich: G. Henle Verlag, 2008. HL.51480830. ISMN M201808307.

14.   Gertsch, Norbert, ed. *Iberia* (Book 1). Urtext ed. Munich: G. Henle Verlag, 2002. HL.51480647. ISMN M201806471.

15.   ———. *Iberia* (Book 2). Urtext ed. Munich: G. Henle Verlag, 2007. HL.51480648. ISMN M201806481.

16.   ——. *Iberia* (Book 3). Urtext ed. Munich: G. Henle Verlag, 2010. HL.51480649. ISMN M201806495.

17.   ——. *Iberia* (Book 4). Urtext ed. Munich: G. Henle Verlag, 2013. HL.51480650. ISMN M201806501.

18.   González, Guillermo, and Jacinto Torres, eds. *Isaac Albéniz's* Iberia: *Facsimile, Urtext, and Performing Editions.* 3 vols. Madrid: Editorial de Música Española Contemporánea (EMEC); Española de Ediciones Musicales Schott (EDEMS), 1998. Reviewed by Walter Aaron Clark, *Notes of the Music Library Association* 56/4 (June 2000): 1011–14. In English; Begoña López, *Revista de musicología* 24/1–2 (2001): 394–95. In Spanish.

Volume I: Integral revision by Guillermo González; facsimile edition of the manuscripts and historical-documental essay by Jacinto Torres. Facsim. reprod. (color), 161 p.; acknowledgments in Sp., Eng., p. iii; foreword, pp. v–viii; essay "*Iberia* a través de sus manuscritos"/"*Iberia* through the Manuscripts," pp. ix–xli. Cloth. ISBN 848992113X; ISBN 8492148438; ISMN M540010065; ISBN 3795754674; EDEMS ED 8995; EMEC E00355.

Volume II: Integral edition and Urtext edition by Guillermo González. Madrid: Editorial de Música Española Contemporánea (EMEC); Española de Ediciones Musicales Schott (EDEMS), 1998. [Acknowledgments in Sp., Eng., p. ix; contents, p. xi; foreword, pp. xiii–xix; synoptic table, p. xxi; score, 168 p.; trans. of Fr. expressions, pp. 171–77.] ISBN 8489921148; ISBN 8492148446; ISMN M540010058; EDEMS ED 8994; EMEC E00356.

Volume III: Revised edition by Guillermo González. [Acknowledgments in Sp., Eng., p. ix; contents, p. xi; foreword, pp. xiii–xix; synoptic table, p. xxi; score, 168 p.; trans. of Fr. expressions, pp. 171–77.] ISBN 8489921156; ISBN 8492148454; ISMN M540010041; EDEMS ED 8993; EMEC E00357.

19.   Iglesias, Antonio. *Iberia : 12 nuevas "impresiones" en cuatro cuadernos; La vega; Azulejos; Navarra.* Santiago de Compostela: Música en Compostela, 2006. ISBN 8438104215.

20.   Laufer, Milton Rubén, ed. *La Vega.* Urtext ed. Munich: G. Henle Verlag, 2007. HL.51480823. ISMN M201808239.

21.   ——, ed. *Drei Improvisationen 1903.* With CD recording. Munich: G. Henle Verlag, 2010. Reviewed by Jonathan D. Bellman, "Albéniz Improvisations," *Notes* 68/1 (Sept. 2011): 179–81.

22.   Müllemann, Norbert, ed. *España: Six Album Leaves.* Urtext ed. Fingering by Rolf Koenen. Munich: G. Henle Verlag, 2009. HL.51480857. ISMN 9790201808574.

23.   ——. *Tango.* Urtext ed. Munich: G. Henle Verlag, 2013. HL.51480753. ISMN M201807539.

24.   Pérez, Luis Fernando. *Iberia.* Available at no charge from the Fundación Albéniz, at the Escuela de Música Superior Reina Sofia, Madrid: http://www .classicalplanet.com/iberia/.

25.   Riva, Douglas, and Alicia de Larrocha, eds. *Azulejos* (completed by Enrique Granados). *Enrique Granados: Integral para piano.* Barcelona: Editorial Boileau, 2002. VIII:3. ISBN 8480206829.

26.   Rubio Zamora, Antonio, and Josep Colom, eds. *Revisión pedagógica de la* Suite Iberia. Madrid: Real Musical, 1998. RM 112029. ISBN 8438707122.

27.   Scheideler, Ullrich, ed. *Chants d'Espagne,* op. 232. Urtext ed. Fingering by Rolf Koenen. Munich: G. Henle Verlag, 2004. HL.51480782. ISMN M201807829.

28.   ——. *Suite espagnole,* op. 47. Urtext ed. Fingering by Rolf Koenen. Munich: G. Henle Verlag, 2005. HL.51480783. ISMN M201807836. "Asturias" from this suite published separately, 2013. HL.51480800. ISMN M201808000.

2

Part C: Recent Recordings of Scholarly Value

A comprehensive list of recordings would consume the present volume. Since the discography that appeared in the first edition of this book, in 1998, more than 2,500 commercial recordings have been made of Albéniz's music. That information is now readily available through the online catalog of the Library of Congress (WorldCat) and is not required here. This section is very selective and highlights recordings of particular value to a scholar, largely because of the effort the performer made to become informed about the latest research in this area, and because of the insights contained in the liner notes. The author of the notes is indicated in each entry (liner notes of particular scholarly interest also appear in Chapter 3, Part B: Secondary Sources, under the author's name; these are marked by an asterisk after the author's name below). These choices are not driven by any assessment of the inherent value of the performance, though the standard set by these performers is indeed high. Hence, the absence of, say, Alicia de Larrocha from this list in no way implies a negative assessment of the importance of her recordings. Certainly, any Albéniz scholar will want to become familiar with her interpretations. However, these recordings were made during the past quarter century and reflect important advances in our knowledge and understanding of Albéniz and his music.

STAGE

29.   Eusebio, José de (conductor), and Coro y Orquesta Sinfónica de Madrid. *Henry Clifford*. Decca, 473937-2 (2003). Notes by José de Eusebio* and Walter Aaron Clark.*

30.   Eusebio, José de (conductor), and Coro y Orquesta Sinfónica de Madrid. *Merlin.* Decca, 289467096-2 (2000). Notes by José de Eusebio* and Jacinto Torres Mulas.*

31.   Eusebio, José de (conductor), and Coro y Orquesta Titular del Teatro Real de Madrid. *Merlin.* BBC/Opus Arte DVD, OA 0888D (2004). Notes by José de Eusebio.*

32.   Eusebio, José de (conductor), and Orquesta y Coro de la Comunidad de Madrid. *Pepita Jiménez.* Deutsche Grammophon Gesellschaft, 002894776234 (2006). Notes by José de Eusebio* and Walter Aaron Clark.*

33.   Pons, Josep (conductor), Choeur d'enfants de la Maîtrise de Badalona, and Orquestra de Cambra Teatre Lliure. *Pepita Jiménez* [concert suite in two acts and three scenes]. Harmonia Mundi, HMC 901537 (1995). Notes by Jacinto Torres Mulas.*

ORCHESTRA/CHAMBER ENSEMBLE

34.   Noseda, Gianandrea (conductor), and Orquestra de Cadaqués. "Evocación," "Triana," "Lavapiés" from *Iberia* (orchestration by Jesús Rueda). Tritó, B-51293 (2007). Notes by Luis Suñén.

35.   Galduf, Manuel (conductor), Enrique Pérez de Guzmán (piano), and Orquesta de Valencia. *Concierto fantástico* and *Iberia* (orchestration by Enrique Fernández Arbós). Auvidis Valois, V 4661 (1992). Notes by Gonzalo Badenes.

36.   Martín, Jaime (conductor), and Orquestra Simfònica de Barcelona i Nacional de Catalunya. *Catalonia: Música orquestral d'Albéniz.* Includes *Catalonia; Escenes simfòniques catalanes;* orchestral suite from *Pepita Jiménez* (arranged by José de Eusebio). Tritó, TD-0078 (2010). Notes by Josep Dolcet.

37.   Petrenko, Vasily (director), Isabelle Bres (voice), and Ensemble Orquestra de Cadaqués. *Poèmes d'amour de Paul Armand Silvestre.* Tritó, B-51293 (2007). Notes by Luis Suñén.

SOLO VOICE/CHORUS

38.   Comas, Antonio (tenor), and Mac McClure (piano). *Albéniz integral.* Columna Música, 1CM 0025 (1997). Notes by Frances Barulich.

39.   Díaz Chopite, Mercedes (soprano), and Jorge Robaina (piano). *Albéniz en París y su entorno de la Schola Cantorum.* Several Records, SRD-280 (2004). Notes by Jacinto Torres Mulas.*

40.   Fernández Aransay, Carlos, director, Coro Cervantes. *O Crux: Spanish Choral Music* (includes *Salmo VI: del oficio de difuntos*). Guild, GMCD 7243 (2002). Notes by Carlos Fernández Aransay.

41.   Méndez, Carlos Javier (tenor), and Carlos Javier Domínguez (piano). *Isaac Albéniz: Canciones de concierto.* Sociedad Española de Musicología, DCD292 (2012). Notes by Lourdes Bonnet Fernández-Trujillo.

42.   Pardo, Marina (mezzosoprano), Rosa Torres-Pardo (piano). *The Caterpillar: Albéniz Songs.* Deutsche Grammophon, 0028947431527 (2002). Notes by Andrés Ruiz Tarazona.

PIANO

43.   Baselga, Miguel. *Albéniz: Complete Piano Music,* vols. 1–8: BIS, CD 923 (1998), 1043 (1999), 1143 (2000), 1243 (2003), 1443 (2005), 1743 (2009), 1953 (2011), 1973 (2014). Notes by Tomás Marco (v. 1), Miguel Baselga (v. 2), Álvaro Marías (v. 3), Javier Pérez Senz (v. 4), Walter Aaron Clark (v. 5), Jean-Pascal Vachon (vols. 6–8). (Volume 6 includes *Rapsodia española* with the orchestration by Albéniz, reconstructed by Jacinto Torres Mulas. It also includes the *Concierto fantástico,* both with Lü Jia conducting the Tenerife Symphony Orchestra.)

44.   Baytelman, Pola. *Iberia.* Elan Records, B000006NUV (2005). Notes by the performer.

45.   Pérez, Luis Fernando. *Suite Iberia, Navarra.* Warner Music Spain, 2010. Reissued Verso, B004LP1VDK (2012). Notes by Marco Antonio de la Ossa.

46.   González, Guillermo. *Iberia, Suites españolas nos. 1–2.* Naxos, 8.554311-12 (1998). Notes by Jacinto Torres Mulas.*

47.   ——. *Isaac Albéniz: Evocación de Granada.* Universidad de Granada, CD-09-11; D.L.: M-23670 (2009). Notes by Miriam Perandones Lozano.

48.   Guinovart, Albert. *Albéniz: Sonatas para piano no. 3, 4, 5; L'automne (Valse).* Harmonia Mundi, 1957007 (2003; reissue of a recording made in 1994). Notes by Jacinto Torres Mulas.* Reviewed by Walter Aaron Clark, *Nineteenth-Century Music Review* 3/1 (2006): 136–39.

49.   Hamelin, Marc-André. *Albéniz Iberia.* Hyperion, A67476/7 (2005). Notes by Walter Aaron Clark.

50.   Ish-Hurwitz, Yoram. *Albéniz: Iberia.* 2 vols. Turtle Records, TR-75529 (2009). Notes by the performer and Jacinto Torres Mulas.

51.   Riba, Javier. *Isaac Albéniz: La guitarra soñada* (solo-guitar transcriptions of *Iberia, España: Seis hojas de álbum,* and *Suite española no. 1*). Tritó, TD0050 (2008). Notes by Walter Aaron Clark.

52.   Riva, Douglas. *Azulejos* (completed by Enrique Granados). *Enrique Granados: Piano Music,* vol. 5. Naxos, 8.555325 (2001). Notes by the performer.*

53.   Riva, Douglas, and Jordi Masó. "Triana" from *Iberia* (arrangement for two pianos by Enrique Granados). *Enrique Granados: Piano Music*, vol. 10. Naxos, 8.570325 (2008). Notes by Douglas Riva.*

54.   Ruiz-Pipó, Antonio. *Isaac Albéniz: Unbekannte Klavierstücke*. Koch-Schwann, CD 3-1513-2 (1996). Notes by Jacinto Torres Mulas (the English translation by J & M Berridge is a summary).*

55.   Torres-Pardo, Rosa. *Iberia*. Glossa GSP 98005 (2006). Notes by Antonio Iglesias.

3

Part A: Primary Sources (Holdings and Location of Archives and Albéniz Organizations)

This is not intended as a detailed catalog of the holdings listed below, as the author does not have permission to publish such an inventory and a thorough list would overwhelm the necessary limits of this book (there are over 600 letters in the Biblioteca de Catalunya alone). However, these entries will give any researcher a general understanding of the primary source materials that are currently accessible, their location, and a website to consult. Indeed, most of these websites feature online catalogs that include their Albéniz holdings, with many of the items available in digital format. Precise information about catalog numbers of music manuscripts in the facilities below is available in Chapter 2, Part A: Catalog of Works. NB: facsimiles and reproductions of several manuscripts, reviews, and letters are available in no. 263, Torres/Aguado Sánchez, *Las claves madrileñas de Isaac Albéniz*. Where pertinent here, reproductions in that source are indicated in brackets after the description of contents.

56.   Albéniz family home (residence of his descendants through his daughter Laura)
        San Antonio, 1
        08394 San Vincent de Montalt
        Barcelona
        Spain

        The composer's descendants retain some materials of interest, including his sizable collection of paintings and fans, as well as assorted manuscripts, especially for *Merlin*.

57.   Archivo de la Dirección de Costes de Personal y Pensiones Públicas
        Argumosa, 41
        28012 Madrid
        Spain

Detailed records of Ángel Albéniz's employment in the revenue department of the Spanish government from 1847 to 1881. His personnel file also includes documents pertaining to his retirement in 1881 and the dispensation of his pension after his death in 1903. These documents provide valuable information about the family's residences during Albéniz's early life. [reproduced in no. 263, pp. 34–35]

58.   Biblioteca de Catalunya
       Carrer de l'Hospital, 56
       08001 Barcelona
       Spain
       Website: http://www.bnc.cat/Fons-i-col-leccions/Cerca-Fons-i-col-leccions/
       Albeniz-Isaac

All materials pertaining to the composer are located in the Fons (Fondo) Albéniz, which is available for consultation in the Sala de Manuscrits (manuscript room) and can be consulted online at the address above.

Correspondence: Letters to Albéniz are ordered alphabetically under sig. M986 and include items from such figures as Louis Bertrand, Tomas Bretón, Henri Cain, Ernest Chausson, Edouard Colonne, Alfred Cortot, Mathieu Crickboom, Vincent d'Indy, Paul Dukas, Manuel de Falla, Gabriel Fauré, Enrique Granados, Pierre Louÿs, Joaquim Malats, Camille Mauclair, Francis Money-Coutts (under "C"), Enric Morera, Guillermo Morphy, Joaquín Nin, Felipe Pedrell, Francis Planté, Joseph Ropartz, Dario Regoyos, Déodat de Séverac, Eusebio Sierra, José Tragó, Joaquín Turina, José Vianna da Motta, and Ignacio Zuloaga. Also here is the certificate of his winning first prize in the 1879 piano competition at the Brussels Conservatoire Royal; documents pertaining to his appointment as Comendador Ordinario del Orden de Isabel la Católica (Spanish knighthood); and his comments on auditioning hopefuls at the Paris Conservatoire in 1907. Four letters from Albéniz to Pedrell are in M964.

Newspaper Clippings: Two volumes under sig. M987 contain many reviews of his concerts and operas from the period 1889 to 1894, during his tenure in London. They also include some concert programs. (These are annotated in section C: Contemporary Periodicals.)

Printed materials: Scores from his library, many with dedicatory inscriptions by the composer. Represented are works by Tomás Bretón, Emmanuel Chabrier, Ernest Chausson, Paul Dukas, Manuel de Falla, Vincent d'Indy, Jules Massenet, Enric Morera, Déodat de Séverac, and Joaquín Turina.

Manuscripts: All the operas and operettas and symphonic works. "La vega" from *The Alhambra: Suite pour le piano*; "Evocación," "El Albaicín," "Málaga," "Jerez," and "Eritaña" from *Iberia*; and *Navarra.* Various opera numbers and the incomplete second piano concerto (M985).

59.   Biblioteca del Orfeó Català
      Palau de la Música, 4
      08003 Barcelona
      Spain
      Website: http://bibliotecadigital.palaumusica.org (type Albéniz into the browser
      for direct access to digitized scores, photos, and other items of interest); email:
      biblioteca@palaumusica.cat

      Printed material: Programs from Albéniz's 1888 concerts at the Exposición
      Universal in Barcelona, and from the premiere of *Merlin* in 1950.

      Manuscripts: "Rondeña," "Fête-Dieu à Séville," "Almería," "El polo," and "Triana"
      from *Iberia*; *San Antonio de la Florida* (piano-vocal score in copyist's hand); Act I
      of *Henry Clifford* (piano-vocal score in copyist's hand); "Will You Be Mine?" and
      "Separated," the only extant numbers from *Six Songs*.

60.   Conservatorio Profesional de Música "Francisco Escudero"
      Calle Easo, 45
      20006 San Sebastián
      Gipuzkoa
      Website: http://www.conservatorioescudero.org/es/conservatorio/

      Manuscript score and parts for the *Rapsodia española*, T. 16, probably orches-
      trated by Tomás Bretón.

61.   Museu Isaac Albéniz
      Calle Sant Roc, 22
      17867 Camprodón
      Website: www.albeniz.cat

      Though not a research facility, this small museum will be of interest because of
      the items it contains, including Albéniz's Bernareggi & Gassó piano, as well as
      first editions, photocopies of manuscripts, biographies, books, letters, personal
      items, and photos.

62.   Museu de la Música
      L'Auditori
      Carrer de Lepant, 150
      08013 Barcelona
      Website: http://www.bcn.cat/museumusica/ca/Serveis.html   (follow   Arxiu
      Històric to Colleccions and to the Fons Isaac Albéniz).

      This archive includes some of the most important documentation pertaining to
      his life and work. Most of the materials are kept in large file boxes called *caixas*.
      Correspondence not located in these files is organized numerically and kept in
      folders called *lligalls* (a register is available). Items of interest include:

Correspondence: Letters to him and/or his family from Breitkopf und Härtel, Max Eschig, Enrique Granados, Joaquim Malats, Francis and Helen Money-Coutts (up to 1923), Michel Raux Deledicque (one of his biographers), Juan Valera, and Ignacio Zuloaga. Also includes Albéniz's letters to his wife, Rosina, and letters from Granados to Malats.

Newspaper Clippings: The "Arxiu carpeta premsa" and "Arxiu premsa biogràfic" include newspaper clippings of reviews (many without newspaper title or specific date) of his performances, operas, his reviews of others' works, and articles about him (before and after his death) and his funeral ceremony.

Personal Items: Numerous photographs of him and important figures in his life (Tomás Bretón, Enrique Granados, Guillermo Morphy, Felipe Pedrell); the album he took with him on his early concert tours (containing inscriptions and reviews); journals and diaries; military papers (and those of his maternal grandfather); baptism and death certificates; and other documents pertaining to his death.

Printed materials: Programs of concerts and operas (during and after his life), and of events connected with the centenary of his birth in 1960. Poems by his father, Ángel. His scores and books on music. Journal articles on Albéniz.

Manuscripts: *San Antonio de la Florida* (piano-vocal score in copyist's hand but autographed by Albéniz); *Henry Clifford* and its working version "The Shepherd Lord" (full and vocal scores); *Fantasie espagnole pour le piano* (same as "La vega" from *The Alhambra: Suite pour le piano*); *La Sérénade* (incomplete piano-vocal score); Prelude to *Merlin* (full score); *Launcelot* (incomplete full score of Act II); *Poèmes d'amour* (parts only); and "Lavapiés" from *Iberia*.

63.   Fundación Albéniz
       Escuela Superior de Música Reina Sofia
       Plaza de Oriente s/n
       28013 Madrid
       Spain
       Website: http://www.fundacionalbeniz.com

       This organization was founded by the pianist Paloma O'Shea to promote performance and scholarship devoted to Albéniz (and other composers). It organized a traveling exhibition on Albéniz in 1990 and has issued several important publications. Its archive is not large but includes the photographs that appeared in no. 139, Enrique Franco, ed., *Albéniz y su tiempo*.

64.   Real Conservatorio Superior de la Música, Biblioteca
       Calle Santa Isabel, 53
       28012 Madrid
       Spain
       Website: http://www.rcsmm.eu; email: biblioteca@rcsmm.eu

Manuscripts: Salmo VI, "Cataluña," and "Cuba" from the *Suite española no. 1,* and examination records containing references to Albéniz's studies there *(Actas de los Examenes de 1865–66 a 1871–72 y 72–73 a 77–78).* Numerous first editions. [several items reproduced in no. 263, pp. 13, 22]

65.   Hochschule für Musik und Theater "Felix Mendelssohn-Bartholdy"
Grassistrasse 8
Postfach 100809
04008 Leipzig
Germany
Website: http://www.hmt-leipzig.de/hmt/bibliothek

The Hochschule's library contains Albéniz's record of admission (no. 2513) and Lehrer Zeugniß (also no. 2513), which lists courses taken and provides comments of the professors.

66.   Sociedad General de Autores y Editores
Fernando VI, 4
28004 Madrid
Website: http://www.sgae.es/acerca-de/el-cedoa-de-la-sgae/

First editions of many of Albéniz's works published by Dotesio and Unión Musical Española.

67.   Staatsarchiv Leipzig
Schongauerstraße 1
04328 Leipzig
Germany
Website: http://www.archiv.sachsen.de/106.htm; email: poststelle-l@sta.smi.sachsen.de

The archive of the publisher Breitkopf und Härtel is located here and includes the correspondence to and from Albéniz (the originals of some of the letters from Breitkopf und Härtel are located in the Museu de la Música in Barcelona). There are over fifty letters and cards from 1896 through 1906.

68.   Latymer Archive
Coutts & Co.
440 Strand
London WC2R OQS
United Kingdom
Website: tracey.earl@coutts.com

Retains the 1893 contract between Money-Coutts, Lowenfeld, and Albéniz that became the basis for a much-fictionalized "pact of Faust" between the Spaniard and his wealthy English benefactor. Also contains useful documents pertaining to Money-Coutts's own theatrical investments and speculations, his estate, and his payments to Albéniz.

69.   Conservatoire Royal de Bruxelles (Administration Archives)
       30 rue de la Régence
       1000 Brussels
       Belgium
       Website: http://www.conservatoire.be

       Possesses the Demande d'Admission (numbered 886), listing Albéniz's period
       of study, addresses, and courses taken. (In the final proof stage of this book,
       manuscripts for *L'Hermitage fleuri* were discovered by Belgian scholar Jan de
       Kloe at the Archives de la Ville de Bruxelles, Rue des Tanneurs, 65 1000 Bruxelles;
       website: http://www.bruxelles.be).

70.   Museo Nacional de la Música
       509 e/Bernaza y Villegas
       Habana Vieja CP 10100
       Cuba
       Website: www.museomusica.cult.cu

       Spanish musicologist Emilio Casares discovered orchestral parts for *San Antonio
       de la Florida* in the Fondos del Teatro Tacón, left over from an 1895 production
       at that theater. These provided the basis for José de Eusebio's reconstruction of
       the work for a 2003 production at the Teatro de la Zarzuela in Madrid.

3

Part B: Secondary Sources (Books and Articles)

This bibliography focuses on published materials. Exceptions to that rule are doctoral documents, including unpublished Ph.D. dissertations and D.M.A. theses and dissertations; only master's theses of particular interest appear. It does not include term papers or reviews of recordings and performances. It also does not include short articles (of one to two pages) of no substance. However, longer items of little originality or value are cited so that one can know not to pursue them. Encyclopedia or dictionary entries do not appear unless they are of unusual substance and/or length. Concert programs of scholarly importance are included; moreover, some useful CD/DVD liner notes appear here as well (these are also listed, though not annotated, in Chapter 2, Part C: Discography, along with additional recordings and liner-note authors). Where applicable, entries include the ISBN and Library of Congress call number. Only publications in Catalan, English, French, German, Italian, Russian, and Spanish appear.

71.   Alarcón Hernández, Joana. "Biografía." In *Isaac Albéniz, artista i mecenes.* Catalog of an exhibition organized by the Museu Diocesà de Barcelona, July–September 2009, 47–56. Barcelona: Museu Diocesà de Barcelona, 2009. 284 pp. ISBN 9788493689551. ML410.A3. In Catalan, Castilian, English.

   A year-by-year chronological overview of Albéniz's life, from his birth in 1860 to his death in 1909. This essay is heavily indebted to the latest biographical research and is highlighted by several photographs of the composer, his family, and friends. (Those seeking a very detailed chronology of Albéniz's Madrid years should consult no. 263, Torres/Aguado Sánchez, *Las claves madrileñas de Isaac Albéniz*, pp. 101–31.)

72.   Albéniz, Isaac. *Impresiones y diarios de viaje.* Ed. Enrique Franco. Madrid: Fundación Isaac Albéniz, 1990. 70 pp. ISBN 847506311X. ML410.A3A3 1990.

(Reprinted in no. 222, Ruiz Tarazona, *Albéniz: edición conmemorativa del centenario de Isaac Albéniz.*) In Spanish.

The first publication of Albéniz's travel journals and diaries. The initial entries are from 1880 and record his journey to Budapest in search of Franz Liszt, with whom he hoped to study. The second set of journal entries deals with his journey to Prague in 1897 and the production of *Pepita Jiménez* there in that year. In 1898, Albéniz began a diary in which, until the final entry in 1903, he expatiated on a wide variety of subjects. Unfortunately, this edition was rendered from a typewritten copy made by the composer's daughter Laura. There are some deletions and a number of other discrepancies between this version and the original manuscripts (in the Mm). These errors persist in the printed edition.

73.   Alier, Roger. "Albéniz i l'Òpera." In *Isaac Albéniz, artista i mecenes.* Catalog of an exhibition organized by the Museu Diocesà de Barcelona, July–September 2009, 71–80. Barcelona: Museu Diocesà de Barcelona, 2009. 284 pp. ISBN 9788493689551. ML410.A3. In Catalan, Castilian, English.

Provides a survey of Albéniz's operas, from his English operetta *The Magic Opal* and Spanish operetta (zarzuela) *San Antonio de la Florida,* to his more substantial operatic collaborations with the English librettist Francis Burdett Money-Coutts: *Pepita Jiménez, Henry Clifford,* and the *King Arthur* trilogy. Illustrated with reproductions of letters and programs.

74.   Andrade de Silva, Tomás. "El piano de Albéniz." *Música (Revista de los Conservatorios),* no. 2 (October–December 1952): 71–82. In Spanish.

A treatment of the daunting technical problems posed by *Iberia,* describing it as "anti-pianistic" in its nearly impossible chords, leaps, and rhythms. Proceeds to a brief discussion of the particular challenges of each number in the collection, along with some reflections on their musical style.

75.   Aparici, María Pilar. "'Pepita Jiménez,' Valera-Albéniz." *Boletín de la Real Academia Española* 55/204 (January–April 1975): 147–72. (Reprinted in no. 139, Franco, ed., *Albéniz y su tiempo,* pp. 80–100.) In Spanish.

During the period 1895–98, Albéniz corresponded with the noted Spanish author Juan Valera concerning his plans to convert Valera's novel *Pepita Jiménez* (1874) into an opera. Only Valera's letters have survived, but they reveal his misgivings about the novel's dramatic merits. He declared that even if Mozart were to set it to music, "it would be a disaster." He further insisted that mixing his novel with Albéniz's music would be like "mixing a partridge with custard," a recipe that would ruin both ingredients. Though he did give grudging consent to the project and rejoiced in its success, to the end he believed that there were others of his works more suitable for the stage.

76.   Arbós, Enrique Fernández. *Arbós.* Madrid: Ediciones Cid, 1963. 538 pp. ML410. A73A3 1963. (Excerpt entitled "Santander, 1883" appears in no. 139, Franco, ed., *Albéniz y su tiempo,* pp. 63–67.) In Spanish.

This autobiography provides useful insights into the period when Arbós and Albéniz were students together at the Conservatoire Royal in Brussels (1877–79) and their later collaborations in England during the early 1890s. In this excerpt from his autobiography, Arbós (the renowned violinist and conductor who was a close friend of Albéniz) discusses their joint concert tour in northern Spain in 1883 and makes some amusing observations about Albéniz's mannerisms, especially his eating habits. (Those interested in more detailed information on this topic should definitely consult no. 263, Torres/Aguado Sánchez, *Las claves madrileñas de Isaac Albéniz*, pp. 132–57).

77.   Aviñoa, Xosé. *Albéniz*. Series: Conocer y reconocer la música de. Mexico City: Daimon, 1986. 84 pp. ISBN 9686024867. In Spanish.

This pocket-size work contains a cursory biography and discussion of his music as well as a catalog of his works, discography, chronology, and glossary. Includes only a few footnotes and no musical examples, index, or bibliography.

78.   Barce, Ramón. "Sintesi di folklori professionali in Isaac Albéniz." *Musica/Realtà* 18 (November 1996): 117–30. In Italian.

Albéniz's music is suffused with melodies and rhythms clearly indebted to the folk songs and dances of his native Spain. This insightful article explores the sources of this material that were available to Albéniz and concludes that rather than in the village square, Albéniz came into contact with this folklore in commercial settings, where it was performed by professionals. It was thus urban rather than rural folklore that served as Albéniz's muse.

79.   Barulich, Frances. "Albéniz, Isaac." *Grove Music Online* (accessed August 19, 2014). In English.

Although this is not the longest encyclopedia or dictionary entry available, it is the most accurate and up-to-date; furthermore, it has the online advantage of being revisable and responsive to advances in research.

80.   Baytelman, Pola. *Isaac Albéniz: Chronological List and Thematic Catalog of His Piano Works*. Detroit Studies in Music Bibliography, 72. Warren, MI: Harmonie Park Press, 1993. 124 pp. ISBN 0899900674. ML134.A45A12 1993. In English. Reviewed by Frances Barulich, *Notes of the Music Library Association* 51/3 (1995): 939–42; Gertraut Haberkamp, *Die Musikforschung* 43/1 (1995): 93; Walter Aaron Clark, "Recent Researches in Spanish Music 1800 to the Present," *Inter-American Music Review* 16/1 (Summer–Fall, 1997): 87–88.

A reworking of her doctoral document (Pola Baytelman Dobry, "Albéniz: Chronological Listing and Thematic Catalogue of His Piano Works," D.M.A. thesis, University of Texas, Austin, 1990. 106 pp. UMI AAC 9116798), this is the first thematic catalog of Albéniz's music ever published and the first monograph on him in English. Presents a summary of biographical issues, including recent research casting doubt on some aspects of the existing record. Discusses style periods, publishers, and detailed examination of the piano music in chronological order listing performance, publication information, and special details. The chronology of Albéniz's compositions is often difficult to determine, and some problems persist in her ordering. Concludes with a discography and several other appendices, including a chronology of his life and lists of piano works by collection and by grade of difficulty. Contains many reproductions of cover designs from first editions.

81.   ——. "Style Evolution in the Piano Works of Isaac Albéniz." In *Antes de* Iberia: *de Masarnau a Albéniz*; Pre-Iberia: *From Masarnau to Albéniz*. Ed. Luisa Morales and Walter A. Clark, 151–70. Garrucha, Almería: Asociación Cultural LEAL, 2009. 303 pp. ISBN 9788461353316. ML738.S96 2008. In Spanish and English (Spanish articles include abstracts in English and vice versa).

This article offers a general overview of the stylistic evolution in Albéniz's piano music, from his early imitations of Chopin, Schubert, and Liszt to his character pieces inspired by Spanish folklore as well as his non-Hispanic suites and sonatas. All of these established the necessary foundation for his mature compositions, which included the palpable influence of contemporary French music, with which he became familiar during his Paris years. The culmination of this evolution was, of course, *Iberia*.

82.   Bergadà, Montserrat. "Albéniz, pianista *avant tout*." *Scherzo* 24/240 (April 2009): 118–21. In Spanish.

Although we remember Albéniz first and foremost as a composer, the author is persuasive in reminding us that his art was grounded in his pianism. Indeed, he was one of the greatest pianists during the period in which that instrument's popularity and musical impact were at their zenith. Though he was a renowned interpreter of the Romantic classics, as well as of Scarlatti and Bach, he never made a greater impression than when he played his own works.

83.   Berthelot, Anne. "From Purcell to Albéniz: Merlin at the Opera." *Ars Lyrica: Journal of the Lyrica Society for Word-Music Relations* 15 (2005/06): 57–66. In English.

An intriguing study of the character of Merlin in *King Arthur* by Purcell and *Merlin* (from an incomplete *King Arthur* trilogy) by Albéniz. The author concludes that the character of Merlin in both works is secondary and accessory to Arthurian glory.

84.   Bevan, Clifford. "Albéniz, Money-Coutts and 'La Parenthèse londonienne.'" Ph.D. diss., University of London, 1994. 296 pp. In English. Reviewed by Walter Aaron Clark, "Recent Researches in Spanish Music 1800 to the Present," *Inter-American Music Review* 16/1 (Summer–Fall, 1997): 86–87.

Bevan explores in detail Albéniz's operatic collaboration with the wealthy Englishman Francis Burdett Money-Coutts. The dissertation begins with short biographies of both men up to 1893, with an emphasis on Albéniz's years in London (1890–93) and the formation of the relationship. The three operas

Albéniz composed to librettos by Money-Coutts—*Henry Clifford*, *Pepita Jiménez*, and *King Arthur* (a trilogy)—are examined in a comparative way in terms of their production, reception, textual and musical structure, and influences. Also provides a brief examination of Albéniz's songs on texts of Money-Coutts. The appendices include plot summaries and a thorough catalog of manuscript and published sources. The text is illustrated with numerous musical examples.

85. Bretón, Tomás. "En la muerte de Albéniz." *ABC* (May 21, 1909): 4–5. (Reprinted in no. 139, Franco, ed., *Albéniz y su tiempo*, pp. 121–24; however, this title is an editorial invention. For a reproduction of the original, consult no. 263, Torres/Aguado Sánchez, *Las claves madrileñas de Isaac Albéniz*, p. 227.) In Spanish.

A homage to the recently deceased composer with personal recollections of the author's acquaintance with the young Albéniz. Praises his eventual accomplishments as both a pianist and composer.

86. Bruach, Agustí. "Die Orchesterwerke Isaac Albéniz' nach dem Manuskript 984 der Biblioteca de Catalunya: Versuch einer Einschätzung." *Anuario musical* 54 (1999): 203–14. In Spanish (English abstract).

An examination of the manuscripts of Albéniz's orchestral works now in the Biblioteca de Catalunya (M984). Based on a comparison of drafts with completed works, the author concludes that Albéniz probably received considerable assistance in orchestrating "works in which the orchestral palette appears with a wider range of nuances," such as *Catalonia*. Regrettably, this article reinforces the mistaken notion that Albéniz did not know how to orchestrate. A corrective to this error is found in more recent research in no. 246, Jacinto Torres, "Albéniz ante la orquesta: *Catalonia*."

87. Camín, Alfonso. "De Nueva York a Budapest." *Norte* (Revista mexicana) (1951). (Reprinted in no. 139, Franco, ed., *Albéniz y su tiempo*, pp. 41–49.) In Spanish.

A brief biography of Albéniz that is completely dependent on earlier, often unreliable, secondary sources. The author invents dialogue to make the article a better read. It is useful for some of the historical and cultural background information it contains, including a poem by the Nicaraguan poet Rubén Darío.

88. Carlson, Lindsey. "From Albéniz to Arbós: The Orchestration of 'Iberia.'" Master's thesis, University of Maryland, College Park, 2010. 111 pp. UMI 1478121. In English.

Examines in admirable detail the collaboration between Albéniz and Arbós in the orchestration of *Iberia*. Albéniz actually became a very capable orchestrator but continued to lack confidence in his own ability. He was unsatisfied with his orchestration of "El Puerto" from *Iberia* and approached Arbós to take over. This study concludes that Arbós did not begin afresh but rather revised Albéniz's orchestration; however, the remaining four of his arrangements from *Iberia* were completely his own work.

89.   Chambellan, Charles. *Le Mercure musical* 2/11 (June 1, 1906): 519–20. In French.

        Favorable review of a performance of *Iberia* by Blanche Selva, in which the critic
        had high praise for the young virtuosa. Hails *Iberia* as a work that evokes all of
        Spain, especially its Oriental cultural heritage, but without neglecting Western
        refinements.

90.   Chapalain, Guy. "La Guitare dans l'ecriture d'Isaac Albéniz [part 1]." *Les Cahiers
        de la guitare et de la musique*, n64 (1997): 21–23. In French.

        A brief yet very astute and useful examination of the precise musical ele-
        ments of Andalusian folklore, especially flamenco, that Albéniz deployed in
        his Spanish-style piano works. Imitations of the guitar's characteristic strum-
        ming patterns (*rasgueo*), runs (*picados*), slurred passages (*ligados*), and chord
        progressions are specified and corroborated by representative excerpts from
        Albéniz's music.

91.   ——. "La Guitare dans l'ecriture d'Isaac Albéniz [part 2]." *Les Cahiers de la guitare
        et de la musique*, no. 65 (1998): 34–37. In French.

        A continuation of the previous article, exploring various transcriptions of
        Albéniz's piano works for the guitar, the instrument that he so often and so skill-
        fully evoked at the keyboard. Cites specific musical passages in treating the tech-
        nique of transcription.

92.   Cho, Yoon Soo. "The Spanish Guitar Influence on the Piano Music of Isaac
        Albéniz and Enrique Granados: A Detailed Study of *Granada* and *Asturias*
        of *Suite Española* by Albéniz and *Andaluza* and *Danza Triste* of *Doce Danzas
        Españolas* by Granados." D.M.A., University of Texas, Austin, 2006. 127 pp. UMI
        3221803. In English.

        Explores the manifestation of Spanish nationalist impulses in selected works by
        Albéniz and Granados, particularly evocations of the guitar. In addition to his-
        torical context and biographical information, it presents a comprehensive analy-
        sis of form, harmony, and texture to establish the traits that mark these works as
        Spanish.

93.   Christoforidis, Michael. "Isaac Albéniz's Alhambrism and *fin-de-siècle* Paris." In
        Antes de Iberia*: de Masarnau a Albéniz*; *Pre-*Iberia: From Masarnau to Albéniz.*
        Ed. Luisa Morales and Walter A. Clark, 171–82. Garrucha, Almería: Asociación
        Cultural LEAL, 2009. 303 pp. ISBN 9788461353316. ML738.S96 2008. In Spanish
        and English (Spanish articles include abstracts in English and vice versa).

        The author explores the phenomenon of Alhambrism in Albéniz's music. A fas-
        cination with Granada and its Alhambra as the final redoubt of Arab culture
        in Europe, Alhambrism was pervasive in music, literature, and art of the late
        nineteenth and early twentieth centuries, not only in Spain itself but also in
        France. This article focuses on the interactions between Albéniz, Falla, Turina,
        and Debussy in their musical evocations of the Alhambra.

94. ——. "Research Report: 'Invasion of the Barbarians': Spanish Composers and Challenges to Exoticism in *belle-époque* Paris." *Context*, nos. 29–30 (2005): 111–17. In English.

A nuanced and informative essay on the interaction between Spanish and French music and musicians around 1900. This musical dialogue was mediated by Albéniz, who was the central figure in establishing useful connections and exchanges between Debussy and Ravel, on the one hand, and Falla and Turina, on the other. Though Falla and Turina were Andalusians and somewhat distrustful of Catalan interpretations of flamenco, Turina believed that Albéniz's "soul was completely Andalusian."

95. Clark, Walter Aaron. "A Spaniard in Queen Victoria's Court: Isaac Albéniz, Francis Money-Coutts, and 'The National Trilogy' *King Arthur*." *Nineteenth-Century British Music Studies*, vol. 2. Ed. Bennett Zon, 114–25. London: Ashgate Publishing, 2002. ISBN 0754606414. ML285.5 2002. In English.

Discusses the genesis of Albéniz's Arthurian trilogy with librettos by the English author Francis Burdett Money-Coutts, who provided Albéniz with an ample annual income in exchange for setting his librettos and poems to music. Money-Coutts took a passionate interest in creating an operatic "National Trilogy," consisting of *Merlin*, *Launcelot*, and *Guenevere*. Only the first opera was ever completed, though it was never produced during its creators' lifetimes.

96. ——. "Albéniz en Leipzig y Bruselas: Nuevas luces sobre una vieja historia." *Revista de musicología* 14/1–2 (1991): 213–18. In Spanish.

An examination of records of Albéniz's study at the Hochschule für Musik "Felix Mendelssohn Bartholdy" in Leipzig and at the Conservatoire Royal in Brussels. Contrary to his various claims to having studied 9, 18, or 36 months in Leipzig, he was there for less than 2 months. He began his studies at Brussels in September of 1876, shortly after his departure from Leipzig.

97. ——. "Albéniz in Leipzig and Brussels: New Data from Conservatory Records." *Inter-American Music Review* 11/1 (Fall–Winter, 1990): 113–17. In English.

English version of the above article (slightly condensed). Casts doubt on Albéniz's having met and played for Liszt, who was not in Budapest at the time Albéniz claimed to have met him there.

98. ——. "*Bajo la palmera*: Yradier, Albéniz, and the Lure of the Cuban 'Tango.'" In *Antes de Iberia: de Masarnau a Albéniz*. Ed. Luisa Morales and Walter A. Clark, 141–50. Garrucha, Almería: Asociación Cultural LEAL, 2009. ISBN 9788461353316. ML738.S96 2008. In Spanish and English (Spanish articles include abstracts in English and vice versa).

Albéniz spent part of the years 1875–76 in Cuba, and the island seems to have left an indelible impression on his musical imagination, as there are numerous evocations of the habanera in his works. However, he never used the word "habanera" in any title, preferring instead "tango" or some other designation. This article explores the meaning of the word tango in the context of Albéniz's music and musical epoch and why it refers not to the Argentine variety but rather to the habanera. It also reveals the influence of Sebastián Yradier, to whose habaneras Albéniz's "tangos" owe an obvious debt.

99.   ——. "'Cavalleria Iberica' Reassessed: Critical Reception of Isaac Albéniz's Opera *Pepita Jiménez." Actas del XV Congreso de la Sociedad Internacional de Musicología,* in *Revista de musicología* 16/6 (1993): 3255–62. In English.

A reception history of Albéniz's best-known and most successful opera, which was produced in Barcelona, Prague, Brussels, Paris, again in Barcelona, and finally in Madrid. Although reviewers praised its local color and rhythmic vitality, they faulted Albéniz's preference for the orchestra over the voices and the libretto's lack of dramatic interest.

100.   ——. "Francisco Tárrega, Isaac Albéniz, and the Modern Guitar." *Soundboard Magazine: The Journal of the Guitar Foundation of America* 36/1 (2010): 5–13. In English.

Tárrega was the first to transcribe Albéniz's piano music for the guitar, thus establishing a precedent followed by innumerable later guitarists. This process has enriched the guitar's repertoire and focused attention on many of Albéniz's works that pianists rarely perform in concert. The process of transcription from the piano to the guitar poses special difficulties, which Tárrega overcame to the original composer's satisfaction.

101.   ——. *Isaac Albéniz: A Guide to Research.* Composer Resource Manuals, 45. New York: Garland Publishing, 1998. In English. Reviewed by *American Reference Books Annual* 30 (1999), 469; Carol Hess, *Notes of the Music Library Association* 56/3 (March 2000), 697–99.

The first edition of the present volume was also the first of its kind and presents a summary biography followed by bibliographies of both primary and secondary sources as well as periodical literature during the composer's life. These are followed by a catalog of works, a complete discography, and a chronology of Albéniz's life. The book concludes with three indexes, by proper names, works, and performers.

102.   ——. *Isaac Albéniz: Portrait of a Romantic.* Oxford: Oxford University Press, 1999. 336 pp. ISBN 019816369X. ML410.A42C53 1999. In English.

Reviewed by Rafael Andia, *Les Cahiers de la guitare,* nos. 79–80 (2001): 72–73; *Chamber Music* 17 (October 2000): 194; Michael Christoforidis, *Context: Journal of Music Research* 18 (Winter 2000): 88–89; Jessica Duchen, *BBC Music Magazine* (September 1999): 84; F. Goosen, *Choice* 37/4 (December 1999): 731–32; Carol Hess, *Notes of the Music Library Association* 56/4 (June 2000): 946–48; Allan

Clive Jones, *Classical Guitar* 17/12 (August 1999): 50; Tess Knighton, *Times Literary Supplement*, September 24, 1999, 21; Gavin Meredith, *Online Journal, MusicTeachers.co.uk* 2/8 (February 2001); Bettina Neumann, *Piano* 15/6 (November–December 2007): 33; Robert Sargant, *Classical Music*, September 4, 1999, 34; Andrew Thomson, *The Musical Times* 141/1870 (Spring 2000): 70–71; Jacinto Torres, *Revista de Musicología* 22/2 (1999): 294–302.

The first book-length examination in English of the life and works of the composer. Begins with a history of Albéniz's biography and confronts the issue of Albéniz's prevarications about his early career and the inconsistencies and discrepancies that, as a result, plague all biographical accounts. The biography traces his family history and then attempts, on the basis of much new and previously overlooked documentation, to provide an accurate account of Albéniz's remarkable early career as a touring prodigy and his metamorphosis into a full-time composer of considerable importance. Includes a critical examination of his major compositions for piano, voice, orchestra, and the stage, with an emphasis on his handling of folkloric material. Study of his music's critical reception is supported by ample citation of press notices. Also amply cited are letters to and from the composer and his own diary entries, which tell a great deal about his relationships and inner life. The biography concludes with a critique of his legacy, his role in Spanish music history, and his status in Spain today. Contains a genealogical chart and list of works as well as numerous musical examples.

103.   ——. *Isaac Albéniz: Portrait of a Romantic.* Oxford: Oxford University Press, 2002. ISBN 0199250529. ML410.A42C53 2002. In English.

Paperback edition of the above volume, with minor emendations and corrections.

104.   ——. *Isaac Albéniz: Retrato de un romántico.* Trans. Paul Silles. Madrid: Turner Publicaciones, 2002. 432 pp. ISBN 8475065066. ML410.A3. In Spanish. Reviewed by *El Mundo*, February 28, 2002; José Luis García del Busto, *ABC*, March 23, 2002; Susana Gaviña, *ABC*, February 28, 2002; *La Razón*, February 28, 2002; Jorge de Persia, *La Vanguardia*, August 3, 2002; Jesús Ruiz Mantilla, *El País*, February 28 and March 29, 2002.

Spanish translation of the above biography, with emendations and corrections also found in the English paperback edition of the same year.

105.   ——. "Isaac Albéniz's Faustian Pact: A Study in Patronage." *The Musical Quarterly* 76/4 (December 1992): 465–87. In English.

Examines in detail Albéniz's relationship with the wealthy Englishman Francis Burdett Money-Coutts, the inheritor of a banking fortune who became a writer of poetry and librettos and hired Albéniz to set them to music. All biographers have railed at Money-Coutts for seducing Albéniz into a "pact of Faust," which supposedly forced him to expend his energy on projects that were alien to his nature. This article debunks that view and shows, through their correspondence and other documentation, that there was no compulsion in the arrangement and that it emanated from a deep bond of friendship between the two men. Albéniz benefited to the extent that he did not have to worry about money and was therefore able, during his final, illness-ridden years, to devote himself to composing his *chef d'oeuvre*, *Iberia*.

106. ———. "King Arthur and the Wagner Cult in Spain: Isaac Albéniz's Opera *Merlin.*" *King Arthur in Music.* Ed. Richard W. Barber, 51–60. Woodbridge, Suffolk: Boydell & Brewer, 2002. 198 pp. ISBN 0859917673. ML3849.K55 2003. In English.

As elsewhere in the late 1800s, Wagner's operas provoked extreme reactions of attraction and repulsion in Spain. However, in Barcelona there was virtual unanimity in favor of Wagner, whose operas were regularly performed there, usually in Catalan translation. This is the proper context for analyzing Albéniz's composition of a Wagnerian *King Arthur* trilogy, only the first opera of which, *Merlin*, was ever completed. Though using an English libretto by his friend and librettist Francis Burdett Money-Coutts, *Merlin* could well have been a success in Barcelona or even Madrid, had Albéniz succeeded in arranging a production there. Alas, it was never produced during his lifetime.

107. ———. "La España de Albéniz y Granados: Dos pasados, dos futuros." In *Música y cultura en la Edad de Plata, 1915–1939.* Ed. María Nagore, Leticia Sánchez de Andrés, and Elena Torres, 129–41. Madrid: Instituto Complutense de Ciencias Musicales, 2009. 663 pp. ISBN 9788489457423. ML315.5 2009. In Spanish.

This essay reflects on the political inclinations of both Albéniz and Granados and speculates how they might have reacted to political developments during the so-called Silver Age of the 1920s and 30s, had they lived long enough to witness them. It concludes that Albéniz, a socialist and liberal reformer, might have sided initially with the Republic, whereas Granados, the son and grandson of career army officers and an opponent of Catalan separatism, might have found the nationalists to be the lesser of two evils. In *Iberia* and *Goyescas*, each presented a different musical vision of Spain's past and hence its future.

108. ———. "'Música espanyola amb accent universal: Isaac Albéniz i el seu món." In *Isaac Albéniz, artista i mecenes.* Catalog of an exhibition organized by the Museu Diocesà de Barcelona, July–September 2009, 57–69. Barcelona: Museu Diocesà de Barcelona, 2009. 284 pp. ISBN 9788493689551. ML410.A3. In Catalan, Castilian, English.

Provides a narrative overview of Albéniz's life, times, and music, with special emphasis on the thoughts and feelings he expressed in his letters and diaries, a rich source of information about the composer's interior life and psychology, especially his disenchantment with the politics, culture, and religion of his homeland.

109. ———. "*Pepita Jiménez* and the Rise of *ópera española.* Liner notes for *Pepita Jiménez.* José de Eusebio conducting the Orquesta y Coro de la Comunidad de

Madrid. Deutsche Grammophon Gesellschaft, 002894776234 (2006). In English, Spanish, French.

The author delves into the phenomenon of Spanish opera, a movement that gained momentum in the late nineteenth and early twentieth centuries but never achieved a critical mass. Albéniz made important contributions to this development, especially with his *Pepita Jiménez*, to a libretto by Francis Burdett Money-Coutts based on the eponymous novel by Juan Valera (pub. 1874). Eusebio's scrupulous attention to the composer's original intentions increases our admiration for this work (see no. 32).

110.   ———. "Piano Works by Albéniz Completed or Arranged by Granados." In *Antes de* Iberia: *de Masarnau a Albéniz*; *Pre-*Iberia: *From Masarnau to Albéniz*. Ed. Luisa Morales and Walter A. Clark, 201–06. Garrucha, Almería: Asociación Cultural LEAL, 2009. ISBN 9788461353316. ML738.S96 2008. In Spanish and English (Spanish articles include abstracts in English and vice versa).

Albéniz and Granados were close friends and greatly admired one another's work. Granados in particular looked on Albéniz as a sort of elder brother and considered him a guiding light in Spanish music. Granados arranged Albéniz's "Triana," from *Iberia*, for two pianos, and at the request of Albéniz's widow, he also completed *Azulejos*, which Albéniz had left incomplete upon his death in 1909.

111.   ———. "Prophet with Honour: Isaac Albéniz and *Henry Clifford*." Liner notes for *Henry Clifford*. José de Eusebio conducting the Coro y Orquesta Sinfónica de Madrid. Decca, 473937-2 (2003). In English, French, Spanish.

These notes lay out a summary of Albéniz's career on the stage and his collaboration with Money-Coutts, with whom this opera was the composer's first collaboration (see no. 29). It then presents the genesis and premiere of the work, which was a qualified success but has never again been produced on stage. J. Roca y Roca, writing for *La Vanguardia*, believed that "Albéniz, finally, has succeeded in becoming a prophet in his own country" (see no. 619). Well, not quite yet, but he was on his way.

112.   ———. "Selected Bibliography/Discography of Recent Research on Albéniz, 1994–2009." In *Antes de* Iberia: *de Masarnau a Albéniz*; *Pre-*Iberia: *From Masarnau to Albéniz*. Ed. Luisa Morales and Walter A. Clark, 255–62. Garrucha, Almería: Asociación Cultural LEAL, 2009. ISBN 9788461353316. ML738.S96 2008. In Spanish and English (Spanish articles include abstracts in English and vice versa).

An overview of important advances in scholarship and recorded performances from 1994 to 2009. All of those citations are contained in the present volume.

113.   ———. "'Spanish Music with a Universal Accent': Isaac Albéniz's Opera *Pepita Jiménez*." Ph.D. diss., University of California, Los Angeles, 1992. 380 p. UMI AAC 9317432. In English.

An in-depth study of Albéniz's most successful opera. Begins with an examination of problems in the biography of Albéniz's early life, then an overview of his career as an opera composer and his relationship with Francis Burdett Money-Coutts, the librettist. Chapters on the transformation of the novel into a libretto and on manuscript and published sources are followed by an analysis of the music and the opera's critical reception. The final chapters treat the work's significance in the context of Albéniz's evolution as a composer and in the development of Spanish national opera. Appendices include the English libretto of the 1896 version and a catalog of his stage works. Concludes with an index.

114.   ——. "Variedad dentro de la lógica: clasicismo en la obra de Isaac Albéniz." *Actas del Congreso F. J. Haydn (1732–1809) y I. Albéniz (1860–1909): Clasicismo y Nacionalismo en la Música Española*, Festival de Música Española, Cádiz, November 21, 2009. *MAR* (Música de Andalucía en la Red), the online journal of music department of the Universidad de Granada, 2015. http://mar.ugr.es/.

Albéniz once wrote that the proper formula for music was "variety within logic." This essay explores classicizing elements in Albéniz's style, particularly in regard to his love of the eighteenth century, e.g., Scarlatti, Bach, and Viennese classicism. Albéniz's composition of chaconnes, minuets, and sonatas owes a clear debt to that earlier period and demonstrates that, despite his modernizing tendencies in *La vega* and *Iberia*, he felt a profound reverence for tradition.

115.   Clark, Walter Aaron, and Borja Mariño. Program notes for a concert version of Isaac Albéniz's operetta *The Magic Opal*, Auditorio Nacional (Madrid), February 27, 2010.

Many commentators, especially Gabriel Laplane, considered Albéniz's stage works a waste of time and effort, especially his English operetta *The Magic Opal*. Clark's essay, "'Muy por delante de sus rivales': Isaac Albéniz y su opereta inglesa *The Magic Opal*" (pp. 6–7), reveals that though it is still no competition for *The Mikado*, Albéniz's operetta exhibits considerable craft and wit, something even George Bernard Shaw conceded (see no. 548.). Borja Mariño's commentary, "Reflexiones sobre la recuperación de *The Magic Opal*" (8), touches on the difficulties he faced in reconciling the existing scrum of manuscripts to create a coherent work, one faithful to the composer's original intentions (see no. 3).

116.   Clark, Walter Aaron, José de Eusebio, and Justo Romero. Program notes for a production of Isaac Albéniz's zarzuela *San Antonio de la Florida* and Enrique Granados's *Goyescas*, Teatro de la Zarzuela (Madrid), April 4, 2003. NIPO 184030295.

These three authors contributed essays to the program notes for the most recent incarnation of Albéniz's only extant zarzuela. Clark's essay, "La vida artística de Isaac Albéniz: innovación y renovación" (pp. 9–19), pays special attention to the spirit of innovation and renovation that informs his stage works. Albéniz sought to enlarge the musical resources of the *género chico* (light zarzuela) in both quality and quantity, an approach that angered the critics in Madrid, who felt that the expatriate composer was "putting on airs." In his "'San Antonio' . . . de La Habana" (pp. 31–40), Eusebio describes the orchestral parts that Emilio Casares discovered at the Museo Nacional de Música (Fondos del Teatro Tacón) in Havana, and then explains how he, Eusebio, used these in reconstructing the work for this production. Finally, Justo Romero's notes, "Entre majos y majas" (pp. 61–69), explores Granados relationship to Albéniz and then surveys the latter's career as a composer of musical theater.

117. Collet, Henri. *Albéniz et Granados.* Paris: Librairie Félix Alcan, 1926 (slightly revised edition, 1929). Rev. ed., Paris: Éditions Le Bon Plaisir, 1948. 233 pp. ML390.C69 1948. Spanish trans. by P. E. F. Labrousse, Buenos Aires: Tor-S. R. L., 1948. Reprint of 1929 ed., Paris: Éditions d'Aujourd'hui, 1982. 244 pp. ISBN 2730701958. ML390.C69 1929. In French.

This was a groundbreaking work that set the standard for all biographies to follow. Collet was the first to examine Albéniz's life and works in their entirety. The biographical section includes many anecdotes by acquaintances of the composer who were still alive when Collet wrote the book. Collet also borrows heavily from Guerra y Alarcón (no. 151), Albéniz's first biographer. The section on his music was the first to form a comprehensive overview of his oeuvre and includes a cursory analytical appraisal of the major works and an estimate of their critical reception. Collet, however, had limited access to primary sources and did not consult closely with the Albéniz family in the final stages of preparation. Thus, it contains many errors, which most succeeding biographers were unsuccessful in correcting.

118. ——. "Isaac Albéniz y Joaquín Malats." *Revista musical catalana* 6/72 (December 1909): 377–79. In Spanish.

Examines the relationship between Albéniz and the illustrious Catalan pianist Joaquim Malats, who premiered several numbers from Albéniz's *Iberia.* The correspondence between the two men reveals the uncommon respect and affection Albéniz, himself a pianist of the highest caliber, felt for Malats. It also makes it clear that Albéniz wrote *Iberia* for him and with his special abilities in mind.

119. Colomer i Ràfols, Josep. "Albéniz, un amfitrió fantàstic." In *Isaac Albéniz, artista i mecenes.* Catalog of an exhibition organized by the Museu Diocesà de Barcelona, July–September 2009, 9. Barcelona: Museu Diocesà de Barcelona, 2009. 284 pp. ISBN 9788493689551. ML 410.A3. In Catalan, Castilian, English.

The author is the President of the Caixa Penedès, which provided financial support for an exhibition devoted to Albéniz and the little-known role he played as a patron of the visual arts. Provides insights into the genesis and organization of the exhibition at the Diocesan Museum of Barcelona.

120. Condesa de Castellà (Isabel María del Carmen de Castellví y Gordon). "Albéniz y su *Iberia.*" *Hojas Musicales de* La Publicidad, no. 32 (Barcelona), May 3, 1917. Also in *Tribuna* (Barcelona), April 30, 1917. In Spanish.

This booklet presents brief summations of the twelve numbers of Albéniz's masterpiece for piano. They are aimed at the general reader but present a few genuine insights into the music. Mostly of limited value to the specialist.

121.   Cooper, Colin. "Albéniz and Shaw." *Classical Guitar* 25/1 (September 2006): 30–31. In English.

A brief but intriguing examination of the intersection of Albéniz's career with that of the celebrated author George Bernard Shaw. Though the two men never actually met, this article surveys Shaw's several reviews of Albéniz's performances and stage productions during his tenure in London, 1890–93. This useful article is clearly indebted to earlier research but includes no citation of sources.

122.   Cortès, Francesc. "Para empezar con las obras líricas." *Scherzo* 24/240 (April 2009): 122–27. In Spanish.

A very useful overview of Albéniz's stage works and their reception, from the early zarzuelas through *Merlin*. This is an aspect of the composer's output that received short shrift from nearly all biographers; however, the reemergence of these works on recordings and in productions during the last 15 years or so has compelled us to reevaluate Albéniz's stature and contributions as a composer.

123.   Debussy, Claude. "Concerts Colonne—Société des Nouveaux Concerts." *Bulletin français de la Société Internationale de Musique* 9/12 (December 1, 1913): 42–44. In French.

In 1913, Debussy attended a concert of Spanish works performed by Spanish musicians. Albéniz's *Iberia*, a work with which he had long been familiar, was on the program, and he singles it out for special honors. Of particular merit is "Eritaña": "Never has music attained to such diverse, such colorful impressions." He goes on to state that "in this *Iberia* collection . . . Albéniz has given his best."

124.   De Kloe, Jan. "Albéniz in Brussels." *Soundboard* 30/4 (2004–05): 7–16. In English.

A superb examination of Albéniz's connections with the Belgian capital, first as a student at the Conservatoire Royal (1876–79) and later, in 1905, during the production of his opera *Pepita Jiménez* at the Théâtre Royal de la Monnaie. Corrects and expands factual data previously available in biographical accounts. The article is enhanced by helpful illustrations.

125.   Domenech Español, M. "Isaac Albéniz." *Revista de música* (Buenos Aires), no. 2 (1928): 150–55. In Spanish.

Begins with a discussion of Spain's curious lack of preeminence in music (a questionable assertion, to be sure), given its illustrious history in literature and the visual arts. Focuses on Albéniz as one of the "geniuses" of Spanish music who helped create a distinctive national style. Briefly surveys his life and works, with special attention to the nationalist piano music, especially *Iberia*.

126. Escalas, Romà. "El legado de Albéniz en el Museu de la Música de Barcelona." *Scherzo* 24/240 (April 2009): 132–36. In Spanish.

Much of the Albéniz family archive was donated to the Museu de la Música during the late 1970s and early 1980s. It might have been better if the entire archive had been deposited in one place, but instead, it was divided up among several facilities in Barcelona. Some of it remains in the family home north of the city. This useful article summarizes the contents of that part of the archive now residing in the Museu de la Música, which has experienced a few changes of location over the past two decades. Now that the Museu is in a permanent location (see no. 62), the collection will continue to be of inestimable value to researchers in this area of study.

127. Eusebio, José de. "Albéniz's Excalibur." Liner notes for *Merlin*. José de Eusebio conducting the Coro y Orquesta Sinfónica de Madrid. Decca, 289467096-2 (2000). In English.

Conductor José de Eusebio has been responsible for reviving Albéniz's stage works, parting company with earlier revivalists by adhering to the composer's original intentions rather than undertaking revisions in the belief that Albéniz needed a little help, especially with orchestration. In these notes (see no. 30), he provides useful background on Albéniz's *Merlin*, its genesis, manuscript sources, and the arduous process of revival. Although it remains to be seen whether *Merlin* will, as Eusebio predicted, "become part of the major international operatic repertoire," it has certainly been "a continual surprise to all those drawn to its history and sound-world."

128. ——. "Albéniz Reaches Camelot at Last." Liner notes for *Merlin*. José de Eusebio conducting the Coro y Orquesta Titular del Teatro Real de Madrid. BBC/Opus Arte DVD, OA 0888D (2004). In English, French, German.

Offers a detailed background of the genesis and revival of this remarkable work, one that is complementary to the above notes and should be consulted by any serious student of *Merlin*. This DVD (see no. 31) was a landmark recording not only in the history of Albéniz research and reception but also in the history of Spanish opera, as it completely upends conventional notions of the nature and extent of *opera española* around 1900.

129. ——. "From Myth to History." Liner notes for *Henry Clifford*. José de Eusebio conducting the Coro y Orquesta Sinfónica de Madrid. Decca, 473937-2 (2003). In English, French, Spanish.

Conductor José de Eusebio provides useful background on Albéniz's stage works and insights into the methodology of his reconstruction of this work from manuscript sources (see no 29).

130. ——. "Prophets and Prophecies." Liner notes for *Pepita Jiménez*. José de Eusebio conducting the Orquesta y Coro de la Comunidad de Madrid. Deutsche

Grammophon Gesellschaft, 002894776234 (2006). In English, Spanish, French.

In these notes, Eusebio provides valuable insights not only into the history of Albéniz's best-known and most successful opera but also the difficulties Spanish composers faced in trying to launch the phenomenon of *ópera española*. He devotes considerable attention to his methodology in reviving the work, its various manuscript sources and language options, and he relates the history of previous revivals, in which changes in orchestration and even the plot were deemed necessary (see no. 32).

131.   Falces Sierra, Marta. "Albéniz en Inglaterra, una etapa oscura." *Revista de musicología* 14/1–2 (1991): 214–19. In Spanish.

Examines Albéniz's years in London (1890–93) to shed light on a period of his career that biographers have either given short shrift or misunderstood altogether. Focuses on his relationship with Money-Coutts, the wealthy financier who aspired to write poetry and librettos.

132.   ——. *El pacto de Fausto: Estudio lingüístico-musical de los lieder ingleses de Albéniz sobre poemas de Francis Money-Coutts*. Granada: Universidad de Granada, 1993. 247 pp. ISBN 8433816438. ML410.A3.F35 1993. In Spanish. Reviewed by Walter Aaron Clark, "Recent Researches in Spanish Music 1800 to the Present," *Inter-American Music Review* 16/1 (Summer–Fall, 1997), 85–86.

The first thorough study of an overlooked portion of Albéniz's output. She begins with an examination of the sources and biographical problems, and then continues with a look at Albéniz's London period during the early 1890s. This establishes the foundation for a critical examination of the socalled "pact of Faust" and Albéniz's relationship with Francis Burdett Money-Coutts. For it was to poems of Money-Coutts that Albéniz composed most of his songs, and an analysis of these forms the principal substance of the rest of the book. After presenting the manuscript and published sources, she focuses on the relationship between musical phrasing and poetic structure. (Falces is a professor of philology at the University of Granada, where she received her doctorate.) The book concludes with several appendices, including a copy of Albéniz's contract with Money-Coutts and reproductions of the songs treated in the book.

133.   Fernández Marín, Lola. "El flamenco en la música nacionalista española: Falla y Albéniz." *Música y educación* 19/1 (March 2006): 29–64. In Spanish.

A fascinating and quite original examination of precise harmonic, melodic, and rhythmic elements in flamenco that inform various works by Albéniz and Falla. Not only does this study shed light on Spanish nationalist works inspired by flamenco, but it also sheds light on flamenco itself, which was otherwise not written down during the period in which these men were composing.

134.   Fernández-Cid, Antonio. "Matices diferenciales y nexos afectivo-musicales de Enrique Granados e Isaac Albéniz." *Notas de música (Boletín de la Fundación Isaac Albéniz)* 1 (December 1988): 16–19. In Spanish.

Examines the relationship between the two dominant figures in Spanish music ca. 1900, based on personal recollections of friends and family. Points out the affectionate respect and admiration the two Catalan musicians felt for one another.

135.   Ferrer, Victoria Alemany. "La estancia de Isaac Albéniz en Valencia en 1882." *Anuario musical* 66 (January–December 2011): 235–61. In Spanish (English abstract).

Albéniz toured throughout the length and breadth of Spain during his youth and early adulthood, including appearances in Valencia during the summer of 1882. This article documents those performances, part of a concert tour that also took him to nearby Alicante, Cartagena, and Alcoy. It explores the welcome he received in Valencia, the social and cultural impact of his performances, and the relationships he forged there with other aspiring musicians, as well as painters and sculptors.

136.   Figuerola i Rotger, Pere Jordi. "Introducció." In *Isaac Albéniz, artista i mecenes.* Catalog of an exhibition organized by the Museu Diocesà de Barcelona, July– September 2009, 15–46. Barcelona: Museu Diocesà de Barcelona, 2009. 284 pp. ISBN 9788493689551. ML410.A3. In Catalan, Castilian, English.

A vivid overview of the exhibition devoted to Albéniz and his contributions to Catalan culture around 1900. Explores Albéniz's personality, his art, and his patronage of fellow musicians and of painters, including his daughter Laura, who was a gifted artist. Letters, programs, music, memorabilia, photographs, drawings, and paintings were among the rich offerings in this exhibition, and many of them illustrate this article.

137.   Font Batallé, Montserrat. "Blanche Selva y la première de *Iberia* en Paris: del virtuosismo francés al andalucismo." In *Antes de* Iberia: *de Masarnau a Albéniz;* Pre-Iberia: *From Masarnau to Albéniz.* Ed. Luisa Morales and Walter A. Clark, 183–200. Garrucha, Almería: Asociación Cultural LEAL, 2009. 303 pp. ISBN 9788461353316. ML738.S96 2008. In Spanish and English (Spanish articles include abstracts in English and vice versa).

Blanche Selva was the first to premiere the entire *Iberia* collection, but what is sometimes overlooked is the extent to which she participated in the work's genesis as well as its presentation. This article explores her role in the creation and performance of *Iberia*, as well as the impact that her renditions had in France, and the contribution she made to Albéniz's legacy through her piano teaching as well.

138.   Fornet, Emilio. *Isaac Albéniz.* Series: Figuras de la raza 2/24. Madrid: A. Marzo, 1927. 55 pp. ML410.A328 F72. In Spanish.

An insubstantial biography intended for a general readership with limited knowledge of music.

139.   Franco, Enrique, ed. *Albéniz y su tiempo.* Madrid: Fundación Isaac Albéniz, 1990.
        152 pp. ISBN 8475063136. ML141.A5 1990. In Spanish and Catalan.

        A catalog of the 1990 traveling exhibition organized by the Fundación. It con-
        tains articles and essays about Albéniz and his times. This was clearly an out-
        growth of the earlier *Imágenes de Isaac Albéniz* (see no. 140 below) but includes
        much additional material, as well as some items previously published. Richly
        illustrated with photographs and drawings of Albéniz and important figures and
        locales in his life story. (The articles and essays about Albéniz appear singly in
        this bibliography.) This seminal volume did much to stimulate research over the
        intervening years, and any Albéniz scholar will definitely want to consult more
        recent publications for updates and corrections to the information this book
        contains. Especially useful in this regard is no. 263, Torres/Aguado Sánchez, *La
        claves madrileñas de Isaac Albéniz.*

140.   ——, ed. *Imágenes de Isaac Albéniz.* Madrid: Fundación Isaac Albéniz, 1988.
        50 pp. ISBN 8475062504. ML410.A314 1988. In Spanish.

        A collection of essays, articles, and poems dealing with Albéniz. Includes many
        photographs as well as passages from his travel diaries. This was the first major
        publication of the Fundación and includes some items not found in their subse-
        quent publications (these appear singly in this bibliography).

141.   Franco, Enrique. "La Suite *Iberia* di Isaac Albéniz." *Nuova rivista musicale itali-
        ana* 7 (1973): 51–74. In Italian.

        Offers useful insights into each of the numbers of the famous collection. Traces
        the folkloric origin of some of the thematic material and touches on salient
        aspects of Albéniz's handling of the piano.

142.   Gallego, Antonio. "Isaac Albéniz y el editor Zozaya." *Notas de música (Boletín de
        la Fundación Isaac Albéniz)* 2–3 (April–June 1989): 6–14. In Spanish.

        Explores Albéniz's relations with the Madrid editor Benito Zozaya, who pub-
        lished much of Albéniz's piano music during the 1880s, when Albéniz was resid-
        ing in the capital. Zozaya was also the publisher of *La Correspondencia Musical,*
        in which notices of Albéniz's concerts regularly appeared and which is one of the
        most important sources of information about his activities during this period.

143.   ——. "Triana: Un ballet de Antonia Mercé "Argentina." *Scherzo: Revista de música*
        4/35 (June 1989): 70–72. In Spanish.

        A brief but fascinating history of the balletic interpretation of "Triana" from
        Iberia. Antonia Mercé, whose stage name was "La Argentina" (she was born to
        Spanish parents living in Buenos Aires), was a renowned Spanish dancer of the
        early 1900s and took a special interest in choreographing Albéniz's music, par-
        ticularly the orchestrations by Enrique Fernández Arbós (see no. 212).

144.   Gallego, Julián. *"Albéniz: La España que (acaso) fue."* *Música (Boletín de la
        Fundación Isaac Albéniz)* 1 (December 1988): 27–28. In Spanish.

Deals with Albéniz's romantic longing for a Spain that existed mostly in the realm of idealized reminiscence. This longing finds poignant expression in *Iberia,* whose musical depictions of various locales in Spain such as "Málaga" and "Almería" do not correspond to present or historical reality.

145. García, Desirée. "La otra estética de la música para piano catalana: Comparación entre la técnica pianística de la suite *Iberia* de Isaac Albéniz y las primeras obras para piano de Frederic Mompou." In *Antes de Iberia: de Masarnau a Albéniz, Pre-Iberia: From Masarnau to Albéniz.* Ed. Luisa Morales and Walter A. Clark, 239–54. Garrucha, Almería: Asociación Cultural LEAL, 2009. 303 pp. ISBN 9788461353316. ML738.S96 2008. In Spanish and English (Spanish articles include abstracts in English and vice versa).

An interesting comparison of Albéniz with another Catalan pianist and composer, Frederic Mompou (1893–1987). Though both studied in Paris and composed mainly for the piano, their aesthetics and compositional techniques were quite different, differences which the article explores by comparing and contrasting Albéniz's *Iberia* with various keyboard works by Mompou.

146. García, Laura Sanz. "Isaac Albéniz y la difusión de la cultura española en París, a través del género epistolar." *Anuario musical* 65 (January–December 2010): 111–32. In Spanish (English abstract).

This article makes excellent use of surviving correspondence at the Biblioteca de Catalunya to flesh out the central role Albéniz played in establishing crucial connections between Spanish (particularly Catalan) musicians, artists, and writers active in Paris around 1900 and their French counterparts. The author compares and contrasts Spanish and French cultures at that time, as reflected in the interaction of these two groups.

147. Gauthier, André. *Albéniz.* Translated from French to Spanish by Felipe Ximénez de Sandoval. Madrid: Espasa-Calpe, 1978. 123 pp. ISBN 8423953300. ML410. A3G38 1978. In Spanish.

Gauthier succeeded Laplane as the foremost French biographer of Albéniz. The biographical material is completely dependent on earlier secondary sources. Offers helpful synopses of Albéniz's stage works as well as a balanced discussion of *Iberia.* The discography and bibliography, however, are so cursory as to appear mere afterthoughts.

148. Gilson, Paul. "Albéniz à Bruxelles." *Notes de musique et souvenirs.* Brussels: Collection Voilà, 1924. Pp. 11–19. Reprinted Brussels: Éditions Ignis, 1942. (Reprinted in no. 139, Franco, ed., *Albéniz y su tiempo,* pp. 29–32, in Spanish.) In French.

Gilson was a friend of Albéniz and recorded his impressions of their first meeting in this article. Must be taken with a grain of salt, as the author declares that Albéniz did not introduce himself until after they had had supper together. But his recollections of Albéniz's loquacity and vivacity agree with other accounts.

149.   Gómez Amat, Carlos. *Historia de la música española*. Vol. 5: Siglo XIX. Madrid: Alianza Música, 1984. Pp. 305–17. ISBN 8420685054. ML315.A48. In Spanish.

Amat devotes an entire chapter to Albéniz, but from a biographical standpoint it suffers from reliance on accounts that are not altogether accurate. The discussion of the music is very limited and not furnished with any musical examples.

150.   Grew, Sydney. "The Music for Pianoforte of Albéniz." *The Chesterian* 6/42 (1924): 43–48. In English.

Surveys the piano works of the composer and treats the "startling difference" between his earliest works and *Iberia*. Lauds the genuineness of his Spanish style, declaring that the works of non-Spaniards in that vein have "either perverted our taste for Spanish music or obscured our vision, the incomplete or false making us unable to apprehend the character of the true and absolute." Recommends that musicians familiarize themselves with Spanish folklore to gain a fuller appreciation of Albéniz's music, claiming that "he will always most please men and women of high intellectual ardour."

151.   Guerra y Alarcón, Antonio. *Isaac Albéniz, notas crítico-biográficas de tan eminente pianista*. Madrid: Escuela Tipográfica del Hospicio, 1886. Extract in G. Arteaga y Pereira, ed., *Celebriades musicales* (Barcelona: Centro Editorial Artístico, 1886), 650–52. Original reprinted Madrid: Fundación Isaac Albéniz, 1990. 47 pp. ISBN 8475063136. ML410.A3G84 1990. In Spanish.

The first biographical account of Albéniz, issued in conjunction with his sensational concerts in Madrid in 1886. Information for the booklet came straight from Albéniz but does not agree in many particulars with accounts he later dispensed to other journalists, friends, family members, and biographers, or with the actual historical record as revealed in primary sources. In fact, this publication was a sort of propaganda, and the self-mythologizing fantasies it contains found their way into many subsequent biographical accounts because later writers were reluctant to doubt Albéniz's own word. Includes useful lists of his repertoire, compositions, and his extraordinarily ambitious program at the Salón Romero on January 24 of that year.

152.   Halbreich, Harry. "Análisis de *Iberia*." *Scherzo: Revista de música* 4/35 (June 1989): 78–81. In Spanish.

Presents brief but insightful descriptions of each of the movements from Albéniz's *chef d'oeuvre*, with useful emphasis on the work's favorable reception in France among members of the avant-garde, especially Messiaen. Despite its title, it does not present so much of a musico-theoretical analysis as it does an aesthetic one.

153.   Haller, Robert S. "Malory Meets Wagner in Madrid: Albéniz's *Merlin* and the Mythologizing of Arthur." *Ars Lyrica* 15 (2005–06): 67–78. In English.

A very astute analysis of the opera *Merlin*, especially its textual sources and Money-Coutts's transformation of them into a libretto of questionable utility. Particularly useful here is a chart comparing the sorcerer Merlin's scenes with their sources in Wagner and Malory. This article was written in the wake of *Merlin*'s revival in 2003 at the Teatro Real in Madrid (see nos. 711–13) and somewhat skeptically concludes that "the disparate elements brought together in this opera could never make consistent artistic sense no matter what principles of composition and dramatization were followed."

154.   Harding, James. "Isaac Albéniz." *BBC Music Magazine* 8/9 (May 2000): 36–40. In English.

Albéniz was the BBC's Composer of the Month in this issue, and the author presents a skillful summary of new information recently made available in the Clark biography (nos. 102–04). Includes a nicely illustrated Life & Times chronology, as well as a sidebar recommending particular recordings and books.

155.   Harper, Allanah. "Isaac Albéniz." *The Gramophone* (December 1927): 265–68. In English.

A brief but well-written overview of the composer's life and work. Contains some accurate and even useful information, in addition to the usual fables.

156.   Heras, Antonio de las. *Vida de Albéniz.* Barcelona: Ediciones Patria, 1940. 182 pp. ML410.A3H3. In Spanish.

Superficial biography consisting of short chapters and providing no footnotes or bibliography. Distillation of secondary sources with little discussion of the music and no musical examples.

157.   Iglesias, Antonio. *De la dificultad del gran piano de Isaac Albéniz.* Madrid: Editorial Alpuerto, 1988. 25 pp. (Offprint of an article that appeared in the III. *Boletín de la Reial Acadèmia Catalana de Belles Arts de Sant Jordi* in Barcelona.) In Spanish.

Intriguing study of the technical difficulties that abound in Albéniz's piano work *Iberia*. Among these problems are frequent hand crossings, intertwining of the fingers of both hands, superabundant accidentals (especially double flats), and the exaggerated use of tempo and dynamic markings. Yet, for all his specificity in these respects, Albéniz neglected to include metronome markings and was stingy with fingerings, leaving that job for performers and editors. Thus, every performer must arrange certain passages of the work to make it playable, says Iglesias.

158.   ——. *En torno a Isaac Albéniz y su "Iberia."* Madrid: Real Academia de Bellas Artes de San Fernando, 1992. 46 pp. In Spanish.

The text of a lecture given at the Real Academia de Bellas Artes de San Fernando on April 5, 1992. Presents an overview of Albéniz's career and accomplishments and treats the particular significance of his greatest work, *Iberia*. Deplores the ongoing neglect, both official and scholarly, of Albéniz in his homeland and calls for greater recognition of his importance. Includes the text of a response by Antonio Fernández-Cid, who concurs with and elaborates upon themes presented by Iglesias. The 15 pages of footnotes contain some useful information.

159.   ——. *Enciclopedia Salvat de los grandes compositores.* Volume 4: La música nacionalista. Pamplona: Salvat S.A. de Ediciones, 1982. Pp. 230–50. ISBN 8471374617 (v. 4). In Spanish.

A remarkably lengthy entry for its time. Though the biography is based on the canon and has now been superseded, it is very detailed and still contains some valuable data. Includes many photographs and illustrations as well as a list of works.

160.   ——. *Isaac Albéniz (su obra para piano).* Madrid: Editorial Alpuerto, 1987. 2 vols. 425 pp. (v. 1) and 488 pp. (v. 2). ISBN 8438101119 (v. 1) and 8438101208 (v. 2). ML410.A3 I3 1987. In Spanish.

Another in this author's series of studies of Spanish piano music and composers. Presents detailed examination of Albéniz's large piano output. The works are placed in alphabetical rather than chronological order. The books are enhanced by musical examples, poems, and photographs and conclude with a list of works, discography, and bibliography.

161.   Iglesias, Antonio, and Jacqueline Kalfa. "Albéniz, Isaac." *Diccionario de la música española e hispanoamericana.* Ed. Emilio Casares, i:188–201. Madrid: Sociedad General de Autores y Editores, 1999. ISBN8480483040. ML101.S7 D53 1999. In Spanish.

A very substantial article richly illustrated with photos and concluding with an ample bibliography. Still, the authors persist in perpetuating Albéniz's self-mythology, even in the face of contradictory evidence presented in several of the items listed in the bibliography. Not a reliable source of information.

162.   *Isaac Albéniz, artista i mecenes.* Catalog of an exhibition organized by the Museu Diocesà de Barcelona, July–September 2009. Barcelona: Museu Diocesà de Barcelona, 2009. 284 pp. ISBN 9788493689551. ML410.A3. In Catalan, Castilian, English.

Contains articles by the following (see separate entries): Joana Alarcón Hernández, Roger Alier, Walter Aaron Clark, Josep Colomer i Ràfols, Pere Jordi Figuerola i Rotger, Josep Marti i Bonet, and Julio Samsó Moya.

163.   Istel, Edgar. "Isaac Albéniz." Trans. Frederick H. Martens. *The Musical Quarterly* 15 (1929): 117–48. In English.

A summary of Albéniz's life and works, based in part on Collet (no. 117) and in part on the author's acquaintance with the composer's widow, Rosina. Istel deprecates Albéniz's attempts to compose opera, especially *Merlin,* and finds *Iberia* to be unconvincing in its complexity and hence mere "studio music." Albéniz was best at "singing his little song beneath the eternally smiling sun of Spain, freely and happily, with no concern for academic demands." As patronizing and inaccurate as this assessment clearly is, Istel reserves his most lethal venom for Money-Coutts and the "Faustian pact," which he holds "responsible for Albéniz's untimely end." Despite all this, the article contains musical examples and some useful insights into the music.

164. Jankélévitch, Vladimir. "Albéniz et l'État de verve." *Mélanges d'histoire et d'esthétique musicales. Offerts à Paul-Marie Masson*, vol. 1, pp. 197–209. Paris: Bibliothèque d'Études Musicales, 1955. In French.

Essay on Albéniz's musical style. Ideas are often couched in lyrical prose that seems specific but offers few substantial insights. Though there is a minimum of modern theoretical terminology, the text is illustrated with musical examples.

165. ——. *La Présence lointaine. Albéniz, Séverac, Mompou*. Paris: Éditions du Seuil, 1983. 158 pp. ISBN 2020064510. ML390.J24 1983. In French.

An expansion of the above article. He states that "the distance is great between the charming 'tiles' of the second act of *Pepita Jiménez*, which relies on enumerative and amplified juxtaposition, and the third and fourth books of *Iberia*, which develop through a kind of organic growth, like tropical plants." Albéniz is the "poet of mystery" and the "magician of flat keys." Resorts to the standard observation that in his compositions for the stage Albéniz, a "phenomenal pianist, . . . never ceased to feel and think through his rapport with the keys."

166. Jean-Aubry, Georges. "Isaac Albéniz (1860–1909)." *Musical Times* 58 (1917): 535–38. In English.

Presents a biographical summary interlaced with personal recollections of the composer. Extensive treatment of *Iberia* and its merits in relation to piano warhorses of the nineteenth century by Chopin, Liszt, Schumann, Franck, and so on. Explores Spain's indifference to much of his work. "The life-work of Albéniz is perhaps the only image around which all Spain, whether from North or South, assembles. One and all of the young composers of Spain owe to him a debt."

167. Jiménez, Lourdes. "Isaac Albéniz, artista i mecenes." In *Isaac Albéniz, artista i mecenes*. Catalog of an exhibition organized by the Museu Diocesà de Barcelona, July–September 2009, 117–30. Barcelona: Museu Diocesà de Barcelona, 2009. 284 pp. ISBN 9788493689551. ML410.A3. In Catalan, Castilian, English.

A survey of Albéniz's relationship with the art and artists of his own time, especially those associated with the modernist movement. Treats photographs and paintings of the composer himself and then discusses his sizable collection of paintings, including canvases by Ramon Casas, Santiago Rusiñol, Ignacio Zuloaga, and Darío de Regoyos, as well as several lesser-known but excellent painters. This article is followed by color reproductions of paintings and drawings by these artists, including works by Laura Albéniz, the composer's daughter.

168. Kalfa, Jacqueline. "Isaac Albéniz à Paris." *Revue internationale de musique française* 9/26 (June 1988): 19–37. In French.

Treats in detail Albéniz's Paris years (1894–1909) and his relationship with notable musicians and institutions, including Chausson and d'Indy, the Société Nationale de Musique, and the Schola Cantorum. Discusses his relationship with Debussy and the influence they exerted on one another. Albéniz was no mere hanger-on but rather an active participant in the Parisian musical scene around 1900 and was greatly admired for his virtuosity and the vibrant originality of his music.

169. ——. "Inspiration hispanique et ecriture pianistique dans *Iberia* d'Isaac Albéniz." Thèse de 3e cycle de musicologie, Université de Paris-Sorbonne, 1980. 624 pp. In French.

An exhaustive study of the pianistic style of Albéniz's most important composition. It begins with a general introduction to the work, followed by five chapters devoted to Spanish music from the era of Domenico Scarlatti through the revival of the zarzuela, with an emphasis on folk music and nationalism. Chapters 6 through 20 deal with Albéniz's handling of local color, articulation, notation, modality, evocation of the guitar, and his harmonic language, particularly the use of nonharmonic tones. Chapters 21 through 23 treat the form of the pieces, particularly in relation to the use of variation and improvisation in Spanish folk music. The final three chapters discuss the performance and reception of the work as well as its influence on other composers (Granados, Turina, Falla, and Ohana). The dissertation concludes with appendices pertaining to documentation (programs, correspondence, transcriptions, and press reviews) and terminology. The bibliography is followed by a discography, tables of musical examples and illustrations, and an index of names.

170. ——. *Isaac Albéniz (1860–1909): la vocation de l'Espagne.* Paris: Séguier, 2000. 124 pp. ISBN 2840491826. ML410.A3. In French.

A brief biography intended for a general readership, without analysis of the composer's music. Eschews any engagement with the world of Albéniz scholarship, despite a florescence in this area during the 1990s. Thus, this book recycles the same old legends about Albéniz's escapades as a stowaway and his improbable studies with Liszt, among many other things. Includes a works list, now superseded by Torres's *Catálogo* (no. 241), but no bibliography or index. Useful only for the author's occasional insights into Albéniz's Parisian milieu and the circles in which he moved.

171. Laplane, Gabriel. *Albéniz, sa vie, son oeuvre.* Preface by Francis Poulenc. Geneva: Éditions du Milieu du Monde, 1956. 222 pp. ML410.A3L3. In French. *Albéniz: vida y obra de un músico genial.* Translated into Spanish by Bernabé Herrero

and Alberto de Michelena. Paris: Editorial Noguer, 1958. 240 pp. ML410.A3L318 1958.

Laplane's biography was the most thorough effort ever undertaken. Its 3 sections and 19 chapters include not only a biographical discussion but also an excellent treatment of his musical style and a survey of his works. It concludes with a useful bibliography (a rarity in this field), as well as the customary discography and chronology of Albéniz's life. Still, it is far from a reliable source of information and is rife with errors and the usual misconceptions, the result of too great a reliance on secondary sources and a reluctance to treat the composer's autobiographical dispensations with the necessary circumspection.

172.   Laufer, Milton Rubén. "Isaac Albéniz and *La Vega*: A Publication History and New Edition." D.M.A. thesis, Rice University, 2003. 106 pp. UMI 3090167. In English.

La vega is a transformative work in Albéniz's output, in both its formal/harmonic complexity and its stylization of folkloric materials. This groundbreaking thesis establishes the history of its publication through a careful examination of primary sources and offers a cleaned-up version, one free of the editorial errors that plagued many of Albéniz's works.

173.   Laufer, Milton Ruben, and John Q. Walker. "Musical Archaeology: The Recovery and Re-performance of Isaac Albéniz's Improvisations." In *Antes de* Iberia: *de Masarnau a Albéniz*, Pre-Iberia: *From Masarnau to Albéniz*. Ed. Luisa Morales and Walter A. Clark, 207–14. Garrucha, Almería: Asociación Cultural LEAL, 2009. 303 pp. ISBN 9788461353316. ML738.S96 2008. In Spanish and English (Spanish articles include abstracts in English and vice versa).

Albéniz made three surviving wax cylinder recordings in 1903, consisting of his improvisation of three "Impromptus." Using the latest technology, these works have been transcribed and then re-performed by Zenph Studios, providing likenew renditions of what are some of the composer's final works. The transcriptions have been published by G. Henle (see no. 21). This article explains the fascinating process by which these works have been restored.

174.   Lebrun, Vera. "A Great Spanish Composer." *Radio Times* (April 17, 1936): 11. In English.

Discusses Albéniz's London connections and presents the most accurate estimate of the amount of compensation Money-Coutts paid him to set his librettos and poems to music, about £1,200 a year. Lebrun was married to Albéniz's only son, Alfonso.

175.   Lewis, Lisa Michele. "Twelve *nouvelle impressions*: Historical and Cultural Factors Relating to the Performance of Isaac Albéniz's *Iberia* Suite." D.M.A. diss., University of Washington, 1998. 141 pp. UMI 9826344. In English. Reviewed by Hadassah Gallup Sahr, *Bulletin of the Council for Research in Music Education*, no. 150 (Fall 2001): 73–74.

This dissertation examines the indigenous Spanish elements that influenced and inform Albéniz's *Iberia*. Treats the significance of Arabic and Islamic music and culture, the influence and history of Gypsy music in Spain, the legacy of Mozarabic chant, transference to the keyboard of guitar and other idioms, the virtuosic keyboard style of Domenico Scarlatti, and trends of nationalism and use of folk music in early-twentieth-century Spain. Such a broad range of generalizations must always be viewed critically, even skeptically.

176.   Llongueres, Joan. "Como conocí a Isaac Albéniz." *Evocaciones y recuerdos.* Barcelona: Dalmau, 1944. (Reprinted in no. 139, Franco, ed., *Albéniz y su tiempo,* pp. 111–13.) In Spanish.

Relates interesting anecdotes about his acquaintance with Albéniz and confirms, among other things, Albéniz's close relationship with Barcelona modernists and his fluency in Catalan, which some sources deny.

177.   Llopis, Arturo. "En el centenario de Isaac Albéniz." *Destino* (February 13, 1960): 13–17. In Spanish.

An article based on conversations with Mariano Perelló, the Catalan violinist who was a friend of Albéniz. Perelló became acquainted with Albéniz during the final years of the composer's life, and this article's value lies in the credible anecdotes it provides of Albéniz's personality and relationships with others. Albéniz was, by this account, especially eager to help young, aspiring Spanish musicians like Perelló, but he was generous with everyone. Once, while the two were walking down the street together in Barcelona, Albéniz gave a few pesetas to a poor old woman and then exhorted Perelló to "learn to be generous."

178.   Llorens Cisteró, José María. "El 'Lied' en la obra musical de Isaac Albéniz." *Anuario Musical* 15 (1960): 123–40. In Spanish.

The first detailed study of all of Albéniz's art songs. Though the majority of these were written to texts by the English poet Francis Burdett Money-Coutts, Albéniz composed several other songs to Italian and French texts (see nos. 132 and 251). This article examines the songs in chronological order treating their genesis and style, with numerous musical examples. States that Albéniz's songs have not gained the same notoriety as his piano music because he invests most of the musical interest in the piano accompaniment (which is often virtuosic), while the voice declaims the text in a recitative that is often unmemorable. There are exceptions in which the piano is subordinate to a lyrical vocal line, for example, "To Nellie" from *To Nellie: Six Songs* (to poems by Money-Coutts), and the earlier *Seis baladas* (to Italian texts by the Marquesa de Bolaños). These are his most effective works in this genre.

179.   ——. "Isaac Albéniz a través de unas cartas inéditas." *San Jorge,* no. 38 (April 1960): 26–31. In Spanish.

The extant correspondence of Albéniz numbers in the hundreds of letters. Among these are missives from many distinguished contemporaries in France and Spain, and this article presents brief excerpts from several of them. Included are passages by Tomás Bretón, Alfred Bruneau, Gabriel Fauré, Enrique Granados, Joaquim Malats, and Enric Morera concerning both his performances and compositions. Unfortunately, these quotes bear neither the date nor the provenance of the letter; however, they establish the composer's wide range of personal and professional contacts and the high esteem and affectionate regard in which he was held. Pedrell, his erstwhile teacher, asked him to "remember those who love you for your genius, your constant work, and your goodness of heart."

180.   ——. "Notas inéditas sobre el virtuosismo de Isaac Albéniz y su producción pianística." *Anuario Musical* 14 (1959): 91–113. In Spanish.

Excerpts from letters, poems, and articles concerning Albéniz's remarkable gifts as a performer and improviser at the piano. Includes commentary from the album he took on his early concert tours in which admirers inscribed their encomiums. Also provides substantial quotes from letters by Francisco Barbieri, Vincent d'Indy, and Charles-Marie Widor congratulating him on his performances and his own compositions. Albéniz was a notable interpreter of eighteenth-century music, especially Scarlatti and Bach, and he was also a sensitive chamber musician whose rendering of Brahms won particular praise from his fellow musicians. Also includes passages from the correspondence between Albéniz and Joaquim Malats in regard to *Iberia*, as well as from his earlier letters to Enrique Moragas concerning "Granada" from the *Suite española no. 1*. Also represented are Tomás Bretón, Manuel de Falla, Enrique Granados, and the author Camille Mauclair. The article concludes with some dedications to Albéniz found in scores by d'Indy, Lluis Millet, and lgnacy Paderewski.

181.   Longuemare, Anne-Lise. "Nationalism and Exoticism: Performing Isaac Albéniz's *Iberia*." D.M.A. thesis, University of California, Los Angeles, 2004. 69 pp. UMI 3121222. In English.

Examines the various stylistic elements in Albéniz's *Iberia*, including Lisztian Romanticism, French Impressionism, and Spanish folklore. Argues that Albéniz's textures, his layering of voices, constituted a new way of conceiving pianistic sound that had deep roots in Spanish folk music. Makes use of historical recordings of Spanish folk and classical music, especially of flamenco and by Alicia de Larrocha, to shed light on issues of tempo, phrasing, pedaling, and formal structure in *Iberia*.

182.   López, Begoña. "Nuevas aportaciones a *Deux morceaux de prose de Pierre Loti*, de Isaac Albéniz." *Anuario musical* 57 (2002): 241–49. In Spanish (English abstract).

Explores the relationship between Albéniz and the French author Pierre Loti (né Julien Viaud) in the context of two songs that the composer wrote on texts of Loti, *Crépuscule* and *Tristesse*, which the author dates to 1898. The article explores in helpful detail Albéniz's relationship not only with Loti but also with a circle of artists, authors, and musicians called Les Vingt ("The Twenty"), which included Chausson, Debussy, Dukas, Fauré, Regoyos, Rodin, Whistler, and other luminaries. These songs were well known to earlier scholars, though the article treats the discovery of the manuscripts, for which, however, no precise information concerning their location is given. Those interested in all of Albéniz's songs are encouraged to consult no. 12, Torres, *Integral de la obra para voz y piano*, for the most accurate and up-to-date information.

183.   López-Bonastre, Begoña. "Isaac Albéniz: un double ancrage." *Échanges musicaux franco-espagnols XVIIe-XIXe siècles*. Proceedings of the Recontres de Villecroze, October 15–17, 1998. Ed. François Lesure, 335–41. Villecroze: Académie Musicale de Villecroze. ISBN 2252032995. ML270.1. In French.

Albéniz was "anchored" in two different cultures, the Spanish and the French. The Parisian influence on his output becomes more marked in his mature compositions, especially his songs with French texts, on which this essay focuses.

184.   Lucena, Luis Seco. "En la Alhambra." *Cuadernos de la Alhambra*. Granada, 1982. (Reprinted in no. 139, Franco, ed., *Albéniz y su tiempo*, pp. 105–09.) In Spanish.

Fascinating account of Albéniz's concerts in Granada in 1882 and his enthusiasm for the Alhambra. Albéniz created a sensation in the city and later expressed his love of Granada in several of his most popular compositions for the piano.

185.   Maione, Orazio. "Isaac Albéniz: *Iberia* e il problema dello stile." *Rassegna musicale curci* 55 (September 2002): 27–30. In Italian.

A brief and rather derivative (though without citations) overview of the stylistic influences operating in Albéniz's *Iberia*, from Spanish folklore to eighteenth-century keyboard music to French Impressionism.

186.   Marliave, Joseph de. *Études musicales*. Paris: Librairie Félix Alcan, 1917, pp. 119–38. ML60.M16. (Reprinted in no. 139, Franco, ed., *Albéniz y su tiempo*, pp. 33–40, in Spanish.) In French.

Compares Albéniz to Schumann in his Romantic technique but classical restraint, particularly in using folklore. Like Schumann, his inspiration is "noble and elevated." Regards *Merlin* as an error and a waste of time that should have been spent on piano composition.

187.   Marti i Bonet, Josep. "Albéniz, 'un dels nostres, el gran amic.'" In *Isaac Albéniz, artista i mecenes*. Catalog of an exhibition organized by the Museu Diocesà de Barcelona, July–September 2009, 11–13. Barcelona: Museu Diocesà de Barcelona, 2009. 284 pp. ISBN 9788493689551. ML410.A3. In Catalan, Castilian, English.

The author is director of the Diocesan Museum of Barcelona and provides fascinating insights into the organization of an exhibition devoted to Albéniz's activities as a patron of the visual arts. Includes a discussion of Albéniz's relations with many Catalan artists and writers in Barcelona's Art Nouveau movement, or *Modernisme catalan*.

188. Martínez, Julia. *Falla. Granados. Albéniz.* Series: Temas españoles. 2nd ed., pp. 21–30. Madrid: Publicaciones Españolas, 1959. ML390.M3. In Spanish.

Intended for a general readership, it contains no footnotes or other references and is a summary of common secondary sources. Describes his music as "the fruit of an improvisation unaware of the rules and ignorant of technical names," a gross exaggeration of statements by Felipe Pedrell and irrelevant to Albéniz's mature works.

189. Martínez Burgos, Manuel. "Isaac Albéniz: la armonía en las composiciones de madurez para piano solo como síntesis de procesos tonales y modales." Ph.D. diss., Universidad Autónoma de Madrid, 2004. 782 pp. UMI 3148054. In Spanish.

This dissertation explores tonal and modal harmonies in Albéniz's late works, including "Córdoba" from *Chants d'Espagne, La vega, Espagne (Souvenirs), Yvonne en visite!, Iberia, Navarra, and Azulejos.* Albéniz's integration of tonality and modality is accomplished through juxtaposition, superimposition, and integration of chords. Such harmonic procedures have important implications for the formal structures in these works. Includes abundant analysis of specific passages in the mature works.

190. ——. "La armonía en *Iberia* de Isaac Albéniz como síntesis de procesos tonales y modales." *Inter-American Music Review* 18/1–2 (summer 2008): 337–65. In English.

A summary of the preceding dissertation, it presents an analysis of Albéniz's *Iberia* and examines the myriad ways that the composer juxtaposes, superimposes, and integrates chordal structures. Continues with an examination of Albéniz's synthesis of harmonic procedures, focusing on tonality and modality.

191. Mast, Paul Buck. "Style and Structure in 'Iberia' by Isaac Albéniz." Ph.D. diss., University of Rochester, Eastman School of Music, 1974. UMI AAC 7421529. In English.

An exhaustive and detailed analysis of Albéniz's greatest work. Though somewhat dated, it is still very useful. Mast begins with a distillation of secondary sources in presenting a portrait of Albéniz as a man and artist. A chapter on Spanish folk music, mainly flamenco, serves as a necessary introduction to an extensive summary of the work's principal stylistic features. He then proceeds systematically through the four books of *Iberia* in discussing the formal structure of each number, with emphasis on Albéniz's adaptation of sonata form to his folkloric style. The conclusion is a useful recapitulation of the major points. This is followed by a works list, bibliography, discography, and an index to musical examples and Spanish terms.

192. Menéndez Aleyxandre, Arturo. *Albéniz, primer universalizador de la música española.* Barcelona: Graf Valero, 1960. 10 pp. In Spanish.

Text of a lecture given in commemoration of the centennial of Albéniz's birth. Credits Albéniz with elevating Spanish music from the trivial and the commonplace to the level of high art. "The music of Albéniz is folkloric in a lofty and exceptional sense . . . his music is Iberian in its etymology and universal in its potency and destiny."

193.   Mitjana, Rafael. "Merlin." *Revista musical de Bilbao* (October 1902). Reprinted in Rafael Mitjana, *¡Para música vamos!* Valencia: Casa Editorial F. Sempere, 1909. Pp. 202–07. Ml315.5.M5. (Also reprinted in no. 139, Franco, ed., *Albéniz y su tiempo*, pp. 77–80.) In Spanish.

Favorable assessment of Albéniz's Wagnerian opera *Merlin*, the only finished part of a projected trilogy entitled *King Arthur* with librettos by Money-Coutts. Praises the dance numbers in Act III as well as Albéniz's overall mastery of technique, structure, and setting of the text. Compares the "profundity" of its conception with Wagner's *Ring*.

194.   Montero Alonso, José. *Albéniz. España en "suite."* Barcelona: Silex, 1988. 189 pp. ISBN 8477370095. ML410.A3.M6 1988. In Spanish.

Basically a summary of secondary sources, especially Collet (no. 117), Laplane (no. 171), and Ruiz Albéniz (no. 221). Contains little in the way of original research, and the bibliography is largely confined to items in Spanish. Strictly biographical, with no discussion of the music. The concluding works list and chronology are useful; however, there is no index.

195.   Moragas, Rafael. "Epistolario inédito de Isaac Albéniz." *Música* 1/5 (May–June 1938): 38–45. In Spanish.

Letters from Albéniz to his friend Enrique Moragas throw valuable light on the genesis of several of his works, including "Granada" from the *Suite española no. 1*, "La vega" from the incomplete *The Alhambra. Suite pour le piano*, and the reorchestration of *Pepita Jiménez*. Also reveals his plan (unrealized) to set Joaquín Dicenta's play *Juan José* as an opera.

196.   Morales, Luisa, and Walter A. Clark, eds. *Antes de Iberia: de Masarnau a Albéniz; Pre-Iberia: From Masarnau to Albéniz.* Garrucha, Almería: Asociación Cultural LEAL, 2009. 293 pp. ISBN 9788461353316. ML738.S96 2008. In Spanish and English (English articles have Spanish abstracts and vice versa).

The proceedings of a major conference that took place in Garrucha, Spain, in southeast Andalusia near Almería, in the summer of 2008, in anticipation of the centennial of the composer's death. The volume is divided into three main parts: (1) Albéniz and His Historical Context, (2) Albéniz's Musical Style, and (3) Recovery and Rediscovery of Albéniz's Works. Several entries deal with other nineteenth-century piano virtuosos, composers, and teachers. Articles focused mainly on Albéniz are by some of the leading experts in this field, including Pola Baytelman, Michael Christoforidis, Walter Clark, Desirée García, Montserrat

Font Batallé, Milton Laufer, Alfonso Pérez Sánchez, and Jacinto Torres Mulas. These appear as separate entries in this bibliography.

197. Morales, Pedro G. "Notes for an Essay on Albéniz." *Essays on Music*. Ed. by Felix Aprahamian, pp. 5–9. London: Cassell & Co., 1967. ML55.A65. In English.

The author knew Albéniz, who told him that he used to perform the overture to Rossini's *Semiramide* with his back to the piano, and "that trick saved me more than once from starvation." There is some truth to this, but otherwise the account is anecdotal and loose with facts.

198. Morrison, Bryce. "The Essence of Spain, Definitively Captured in Albéniz's Masterpiece." *Gramophone* 90/1084 (June 2012): 96–101. In English.

Focuses on Albéniz's *Iberia* and its outstanding interpreters. Commences with pianist Blanche Selva's feelings about premiering the work and then assays recordings by other artists who have tackled it, including Aldo Ciccolini, Nicholas Unwin, Rosa Torres-Pardo, and Martin Jones, whose interpretation the author finds fluent but overly introspective.

199. "Necrologie." *Bulletin français de la Société Internationale de Musique* 5/7 (July 15, 1909): 717. In French.

This anonymous obituary tribute to the late pianist and composer reveals the tremendous attraction Albéniz had for Parisians, both as a man and a composer. Refers to the possibility of a production of Albéniz's opera *Pepita Jiménez* at the Opéra-Comique, something that would not happen until 1923. Deplores "indolent Spain's" continuing neglect of the "genius of one of its most glorious sons." This was probably a reference to the lack of interest there in his stage works.

200. Nectoux, Jean-Michel. "Albéniz et Fauré. Correspondence inédite." *Tilas (Travaux de l'Institut d'Études Iberiques et Latino-Americaines)*, pp. 159–86. Strasbourg, 1977. In French.

The only complete publication of the extensive correspondence (22 cards and letters) from Fauré to Albéniz and his family (in the Bc, sig. M986, "F"). These make it clear that they were the most intimate of friends and greatly admired one another. In addition, there are three poems by Fauré to Albéniz that reveal not only his wit and humor but also his affection for the Spaniard.

201. Newman, Ernest. "Albéniz and his 'Merlin.'" *The New Witness* 10/254 (September 20, 1917): 495–96. In English.

Though not premiered until 1950 (in Barcelona), Albéniz's opera *Merlin* found an early advocate in Ernest Newman, who extolled the "magical beauty" of the music. He recommended the score "to anyone who is on the look-out for something at once original, strong and beautiful" and who could appreciate with him the fact that "the best opera on our sacrosanct British legend has been written by a Spaniard."

202.   Nommick, Yvan. "Albéniz en París: Recepción y magisterio." *Scherzo* 24/240 (April 2009): 114–17. In Spanish.

An insightful overview of Albéniz's close relationships with leading musicians in *fin-de-siècle* Paris. These included such luminaries as Debussy, d'Indy, Dukas, Fauré, and Ravel, as well as his Spanish compatriots Falla and Turina. Albéniz played a key role in promoting a progressive form of Spanish music and assisting other Spanish composers keen to follow his lead.

203.   Pedrell, Felipe. "Albéniz. El hombre, el artista, la obra." *Músicos contemporáneos y de otros tiempos*. Paris: P. Ollendorf, 1910. Pp. 375–81. ML60.P373. Also in *Revista musical catalana* 6 (May 1909): 180–84 (in Catalan), and *La Vanguardia* (June 15, 1909) (in Spanish) (reprinted in no. 140, Enrique Franco, ed., *Imágenes de Isaac Albéniz*, pp. 20–22, in Spanish). See also Felip Pedrell, "Isaac Albéniz. L'home, l'artista i l'obra," *Revista musical catalana—Bulletí de l'Orfeó Català*, suplemento del no. 65 (June 7, 1909): 180–84. In Catalan.

Albéniz briefly studied composition with Pedrell in Barcelona during the early 1880s. In this article, Pedrell provides fascinating insights into this apprenticeship and Albéniz's distinctive musical personality. Pedrell claims that Albéniz was uncomfortable with the rules and regulations of composition, which only stifled his creativity. Pedrell overstates the case for Albéniz's lack of formal training and unfamiliarity with music theory, but Albéniz was a diffident orchestrator, and Pedrell gently chides him for using the orchestra as an extension of the piano. Pedrell has unqualified praise for Albéniz's pianistic gifts and applauds the "Spanish fragrance, flavor, and color" in *Iberia,* a nationalist impulse that Pedrell had helped inspire in Albéniz. Laments the ingratitude shown to Albéniz by his homeland, a refrain repeated many times by other commentators as well.

204.   Pena, Joaquim. "Musichs que fugen." *Joventut* 3 (1902): 383–85. In Catalan.

Pena recounts a dinner given in Albéniz's honor before his departure from Barcelona for Madrid in 1902. The event was held at the Hotel Sant Jordi de Vallvidrera, and many friends and luminaries were in attendance, including the conductor Crickboom and the critic Suárez Bravo. In spite of the festive mood, Albéniz expressed with some bitterness his reasons for moving to Madrid. He found in Barcelona an environment hostile not only to him but to artists like Morera, Pedrell, and Vives, all of whom had likewise fled to the capital city. The final straw, however, was the Liceu's rejection of *Merlin*. This, perhaps more than any other single reason, impelled him to abandon Barcelona.

205.   Pérez de Guzmán, Juan. "Los Albéniz." *La Época* (May 21, 1909). (Reprinted in no. 139, Franco, ed., *Albéniz y su tiempo*, pp. 23–28; however, the title of this article is an editorial invention. A facsimile reproduction of the original (entitled "Isaac Albéniz") is available in no. 263, Torres/Aguado Sánchez, *Las claves madrileñas de Isaac Albéniz*, p. 228.) In Spanish.

Pérez de Guzmán was a friend of the family, first in Barcelona and then in Madrid during Albéniz's young years. Deals with Albéniz's early education, flight from home, concert tours, and the suicide of his sister Blanca.

206. Pérez Sánchez, Alfonso. "El legado sonoro de *Iberia* de Isaac Albéniz. La grabación integral: un estudio de caso." Ph.D. thesis, Universidad Complutense de Madrid, 2012. In Spanish.

One of the most remarkable doctoral documents ever written on Albéniz, this original and thoroughly researched dissertation examines the recordings of the complete solo-piano version of *Iberia* from several perspectives in order to understand them better as commercial products. It is divided into three main parts: (1) historical information regarding the various interpreters and recordings; (2) album-cover iconography; and (3) musical tempo in the recordings. The author's methodology displays admirable rigor and could well serve as a model for further such investigations.

207. ———. "La presencia de *Iberia* en los distintos soportes sonoros." In *Antes de* Iberia: *de Masarnau a Albéniz*; Pre-Iberia: *From Masarnau to Albéniz*. Ed. Luisa Morales and Walter A. Clark, 125–140. Garrucha, Almería: Asociación Cultural LEAL, 2009. 303 pp. ISBN 9788461353316. ML738.S96 2008. In Spanish and English (Spanish articles include abstracts in English and vice versa).

This fascinating article presents a remarkably detailed overview of the recording history of *Iberia*, focusing on how developments in recording technology and formats have influenced the number of audio recordings available. The recording of certain numbers to the exclusion of other, equally worthy ones seems to have been dictated by that selection's suitability to the recording technology available at the time.

208. Pla, Josep. "El poeta Moréas y Albéniz." *Vida de Manolo contada por el mismo.* Barcelona: Ediciones Destino, 1947. 151 pp. (Excerpt entitled "La generosidad" appears in no. 140, Enrique Franco, ed., *Imágenes de Isaac Albéniz*, pp. 17–19.) In Spanish.

This is Chapter 17 of Pla's book and deals with Albéniz and the renowned Symbolist poet Jean Moréas (né Yánnis Papadiamantópoulos, 1856–1910). In this excerpt from that chapter, Pla recounts the kindness and generosity Albéniz showed to the young Spanish sculptor Manolo Hugué, the subject of the biography. Albéniz's home was a haven of warmth and hospitality for many Spanish writers, artists, and musicians trying to establish their careers in Paris around 1900. Fortunately, *La Vida de Manolo* has appeared in a newer edition (Barcelona: Libros del Asteroide, 2008; ISBN 9788493659738), and this is actually easier to obtain than the source cited here.

209. Raux Deledicque, Michel. *Albéniz, su vida inquieta y ardorosa.* Buenos Aires: Ediciones Peuser, 1950. 437 pp. In Spanish.

Raux Deledicque was a Frenchman who had briefly met Albéniz in 1908, before moving to Buenos Aires in 1914. His is the first and last attempt to write a novelistic biography of Albéniz, in which he invents large amounts of dialogue and fills in the "gaps" with unsubstantiated claims and sheer fiction. The lengthy book includes no serious discussion of the music, and scholarly rigor is lacking (no footnotes, index, or bibliography). The author did correspond with Albéniz's descendants, who obligingly sent him much of the archive to examine. Therefore, the book cannot be entirely disregarded.

210.   Redford, John Robert. "The Application of Spanish Folk Music in the Piano Suite 'Iberia' by Isaac Albéniz." D.M.A. document, University of Arizona, 1994. 75 pp. UMI AAC 9426340. In English.

Heavily indebted to Mast's dissertation (no. 191) and otherwise rather superficial, this work's chief value lies in its examination of folkloric references in *Iberia* through citation of examples from collections of Spanish folk song. Although Albéniz rarely quoted folk songs verbatim, these examples serve as useful points of reference in identifying to which types of song and dance themes from *Iberia* belong.

211.   Reig, Ramon. "Isaac Albéniz." *Revista de Gerona* 5/6 (Primer Trimestre de 1959): 55–56. In Spanish.

Reig relates interesting anecdotes about his meeting with Arthur de Greef, the Belgian pianist who tied for first place with Albéniz in the 1879 piano competition at the Conservatoire Royal in Brussels, where they were both students of Louis Brassin. De Greef declared that the jury could not decide between them, so evenly matched were they, and eventually declared them both winners "with distinction." (There were a total of four contestants on this occasion.) This is an aspect of that competition not revealed in any other account.

212.   Reverter, Arturo. "Albéniz-Arbós: Amistad, relación musical, escenarios." *Notas de música (Boletín de la Fundación Isaac Albéniz)* 2–3 (April–June 1989): 23–27. In Spanish.

Enrique Fernández Arbós (1863–1939) was a celebrated conductor and violinist whose orchestrations of several numbers from *Iberia* have found their way into the standard orchestral literature. Reverter explores the close personal relationship between these two giants of Spanish music, which began when they were students at the Brussels conservatory in the 1870s and ripened during their numerous concerts together in Spain and England during the following two decades.

213.   ——. "Historia de una amistad." *Scherzo: Revista de música* 4/35 (June 1989): 74–76. In Spanish.

Covers much of the same ground as the preceding article, with special emphasis on the two musicians' activities in London during the 1890s and Arbós's career as a conductor and orchestrator after the death of Albéniz in 1909.

214. Riva, J. Douglas. "Master class: Albéniz's 'Malagueña.'" *Virtuoso and Keyboard Classics* 10/4 (1990): 42–43.

Helpful insights into the technical and interpretive dimensions of one of Albéniz's most popular and characteristic works (T. 95C), by one of the leading interpreters of Spanish piano music.

215. ——. Liner notes for *Azulejos* (completed by Enrique Granados). *Enrique Granados: Piano Music*, vol. 5. Douglas Riva, piano. Naxos, 8.555325 (2001). In English, French, Spanish.

American pianist Douglas Riva is, after Alicia de Larrocha herself, the most important modern revivalist of Granados's piano works. Together with Larrocha, he published the first-ever critical edition of the complete works for piano (Barcelona: Boileau, 2002), and this CD is one of his groundbreaking Naxos recordings of the edition. This disc includes *Azulejos*, T. 107, a work Albéniz left unfinished at his death and which his widow requested that Granados finish. As Riva explains, "The 89 measures added by Granados continue *Azulejos* in the style begun by Albéniz, capturing the warmth and mystery alluded to in the title" (see no. 52).

216. ——. Liner notes for "Triana" from *Iberia* (arrangement for two pianos by Enrique Granados). *Enrique Granados: Piano Music*, vol. 10. Douglas Riva and Jordi Masó, pianos. Naxos, 8.570325 (2008). In English.

As Riva explains, "Granados's transcription of . . . *Triana* . . . is his only work scored for two pianos. His transcription respects the construction and details of the original version for piano solo. The only changes Granados made to the work involve filling out the harmonies of some chords and dividing the themes between the two players so as to alternate their presentation and development, producing an impassioned and brilliant dialogue" (see no. 53).

217. Roda, Cecilio de. "La 'Suite' Iberia." *Programas de Conciertos, Sociedad Madrileña* (1911–13). (Reprinted in no. 139, Franco, ed., *Albéniz y su tiempo*, pp. 73–76.) In Spanish.

Program notes for *Iberia* (the excerpt in Franco presents only "Evocación," "El Puerto," and "Triana"). The author's insights into the folkloric references are useful and are supported by brief musical examples. Conveys the fact that Albéniz was no ethnographer and mixed these references in a "capricious" manner without regard to consistency or authenticity.

218. Rodríguez Bermejo, Sonia. "Discovering Isaac Albéniz as a Song Composer." D.M.A. document, University of Cincinnati, College-Conservatory of Music, 2010. UMI 3432350. In English.

This document provides a guide for performers to Albéniz's art songs, of which there are about 30. Argues that these have not received the attention from scholars they deserve, though this is not really true in light of the work by

Jacinto Torres in particular (see nos. 12 and 251), which provides the most detailed and accurate research available. After an overview of biographical issues, the chapters focus on the settings of Gustavo Adolfo Bécquer's poetry; Italian songs; and French songs, with special attention to Wagnerian influence and that of the French *mélodie*. Finally, Albéniz's numerous English songs, with texts by Francis Burdett Money-Coutts, receive attention, concluding with the bilingual *Quatre Mélodies*, which are characteristic of the composer's mature style.

219.   Romero, Justo. *Isaac Albéniz: Discografía recomendada. Obra completa comentada.* Barcelona: Ediciones Península, 2002. 495 pp. ISBN 8483074575. ML156.5.A43. In Spanish.

This unique volume begins with a 60-page biographical summary revealing an admirable awareness of recent advances in Albéniz research by Clark, Torres, and others. This section concludes with opinions on Albéniz by such figures as Debussy, Pedrell, Rubinstein, and Sopeña. The book continues with an annotated catalog of works, organized by genre and medium and providing a brief commentary on each composition. Of special interest is the discography that concludes each entry in the catalog. Though by no means comprehensive, it suggests excellent historic and modern recordings of each work, where available. The book concludes with a chronology and index.

220.   Romero, Justo, Llúcia Gimeno, and Lourdes Jiménez Fernández. *Albéniz, leyendas y verdades.* Catalog of the exhibition organized by Spain's Ministerio de Cultura, the Biblioteca Nacional, and the Sociedad Estatal de Conmemoraciones Culturales in the Centro Cultural del Conde Duque de Madrid, November 11, 2009, to January 31, 2010. Madrid: Ayuntamiento de Madrid, 2009. In Spanish.

Fascinating and richly illustrated guide to the 2009–10 exhibition in Madrid, honoring the centenary of the composer's death and the sesquicentennial of his birth. Explores the fine line between legend and reality in the composer's life story. Comes with a DVD of the exhibition.

221.   Ruiz Albéniz, Victor. *Isaac Albéniz.* Madrid: Comisaria General de Música, 1948. 143 pp. In Spanish.

This brief biography is by Albéniz's nephew (the son of his sister Clementina), a doctor who attended Albéniz on his deathbed and who eventually gave up medicine to work as a music critic in Madrid. It is neither comprehensive nor entirely accurate, but it does present some interesting glimpses into Albéniz's private life based on family records as well as on the author's own relationship with the composer. Of special interest are passages from Albéniz's letters to Clementina. (These letters, located in the Biblioteca Nacional in Madrid, are now available in facsimile and transcription in no. 263, Torres/Aguado Sánchez, *Las claves madrileñas de Isaac Albéniz*, pp. 85–100.) His account of Albéniz's final days is the most detailed and reliable in any biography.

222.   Ruiz Tarazona, Andrés. *Albéniz: edición conmemorativa del centenario de Isaac Albéniz.* Madrid: Sociedad Estatal de Conmemoraciones Culturales, 2009. In Spanish.

A package of several items issued in connection with a special Madrid exhibition organized to commemorate the centenary of the composer's death and the sesquicentennial of his birth. Includes a reprint of Albéniz's travel diaries, *Impresiones y diarios de viaje*, edited by Enrique Franco (see no. 72); a DVD of the film *Iberia* by Carlos Saura, featuring arrangements of Albéniz's masterpiece accompanied by dance; the illustrated screenplay for Saura's *Iberia*; a DVD of José Luis López-Linares's documentary *Isaac Albéniz: El Color de la Música*; and a biographical essay by Andrés Ruiz Tarazona, *Albéniz, Soñar España.*

223.   ——. "*Iberia* en discos." *Notas de música: Boletín informativo bimestral de la Fundación Isaac Albéniz*, B. 2&3 (1989): 42–44. In Spanish.

A short essay surveying the rich tradition of *Iberia* on disc and some of the great pianists who have recorded it. Top honors go to Alicia de Larrocha.

224.   ——. *Isaac Albéniz: Espana soñada.* Madrid: Real Musical, 1975. 75 pp. ISBN 8438700098. ML410.A3.R8. In Spanish.

Another brief biography aimed at a general musical readership, it has no bibliography or index. Still, it is one of the few to stress Albéniz's Basque ancestry on his father's side. Otherwise, the book is very dependent on earlier and often undependable sources.

225.   Saba, Thérèse Wassily. "Walter Aaron Clark: Biographer of Albéniz and Granados." *Classical Guitar* 30/3 (November 2011): 22–29. In English.

An interview with Walter Aaron Clark, who expatiates on his research in Spanish music, particularly Albéniz. Notes the composer's bitterness about the negative reception accorded by Spanish critics to his operettas *San Antonio de la Florida* and *La sortija*, and contrasts that resentment with his enduring love of Spanish literature, history, and regional folklore.

226.   Sagardia, Ángel. *Albéniz.* Series: Gent Nostra, 46. Barcelona: Editions de Nou Art Thor, 1986. 51 pp. ISBN 8423953300. ML410.A3.G38 1978. In Catalan.

A small book intended for the general public, it nonetheless contains some insights into the latter period of Albéniz's life, especially regarding the premieres and reception of his stage works. Of greatest interest, perhaps, are several reproductions of drawings by Albéniz's daughter Laura, a noted artist.

227.   ——. *Isaac Albéniz.* Series: Hijos ilustres de España. Plasencia, Cáceres: Editorial Sánchez Rodrigo, 1951. 120 pp. In Spanish.

A major biographical effort. Though it is reasonably detailed, it lacks the footnotes and bibliography that would enhance its reliability and utility. Nonetheless, the author's placement of Albéniz's life and music in a larger cultural and historical context is informative, though the music itself does not receive a close examination. As with all other biographies, reliance on secondary sources and not on rigorous scrutiny of documentation is a major liability.

228.   Saint-Jean, J. "Isaac Albéniz (1860–1909)." *Revue française de Musique* 10/1 (1912): 3–16; 79–83. In French.

One of the most extensive pre-Collet accounts. Provides a biographical over-view that relies heavily on earlier sources, especially Guerra y Alarcón (no. 151). Stresses the importance of his association with Felipe Pedrell and his leading role in Spanish musical nationalism. Gives an overview of his output and includes a reproduction of the "Zortzico" from *España: Seis hojas de álbum* for piano, dedicated to Albéniz's friend Ignacio Zuloaga, the Basque artist. Concludes with an assessment of his late works, especially *Iberia*, and compares him favorably to Schumann and Debussy, among other notable figures in the arts.

229.   Salazar, Adolfo. "Isaac Albéniz y los albores del renacimiento musical en España." *Revista de Occidente* 12/34 (April–June 1926): 99–107. In Spanish.

Basically a review of Collet's recently issued biography of Albéniz and Granados (no. 117). Questions Albéniz's supposed assimilation of Debussian impression-ism, because Albéniz was too wedded to the "Lisztian rhapsody" style. In addi-tion, he did not possess the technical command of Debussy, and his penchant was for "direct, immediate effect," rather than the subtleties and complexities of impressionism.

230.   Salvat, Joan. "Epistolari dels nostres músics: Isaac Albéniz a Joaquim Malats." *Revista musical catalana* 30/357 (September 1933): 364–72. (Reprinted in no. 139, Franco, ed., *Albéniz y su tiempo*, pp. 129–36.) In Catalan.

The correspondence between these two titans of Catalan pianism reveals Albéniz's uncommon affection and respect for his compatriot. The correspond-ence deals mostly with the creation and interpretation of *Iberia*, several numbers of which Malats premiered in Spain (though Blanche Selva was the first to per-form each book in its entirety). *Iberia* was clearly written with Malats in mind, and his performance of it gave Albéniz complete satisfaction.

231.   ——. "Records musical entorn de l'Exposició de 1888." *La Veu de Catalunya* (July 30, 1929). In Catalan.

The author recounts Albéniz's participation in the Universal Exposition held in Barcelona in 1888. Albéniz gave critically acclaimed performances of his music as well as the standard repertoire; in fact, it was during this period that he was particularly absorbed in the music of Domenico Scarlatti. A substantial report that also covers other musical activities at the Exposition.

232.   Samsó Moya, Julio. "El diari de Laura Albéniz." In *Isaac Albéniz, artista i mecenes.* Catalog of an exhibition organized by the Museu Diocesà de Barcelona,

July–September 2009, 81–116. Barcelona: Museu Diocesà de Barcelona, 2009. 284 pp. ISBN 9788493689551. ML410.A3. In Catalan, Castilian, English.

The first-ever publication of the diary of Albéniz's daughter Laura, with an introductory essay on its genesis, contents, and history by the composer's grandson, who owns the diary and has finally made it public. This very important document sheds important light on Albéniz's family and its enduring presence in Spanish cultural life. Laura was a gifted artist, and her drawings adorned the first edition of Albéniz's *Iberia*. Diary entries are in Spanish and French and speak to the cosmopolitan lifestyle of the Albéniz family. Unfortunately, this edition did not use the original manuscripts by the composer's daughter Laura but rather a later, redacted version, so that an initial part containing many interesting observations by Albéniz from just a year before his death do not appear (I am indebted to Jacinto Torres Mulas for this information, who in turn learned it from Julio Samsó, grandson of Laura). Because Albéniz had progressive, even controversial, views about religion and politics (he was an atheist and socialist), there has been a tendency toward censoring his views in various editions.

233.   Saperas, Miquel. *Cinc compositors catalans: Nicolau, Vives, Mossèn Romeu, Lamote, Albéniz.* Barcelona: Josep Porter, 1975. Pp. 163–200. ML390.S2. In Catalan.

Though he relied heavily on secondary sources, Saperas examined material in the archives as well. His biography offers some information of value, especially in regard to the critical reception of Albéniz's music and his relationship to other major figures in Catalan culture in the nineteenth century. Of special interest is his detailed description of Albéniz's burial on Montjuïc in Barcelona.

234.   Seifert, W. "In Memoriam." *Musica* 13 (June 1959): 402–03. In German.

Assays Albéniz's importance, crediting him with bringing international recognition to Spanish national music and being the most significant predecessor of Manuel de Falla.

235.   Selleck-Harrison, Maria B. "A Pedagogical and Analytical Study of 'Granada' ('Serenata'), 'Sevilla' ('Sevillanas'), 'Asturias' ('Leyenda'), and 'Castilla' ('Seguidillas') from the 'Suite Española', Opus 47 by Isaac Albéniz." D.M.A. essay, University of Miami, 1992. 172 pp. UMI AAC 9314534. In English. Reviewed by Walter Aaron Clark, "Recent Researches in Spanish Music 1800 to the Present," *Inter-American Music Review* 16/1 (Summer–Fall, 1997): 88–90.

The first in-depth study of this portion of Albéniz's output, including not only detailed analyses of the music but useful guidance for the practice and execution of each of the numbers. The biography is a distillation of secondary sources and contains the usual errors. Though the author commendably questions the contradictions she finds, a thorough investigation of purely biographical issues was beyond the scope and focus of her work. Concludes with an extensive discography of this suite.

236.   Serra Crespo, José. *Senderos espirituales de Albéniz y Debussy.* Mexico City: Costa
       Arnie, 1944. 196 pp. ML410.A3.S4. In Spanish.

       A slender volume consisting of short chapters in which the author stresses the
       importance of Wagner and folklore in the nationalist music of Albéniz. In par-
       ticular, Pedrell's *Por nuestra música* (1891) is viewed as an influential manifesto,
       uniting these two elements into a coherent philosophy that had a strong impact
       on Albéniz.

237.   Sobrino, Ramón. "El epistolario inédito de Tomás Bretón a Isaac Albéniz (1890–
       1908): nuevos documentos sobre la música española en torno al 98." *Cuadernos
       de música iberoamericana* 5 (1998): 163–83. In Spanish.

       This is a well-organized and thorough presentation of the unpublished cor-
       respondence sent from composer/conductor Tomás Bretón (1850–1923) to
       Albéniz during the period 1890–1908 and that is located in the Biblioteca de
       Catalunya, Barcelona. It will be of great interest to anyone researching the close
       personal and professional relationship between these two men, and it forms a
       useful complement to Bretón's diary entries on Albéniz, edited by Jacinto Torres
       (no. 261).

238.   Solà-Morales, J. M. de. "La sang gironina-gaditana d'Isaac Albèniz." *Annals de
       l'Institut d'Estudis Gironins* 25/2 (1981): 233–53. In Catalan.

       Detailed study of Albéniz's genealogy, tracing his family on both mother's and
       father's sides back to the seventeenth century. Demonstrates beyond doubt that
       Albéniz's father was Basque and that there was no connection between his family
       and that of Mateo and Pedro Albéniz. Contains records of the military service of
       his maternal grandfather, a war hero who served for four decades in the Spanish
       army.

239.   Sopeña, Federico. "En el juego de las generaciones." *Scherzo: Revista de música*
       4/35 (June 1989): 68. In Spanish.

       An insightful essay regarding Albéniz's status as an expatriate and his feelings
       about Spain. Though Albéniz's music expresses great love for his homeland, he
       remained disillusioned with the political and cultural realities of Spain. He was
       not alone in this regard, as disaffection and desire for reform were characteristic
       of the generation that experienced the 1898 war with the United States.

240.   ———. "Gracia y drama en la vida de Isaac Albéniz." *Historia y vida* 2/12 (March
       1969): 122–33. In Spanish.

       Biographical summary making extensive use of correspondence already avail-
       able in Víctor Ruiz Albéniz's monograph (no. 221).

241.   Torres Mulas, Jacinto. *Catálogo sistemático descriptivo de las obras musicales de
       Isaac Albéniz.* Preface by Robert M. Stevenson. Madrid: Instituto de Bibliografía
       Musical, 2001. 521 pp. ISBN 8460728544. In Spanish. Reviewed by Walter Aaron
       Clark, *Notes of the Music Library Association* 59/2 (December 2002): 332–33.

Torres surveys previous attempts to catalog Albéniz's oeuvre and delves into the documentary sources that permit a reappraisal of his output. Of special utility is a list of all the archives (with addresses) holding materials used in assembling this catalog. Torres modestly refrained from assigning "T" numbers to Albéniz's works, though most scholars have since adopted that procedure, including the present author in this volume. The systematic portion of the catalog presents the works numbered continuously throughout and grouped by genre/medium: stage, orchestra, chamber, vocal, and piano. It continues with assorted arrangements, exercises, and improvisations, and concludes with titles for projected as well as spurious and wrongly attributed works. This section is noteworthy for its intelligent deployment of incipits, providing where necessary not only the first few measures of the piece but of the main theme as well, which often does not appear for many measures into the composition. Stage works feature incipits from all the principal numbers of the opera or zarzuela, laid out in order of their appearance. The detailed annotations for each work include information about the basic musical traits (key, meter, tempo), duration, dedication (if any), date and place of composition, manuscript sources (if any; usually there are none) and their present location, date, and venue of premiere, and additional notes and bibliography (where relevant). The text is enhanced by reproductions of manuscript pages, concert programs, and first-edition covers. Of real value are the six indexes, which list: abbreviations; publishers and plate numbers; dedicatees; two works indexes, one organized by medium, the other alphabetically; and a summary index. Remarkable for its wealth of detailed and accurate information, this is the definitive catalog and will stand the proverbial test of time.

242.   ——. "Concentración vs. dispersión de fondos documentales. El desdichado caso de Isaac Albéniz." In *El patrimonio musical: Los archivos familiares (1898–1936)*. Ed. Jorge de Persia and María García Alonso, 55–77. Trujillo (Cáceres): Ediciones de La Coria. Fundación Xavier de Salas, 1997. 151 pp. ISBN 8488611048. In Spanish.

Overview of the state of primary resources in Albéniz research, particularly in regard to the family archive and its dispersal to several libraries and archives, mostly in Barcelona. This is basically a case study in how *not* to handle such a priceless collection of materials.

243.   ——. "El Conservatorio de Madrid en la trayectoria vital y artística de Isaac Albéniz [I]." In *Música. Revista del Real Conservatorio Superior de Música de Madrid*, nos. 16–17 (2009–10): 213–65. In Spanish.

Despite conventional notions about Albéniz's supposed lack of technical and theoretical instruction, this essay reveals his early studies in regular classes at the Real Conservatorio Superior de Música de Madrid. The research is based on hitherto unknown documentation, reproduced here in its entirety for the first time. It also looks at how important the period in which Albéniz lived in Madrid was for the subsequent evolution of his artistic career. This first part focuses on his childhood and adolescence.

244.   ——. "Génesis y avatares de una opereta camaleónica: *The Magic Opal,* de Isaac Albéniz." In *Isaac Albéniz: The Magic Opal. Òpera còmica en dos actes. Llibret d'Arthur Law.* Ed. Borja Mariño, 36–42. Barcelona: Tritó, 2011. ISBN 9788492852079. M1503.A332 M3 2011. In Spanish.

This insightful essay clarifies the supposed involvement of Enrique Fernández Arbós in editing several numbers in this operetta. Torres's research establishes the dates and circumstances of its creation, revision, and premieres, as well as documenting the reception of the work in London and various cities in Britain.

245.   ——. "Influencias estilísticas y fuentes temáticas en la obra de Isaac Albéniz." In *Antes de* Iberia: *de Masarnau a Albéniz;* Pre-Iberia: *From Masarnau to Albéniz.* Ed. Luisa Morales and Walter A. Clark, 125–40. Garrucha, Almería: Asociación Cultural LEAL, 2009. 303 pp. ISBN 9788461353316. ML738.S96 2008. In Spanish and English (Spanish articles include abstracts in English and vice versa).

The author emphasizes various thematic and stylistic elements that are ubiquitous in Albéniz's works, from his earliest essays to his final compositions, which feature increasing stylization of his customary materials. The influence of Scarlatti and Chopin is readily apparent, interwoven with a process of Romantic "invention" in regard to Spanish folklore.

246.   ——. "Isaac Albéniz ante la orquesta: *Catalonia.*" In *Catalonia: rapsòdia simfònica,* T. 24. Ed. Jacinto Torres y Arnau Farré, 3–11. Barcelona: Tritó Edicions, 2010. ISBN 9790692047094. M1045.A53. In Catalan, Spanish, English.

Over the decades, many commentators have criticized Albéniz's supposed inadequacies as an orchestrator, arguing that he required the assistance of others or that it was a mere projection of his pianistic conceptions. This essay rebuts such critiques by providing evidence for the considerable skill that Albéniz acquired in writing an orchestral score, without any prior pianistic scheme or model. It also analyzes the work's thematic ingredients, its genesis, and diffusion.

247.   ——. "Isaac Albéniz en los infiernos." *Scherzo: Revista de Música,* no. 80 (December 1993): 150–53. In Spanish.

This first appeared as the prologue to the dissertation by Marta Falces Sierra (no. 132). It deals with the issue of Albéniz's supposed Faustian pact, in which biographers have portrayed Money-Coutts as Mephistopheles, Albéniz as Faust, and Rosina as Marguerite. Also touches on the subject of Albéniz's connection to Freemasonry (see no. 248). This includes a transcription of a lengthy and humorous poem by the singer E. Alzamora, which is dated London, May 7, 1893. It was previously unpublished and is of considerable biographical interest.

248.   ——. "Isaac Albéniz y los hermanos francmasones." In *La masonería española. Represión y exilios. XII Symposium Internacional de Historia de la Masonería*

Española (Almería, 8–10 octubre 2009), vol. 1. Ed. J. A. Ferrer Benimeli, 601–25. Zaragoza: Gobierno de Aragón, 2010. In Spanish.

Offers a very detailed investigation concerning all aspects of Albéniz's lifelong relationships with freethinkers and Freemasons, including the Masonic membership of many of the people who played a decisive role in his life and the very close connections he established with them, not only in Spain but also in Belgium, Cuba, England, and France.

249. ——. "Isaac Albéniz's Elusive Grail." Liner notes for *Merlin*. José de Eusebio conducting the Coro y Orquesta Sinfónica de Madrid. Decca, 289467096-2 (2000). In English.

Albéniz's collaboration with his English librettist, patron, and friend Francis Burdett Money-Coutts resulted in a truly monumental project, that is, an operatic trilogy based on Malory's Arthurian romance. In these insightful notes, the author explores Albéniz's fascination with Wagner in particular and the evolution of his works for the stage, from *The Magic Opal* to this trilogy, of which only the first installment, *Merlin*, was ever completed. Torres takes to task those commentators who have disparaged Albéniz's efforts in this arena, averring that *Merlin* is, in fact, "a vast and noble achievement from the greatest Spanish composer of his age" (see no. 30).

250. ——. "La inspiración 'clásica' de Isaac Albéniz." Liner notes for *Albéniz: Sonatas para piano no. 3, 4, 5; L'automne (Valse)*. Albert Guinovart, piano. Harmonia Mundi, 1957007 (2003; reissue of a recording made in 1994). In Spanish, French, English. Reviewed by Walter Aaron Clark, *Nineteenth-Century Music Review* 3/1 (2006): 136–39.

Utilizing highly original research, these notes present the interesting story behind the genesis and publication history of Albéniz's piano sonatas from the 1880s. Though of high quality, they lie outside his nationalist style and have received scant attention from performers (see no. 48).

251. ——. "La obra vocal de Isaac Albéniz: songs, mélodies y canciones." *Revista de musicología* 22/2 (1999): 165–219. In Spanish.

The most thorough survey undertaken to that time of the most neglected aspect of Albéniz's oeuvre: his songs. Albéniz wrote 30 songs, in Spanish, French, and English, beginning in the 1880s and continuing to the end of his life. Thus, one can trace his stylistic development through the study of these compositions, the final ones of which exhibit the advanced harmonic and formal procedures of *Iberia* and other late works. It includes an exhaustive examination of the documentary sources, both literary and musical, a catalog of the various works, and critical commentary on the technical and aesthetic characteristics of this music. A greatly expanded and more up-to-date version of this article is available in no. 12, Torres, *Integral de la obra para voz y piano*, pp. 4–35 (Catalan); pp. 38–71 (Spanish); and pp. 74–105 (English).

252.   ——. "La pasión cervantina de Isaac Albéniz." Discurso pronunciado por el Exemo. Sr. Dr. D. Jacinto Torres Mulas en el acto de su toma de posesión como Académico de Número el día 26 de octubre de 2005 y contestación del académico Excmo. Sr. Dr. D. Fernando Aguirre de Yraola. Madrid: Real Academia de Doctores de España, 2005. In Spanish.

Speech read on the occasion of Dr. Jacinto Torres Mulas's induction into the prestigious Royal Academy of Spanish Doctors. Explores Albéniz's intriguing fascination with Cervantes, especially the composer's unrealized plans to write an opera based on the novel *Rinconete y Cortadillo*, in addition to a programmatic orchestral work entitled *Aventura de los molinos*, inspired by Don Quijote's tilting at windmills. It concludes by suggesting a parallel between the failure of these Cervantine operatic endeavors and his final intense dedication to composing *Iberia*. This was a timely essay, intended in part to celebrate the 400th anniversary of the publication of the first part of *Don Quijote*. A revision was published under the title "La jamás imaginada 'Aventura de los molinos', de Isaac Albéniz," in *Cervantes y el Quijote en la Música* (Madrid: Ministerio de Educación y Ciencia, Centro de Estudios Cervantinos, 2007), 345–71.

253.   ——. "La producción escénica de Isaac Albéniz." *Revista de Musicología* 14/1–2 (1991): 167–212. In Spanish.

This was the first systematic study of the stage works of Albéniz, including their genesis, production history, alternate titles, and sources. It was first presented as a paper at the 1990 national meeting of the Spanish Musicological Society in Granada. Its enormous impact has been felt in the subsequent revival, in both recordings and productions, of several of Albéniz's numerous musico-dramatic works, which have been ignored or disparaged by the majority of commentators over the past century. Based on a rigorous examination of documentary evidence, this article helped revolutionize our understanding of Albéniz as a composer.

254.   ——. "La Schola Cantorum de Isaac Albéniz." Liner notes for *Albéniz en París y su entorno de la Schola Cantorum*. Díaz Chopite, Mercedes (soprano), and Jorge Robaina (piano). Several Records, SRD-280 (2004); Tañidos SRD-280 (2004). In Spanish and English.

These substantial notes provide valuable information about the cultural milieu in which Albéniz wrote his French songs, which exhibit a style and character that diverge from the *españolismo* he consistently cultivated in his piano works. In particular, Torres focuses on the Schola Cantorum, where Albéniz taught and of whose major figures he was a close friend and colleague, especially d'Indy and Dukas. He also treats Albéniz's immersion in the Parisian musical scene and close contacts with a wide range of musicians, including Chausson, Debussy,

Fauré, and others. They exerted a strong influence on his late style, fully revealed in these songs (see no. 39).

255. ——. "Las voces y los ecos: Un siglo de historiografía albeniciana." *Anales de la Real Academia de Doctores de España* 14/2 (2010): 143–60. In Spanish.

A deeply insightful overview of the history of Albéniz biography, from its tentative beginnings in the late nineteenth century through the florescence of scholarship in the last quarter century. As one of the leading figures in this development, the author is in an excellent position to assay Albéniz historiography and lay out the necessary intellectual parameters that successful research must observe.

256. ——. Liner notes for *Iberia, Suites españolas Nos. 1–2*. Guillermo González, piano. Naxos, 8.554311–12 (1998). In English, French, Spanish.

These brief notes provide nonetheless fascinating reflections on and deep insights into Albéniz's long stylistic evolution, from the early character pieces in the *Suites españolas* to *Iberia*. The author notes that "For Albéniz, surmounting the limits set by musical *costumbrismo* and the aesthetic of the picturesque, formed part of an internal evolution which has more relation with his personal dynamics rather than any alleged advice" from Liszt or Pedrell (see no. 46).

257. ——. *'Pepita Jiménez', cien años de soledad*. Program notes (pp. 3–9) for a reorchestrated concert version (by Josep Pons) of *Pepita Jiménez* at the Auditorio Nacional in Madrid on November 5, 1997. In Spanish.

Upon the premiere of this concert version of Albéniz's only truly Spanish opera, the author wrote that, despite this revival, "the unvarnished truth is that we continue not to know how Albéniz's original work sounded." The new orchestration by Pons "presented by the publisher [Instituto Complutense de Ciencias Musicales] as a historic recovery of the original is in reality just the opposite: a disfiguration that conforms to commercial logic" rather than real musicology. These notes are an example of courageous truth-telling, an example from which many of us could learn.

258. ——. "Reflexiones en torno a la recuperación de *Merlin*, de Isaac Albéniz." *Revista de musicología* 21/2 (1998): 635–41. In Spanish.

Having played a leading role in the recovery and revival of this major work, the author seeks to reassess Albéniz as a composer, emphasizing his considerable achievements in writing not only piano pieces but also songs, orchestral works, and operas. In particular, *Merlin*, part of a projected but incomplete Arthurian trilogy on books by Francis Burdett Money-Coutts, gives evidence of Albéniz's technical skill and stylistic range in late career, particularly the richness of his harmonic palette and effective employment of leitmotiv (under the influence of his idol, Wagner).

259.   ——. "The Long Sleep of 'Pepita Jiménez.'" Liner notes for *Pepita Jiménez* [concert suite in two acts and three scenes]. Josep Pons conducting the Choeur d'enfants de la Maîtrise de Badalona, and Orquestra de Cambra Teatre Lliure. Harmonia Mundi, HMC 901537 (1995). In English, French, German, Spanish.

An informative treatment of the genesis and checkered performance history of Albéniz's most successful opera, for this concert suite of numbers from *Pepita Jimenez,* arranged by Josep Soler (see no. 33).

260.   ——. "The Metamorphosis of Isaac Albéniz: From Performer to Creative Composer." Liner notes for *Isaac Albéniz: Unbekannte Klavierstücke.* Antonio Ruiz-Pipó, piano. Koch-Schwann, CD 3-1513-2 (1996). In Spanish, German, English, French.

From 1886 to 1892, Albéniz made the transition from a brilliant interpreter of music to a noted composer. The recording includes several rarely heard gems from this period (such as the *Siete estudios en los tonos naturales mayores* and *Les Saisons*), and the liner notes provide important and detailed information about the genesis, publication history, and musical style of these pieces (see no. 54).

261.   Torres, Jacinto, ed. *Tomás Bretón: Diario 1881–1888.* 2 vols. Madrid: Acento Editorial, 1995. ISBN 844830084X. ML410.B844 1995. In Spanish.

Although obviously not devoted exclusively to Albéniz, this is a very important resource because of the close professional and personal relationship between these two giants of Spanish music around 1900. Tomás Bretón (1850–1923) was a leading composer of zarzuela as well as a conductor. He conducted and orchestrated various works by Albéniz, and the two exchanged ideas on a number of subjects. These volumes contain over 100 diary entries pertaining to Albéniz, and thus this is a necessary complement to the article by Ramón Sobrino surveying their correspondence (see no. 237). This is the first and only critical edition of Bretón's diary, and it includes expert commentary by Torres, a prolific authority on Albéniz.

262.   ——. "Un desconocido 'Salmo de difuntos' de Isaac Albéniz." *Revista de musicología* 13/1 (January–June 1990): 279–93. In Spanish.

Torres discovered this work in manuscript at the Real Conservatorio in Madrid. It was composed upon the death of Alfonso XII, the Spanish king who had sponsored Albéniz's studies abroad. The article presents its history, salient musical characteristics, and includes a reproduction of the original manuscript. Torres has since published the work in a modern edition through his Instituto de Bibliografía Musical (see no. 11).

263.   Torres Mulas, Jacinto, with the collaboration of Ester Aguado Sánchez. *Las claves madrileñas de Isaac Albéniz.* Madrid: Ayuntamiento de Madrid, 2008. 254 p. ISBN 8478127127. ML410.A42 T65. In Spanish. Reviewed in *Opus Musica* 35

(May 2009); Frances Barulich, *Fontes Artis Musicae* 57/2 (2010): 224–25; Walter Aaron Clark, *Notes of the Music Library Association* 66/3 (March 2010): 533–35; María Santacecilia, *Doce Notas* (April–May 2009; online).

The authors explore in depth Albéniz's connection to Madrid and the crucial impetus his residence there provided to his career. The book and facsimiles are in a handsome case, with individual sleeves for each. The facsimiles include 15 letters from Albéniz to his sister Clementina and nephew Víctor, as well as four scores (jury piece of 1886; "Curranda" and "Capricho cubano" from *Suite española no. 1*; "Lavapiés" from *Iberia*). The text is illustrated with a wealth of images, including drawings, photographs, paintings, and reproductions of letters and other documents; in fact, many of these appear here and in no other source connected with Albéniz. It provides a valuable education for those interested in the history and culture of the capital during this period. The "Madrid keys" in the title refers to the three central chapters, cleverly entitled *Clave de Sol, de Fa,* and *de Do,* or G, F, and C (V, IV, I). These constitute an allegory of the progressive perfection of Albéniz at both technical and human levels. They also have symbolic significance in relation to the personalities and influence of the three persons who were "key" to the three decisive periods in his life: his father, Ángel, during his infancy; Count Guillermo Morphy during his youth; and his sister Clementina during his mature years. It includes a very detailed chronology, virtually day by day, of his years in Madrid, offering a wealth of previously unpublished information.

264. Torres Mulas, Jacinto, and Guillermo González, eds. *Isaac Albéniz's* Iberia: *Facsimile, Urtext, and Performing Editions.* 3 vols. Madrid: Editorial de Música Española Contemporánea (EMEC); Española de Ediciones Musicales Schott (EDEMS), 1998. Reviewed by Walter Aaron Clark, *Notes of the Music Library Association* 56/4 (June 2000): 1011–14; Begoña López, *Revista de musicología* 24/1–2 (2001): 394–95. Volume I: Integral revision by Guillermo González; facsimile edition of the manuscripts and historical-documental essay by Jacinto Torres. Facsimile reproduction (color), 161 p.; acknowledgments in Sp., Eng., p. iii; foreword, pp. v–viii; essay *"Iberia* a través de sus manuscritos"/"*Iberia* through the Manuscripts," pp. ix–xli. Cloth. ISBN 848992113X; ISBN 8492148438; ISMN M540010065; ISBN 3795754674; EDEMS ED 8995; EMEC E00355. ML96.5.A43.

The author's "historical-documental" essay offers a revealing look at the textual origins and genesis of Albéniz's most celebrated work. This is the *sine qua non* of *Iberia* editions and indispensable to any serious interpreter of the work (see no. 18).

265. Tricas Preckler, Mercedes, ed. *Cartas de Paul Dukas a Laura Albéniz.* Bellaterra: Universidad Autónoma de Barcelona, 1983. 77 pp. ISBN 8474880548. In Spanish. Reviewed by Frances Barulich, *Notes of the Music Library Association* 41/3 (1985): 515–16.

Paul Dukas was an intimate friend of the Albéniz family and maintained a close relationship with it for many years after the composer's death. His letters (69 in all, covering the period 1906–35) to Albéniz's daughter Laura (who served as her father's secretary before his death) make clear the affectionate regard in which he held the Spanish composer and shed some light on the 1923 production of *Pepita Jiménez* in Paris.

266.   Turina, Joaquín. "Encuentro en Paris." *Arriba* (January 14, 1949). (Reprinted in no. 139, Franco, ed., *Albéniz y su tiempo*, pp. 115–16.) In Spanish.

Provides interesting anecdotes about Albéniz based on their friendship, which began in 1907. Includes insights into the genesis of *Iberia* and Albéniz's awareness of contemporary trends in harmony and increased use of dissonance. Also makes clear Albéniz's generosity to Turina in helping him to get his Quintette published and in encouraging him to found his composition on the basis on Spanish folk music.

267.   ——. "La música de Albéniz." Paper presented at the Ateneo in Madrid, January 10, 1942. Originally consisting of a 15-page manuscript, it has been transcribed and published in Antonio Iglesias, ed., *Escritos de Joaquín Turina* (Madrid: Alpuerto, 1982), 199–205. ISBN 8438100414. ML410.T94; and Alfredo Morán, *Joaquín Turina a través de sus escritos* (Madrid: Ayuntamiento de Sevilla, 1981), 99–101. ISBN 8450084245. ML410.T94. In Spanish.

Among other interesting observations, Turina warns against the "dangerous custom" of analyzing Albéniz's music by means of "folkloric recipes." "The principal error that I, as a Sevillian, must condemn is appealing to "so-called *cante jondo*." This is a valuable perspective to keep in mind when approaching Spanish music in general.

268.   Ullate i Estanyol, Margarida. "Rarezas de la discografía histórica (1903–1959)." *Scherzo* 24/240 (April 2009): 128–31. In Spanish.

An intriguing overview of historic recordings of Albéniz's music, many of which were not mentioned in the discography of the first edition of this book (no. 101) or the subsequent discography by Justo Romero (no. 219).

269.   Vajsbord, Miron Abramovic. *Isaak Al'benis: ocherk zhizni: fortepiannoe tvorchestvo.* Moscow: Sov. Kompozitor, 1977. In Russian.

For those who read Russian, this is a modest (149 pages) but useful biography of the composer that features some unusual reproductions, especially programs of performances of *Iberia* in Moscow after the composer's death. This is perhaps the only book that surveys Albéniz's impact on Russian music and musicians.

270.   Verastegui, Alejandro de. "Isaac Albéniz, oriundo Vitoriano." *Boletín de la Real Sociedad Vascongada de los Amigos del País* 17/1 (San Sebastián: Museo de San Telmo, 1961): 43–49. In Spanish.

Brief biographical sketch commemorating the centenary of his birth (written in 1960). Notable for the emphasis it places on Albéniz's Basque ancestry, insofar as his father was a native of Vitoria. Contains intriguing details about his early life, especially in Barcelona, but without substantiation.

271. Villalba Muñoz, P. Luis. "Imagen distanciada de un compositor-pianista." *Gaceta de Mallorca* (1909). (Reprinted in no. 139, Franco, ed., *Albéniz y su tiempo*, pp. 51–61.) In Spanish.

Rehash of the usual anecdotes about Albéniz's early career, gleaned from secondary sources. Offers an unflattering (and inaccurate) assessment of the composer, declaring that Albéniz did not possess the "technique of the art of composition" and that counterpoint in particular remained "inaccessible to his character as a free artist." But we should not be too hasty in dismissing Villalba Muñoz's writings. In the considered opinion of Jacinto Torres, Villalba Muñoz's *Últimos músicos españoles del siglo XIX* (Madrid: Ildefonso Alier, 1914), 161–185, presents a biographical portrait of Albéniz that, whatever its factual liabilities may be, "has the merit of being the first to focus attention on the singular Franco-Andalusian mixture in his style."

272. Wade, Graham. "Reflections on 1909." *Soundboard* 36/1 (2010): 14–18. In English.

The author offers reflections on the first decade of the twentieth century, during which Albéniz, Segovia, and Tárrega were all active (and during which the first two would die). Laments what masterpieces might have flowed from Albéniz's pen had he recovered from his kidney ailment, though guitarists have conferred celebrity on many of his works through the process of transcription initiated by Tárrega.

273. Wang, Myungsook. "Isaac Albéniz's *Iberia* and the Influence of Franz Liszt." D.M.A. diss., City University of New York, 2004. 108 pp. UMI 3144150. In English.

This dissertation explores the various influences apparent in Albéniz's *Iberia*, including those of Pedrell and Debussy. Special attention is paid to Liszt, whose impact on Albéniz's style has not received the scholarly consideration it merits. Post-Lisztian virtuosity is a hallmark of Albéniz's mature works for piano, especially *Iberia*. Whether or not Albéniz actually studied with, or even met, Liszt is not the issue here. Albéniz knew Liszt's music very well and was deeply affected by it. An analysis of passages from works by both composers illustrates this point effectively, particularly in regard to harmony, rhythm, melody, sonority, dynamics, and texture.

274. Wolff, Daniel. "Isaac Albéniz: An Essay on the Man, His Music, and His Relationship to the Guitar." *Classical Guitar* 15 (April 15, 1997): 22–29. In English.

Offers some useful insights into the way in which Albéniz evokes certain guitar idioms, particularly various strumming and plucking patterns, on the piano.
The biographical information is dated and unreliable, based on sources that
have since been superseded.

275.   Yates, Stanley. "Albéniz and the Guitar." *Soundboard* 30/4 (2004–05): 18–25. In
        English.

Makes the telling point that were it not for the attentions of guitarists playing
transcriptions of them, many of Albéniz's lesser-known piano works would
remain in relative obscurity. Provides an overview of guitar arrangements of
Albéniz's piano music, a summary biography, and a description of the composer's piano-performance style. Continues on to an insightful examination
of texture, form, melody, and harmony in passages from selected works, as an
introduction to key stylistic features every guitarist playing this music must
comprehend.

3

Part C: Contemporary Periodical Literature (Reviews and Articles of Interest in Newspapers and Journals During Albéniz's Lifetime, Including Reviews of his Stage Works After his Death)

The following is an extensive but necessarily selective compilation based on research conducted for purposes other than tracking down every article and review ever published (an impossible task). The first section deals with reviews of his concerts. Presented in chronological order according to concert date and then alphabetical order according to periodical title, these give us valuable insights into his pianistic technique and style. They also provide generally reliable information about his activities (though the biographical information is usually suspect). The second section is devoted to reviews of his stage works, including productions that took place after his death. The reviews are organized chronologically according to work and production locale, and then alphabetically according to periodical title.

Aside from clippings found in the archives mentioned in Part A, the papers and journals cited below were consulted in the periodical section of the following libraries. Barcelona: Arxiu Històric de la Ciutat and Biblioteca de Catalunya; Brussels: Bibliothèque Royale Albert 1er; London: British Library; Madrid: Biblioteca Nacional, Hemeroteca Municipal, and Hemeroteca Nacional; Paris: Bibliothèque National; Prague: National Library. An indispensable resource in this area is Jacinto Torres Mulas and Ester Aguado Sánchez's landmark publication *Las claves madrileñas de Isaac Albéniz* (no. 263), which includes reproductions of several of the reviews below. These reviews are marked [see no. 263, page number] after the annotation, to indicate their availability in that book. Also very useful to me has been the unpublished manuscript by Jan de Kloe entitled "Albéniz en Bruselas: Estudio documental sobre las actuaciones de Isaac Albéniz en Bruselas" (Brussels, October 21, 2004). This contains an exhaustive compendium of newspaper articles pertaining to Albéniz's activities in the Belgian capital from 1892 to 1908, especially the production of his stage works there in 1905. I am grateful to Jan for sharing his outstanding research with me. A useful source of information concerning Albéniz's concert touring in

Spain is no. 135, Victoria Ferrer, "La estancia de Isaac Albéniz en Valencia en 1882." Finally, all reviews by George Bernard Shaw are reprinted in Dan H. Laurence, ed., *Shaw's Music: The Complete Musical Criticism in Three Volumes* (New York: Dodd, Mead & Co., 1981).

I. REVIEWS AND ARTICLES DEALING WITH HIS CAREER AS A PERFORMER AND COMPOSER FROM 1869 TO 1894, IN CHRONOLOGICAL ORDER (PAGE NUMBER AND AUTHOR GIVEN WHERE AVAILABLE).

276. *Correo de Teatro* (Barcelona) (July 23, 1869). In Spanish.

Account of his meeting with the Vizconde del Bruch to present him with the *Marcha militar*, Albéniz's first published composition, which bears a dedication to the 12-year-old Viscount.

277. *La Correspondencia Teatral* (Valladolid) (February 15, 1874). In Spanish.

Review of his concert at the Teatro Lope de Vega, where he was a sensation. Reports that he has been giving concerts in northern Castile as well as Catalonia and Andalusia. "Words fail us in praising such mastery, such feeling, such perfection . . . he will be one of the glories of Spanish art." Refers to an earlier review in this same journal, dated January 11, 1874, which reported that Albéniz was hailed throughout Spain as a "new Mozart."

278. *Artista de La Habana* (September 23, 1875). In Spanish.

Favorable report on his concerts in Havana, one given on the ship *Manzanillo* for various luminaries, including editors of the paper *La Bandera*.

279. *Artista de La Habana* (October 10, 1875). In Spanish.

Report on a recital given in his home at Amargura 14 in Havana. It was well received by the "distinguished" invitees. Gives notice of an upcoming concert at the Teatro de Tacón.

280. *El Espectador de La Habana* (November 6, 1875). In Spanish.

Review of his concert at the restaurant El Louvre, in which he played several virtuosic numbers, including a fantasy on themes from *The Barber of Seville*, executed with his back to the piano (several accounts report his ability to do this).

281. *La Época* (Madrid) (October 8, 1876), 3. In Spanish.

Glowing review of his performance at a *tertulia* (literary gathering) of María de la Peña the previous evening. Albéniz performed works by Gottschalk, Weber, and Strauss. Announces that he will leave soon for Brussels to study at the conservatory there. [see no. 263, p. 200]

282. *Diario de Cádiz* (August 23, 1878). In Spanish.

Reports on his concert activities in Brussels, where he was a student at the Conservatoire Royal. Rhapsodizes that "under his able and agile fingers, the piano sighs, cries, and sings."

283. *Diario de Barcelona* (August 24, 1879). In Spanish.

    Favorable review of his performance at the Navas piano factory.

284. *Gaceta de Catalunya* (August 24, 1879). In Spanish.

    Also praises his recital at the Navas piano factory.

285. *Publicidad de Barcelona* (September 16, 1879). In Spanish.

    Review of his recent concert at the Teatre de Novetats, in which the reviewer praises his "excellent hand position, clarity and cleanness of execution, admirable contrasts in tone color, and equality in repeated notes, tremolo, and arpeggios."

286. *Publicidad de Barcelona* (September 28, 1879). In Spanish.

    Favorable assessment of his program at the salon of the piano makers Raynard y Maseras, where he gave his standard recital of Bach, Scarlatti, Mendelssohn, Chopin, and Weber.

287. *Crónica de Barcelona* (September 30, 1879). In Spanish.

    States that he is now moving to Madrid. Places Albéniz in the "classical school" of pianists.

288. *Anunciador de Vitoria* (May 4, 1880). In Spanish.

    Rejoices in his concert and hails him as a true "Vitoriano" (his father was from Vitoria). The casino presented him with a set of gold buttons.

289. *Diario de La Habana* (December 1880). In Spanish.

    Review of his concert at El Louvre, a benefit for a local charity. He performed the Liszt *Spanish Rhapsody* as well as a Beethoven trio, which had to be repeated at the audience's insistence.

290. *El Buen Público* (Havana) (February 10, 1881). In Spanish.

    Review of his concert at the Círculo Español in Havana, at which he conducted an orchestra in selections from *Le Pré aux clercs* by Ferdinand Hérold. He also played the Mendelssohn G-minor concerto.

291. *Santiago de Cuba* (February 15, 1881). In Spanish.

    Review of his concert at the Teatro de la Reina, in which the reviewer praises the perfection, taste, and feeling of a "delicate soul."

292. *LCM* 1/14 (April 6, 1881), 6. In Spanish.

    Reports on his concerts in Santiago and states that he had toured Germany and the United States before his arrival in Cuba. (There is no other evidence to support this claim.)

293.   *LCM* 1/31 (August 3, 1881), 6. In Spanish.

Account of his concert in Santander, declaring that under his hands "the instrument reveals all of the divine mysteries of music."

294.   *LCM* 1/46 (November 16, 1881), 7. In Spanish.

Report of his concert in Zaragoza on November 11, 1881, which was "applauded frenetically." Liszt's *Rigoletto Paraphrase* was the high point of the concert.

295.   *LCM* 1/49 (December 7, 1881), 7. In Spanish.

Account (taken from *El Navarro)* of his December 3 concert in Pamplona in which his program of Scarlatti, Liszt, Mendelssohn, and his own works was "listened to until the final note amidst the most religious silence."

296.   *LCM* 2/57 (February 1, 1882), 6. In Spanish.

Quotes from *El Porvenir Vascongado* (January 25, 1882) that Albéniz performed in between acts of Joaquín Gaztambide's zarzuela *El juramento* ("The Judgement") in Bilbao, which was a benefit for a local charity. His music was well received, though the numbers are not specified.

297.   *LCM* 2/61 (March 21, 1882), 6. In Spanish.

States that Albéniz has just returned from a successful tour of various provincial capitals.

298.   *Diario de Córdoba* (May 20, 1882). In Spanish.

Favorable review of his performance, at the Gran Teatro de Córdoba, of works by Weber, Liszt, Raff, Wagner, and his own *Pavana capricho.*

299.   *LCM* 2/73 (May 24, 1882), 6. In Spanish.

Reports on Albéniz's concerts at the Gran Teatro de Córdoba, which were well received.

300.   *LCM* 2/76 (June 14, 1882), 7. In Spanish.

Account (from the Cádiz *La Palma* of June 10) of his concert at the casino in San Fernando, where he played 12 works and 3 improvisations on melodies submitted by the audience.

301.   *LCM* 2/77 (June 21, 1882), 6. In Spanish.

Review of his concert at the Academia de Santa Cecilia in Cádiz, for a gathering of "famous artists and well-known aficionados." He organized the successful concert himself.

302.   *El Porvenir* (Seville) (June 23, 1882). In Spanish.

Glowing account of his appearance at the Jardines de Eslava de Sevilla, where he presented his well-rehearsed repertoire.

303. *LCM* 2/80 (July 12, 1882), 8. In Spanish.

Glowing report of his concerts in Seville at the Jardines de Eslava.

304. *LCM* 2/81 (July 19, 1882), 6. In Spanish.

Encomiastic account of further concert triumphs in Cádiz.

305. *El Mercantil Valenciano* (July 28, 1882), 2. In Spanish.

Anonymous review of his first concert in Valencia, at the Salón Gómez y Hijos. His great reputation had preceded him, and he did not disappoint the audience during a 4-hour concert that included repertoire from Bach to Beethoven, Liszt, and Wagner.

306. *El Mercantil Valenciano* (August 3, 1882), 3. In Spanish.

Announces Albéniz's concert at the Teatro Principal in Valencia, on the same day as the concert itself, detailing the program and singing the artist's praises.

307. *El Mercantil Valenciano* (August 4, 1882), 2. In Spanish.

Reports that despite Albéniz's impressive rendering of works by Chopin, Scarlatti, Bach, Boccherini, Weber, Liszt, Wagner, and Albéniz himself, the audience was small due to the summer heat and competition from the beach.

308. *El Mercantil Valenciano* (August 6, 1882), 2. In Spanish.

Reports that the local painter Enrique Valls was putting the finishing touches on an oil portrait of Albéniz. This remains the only such portrait from his youth.

309. *El Mercantil Valenciano* (August 9, 1882), 2. In Spanish.

Review of his second concert at the Teatro Principal, another *tour de force* featuring more Chopin as well as Raff, Tosti, Rubinstein, Schubert, Liszt, and Albéniz himself. The weather was not as hot as it was during the first concert, and the audience was somewhat larger for this program.

310. *El Mercantil Valenciano* (August 10, 1882), 2. In Spanish.

Announces that Albéniz will give yet another concert, this time at La Florida, a more pleasant locale than the Teatro Principal.

311. *El Mercantil Valenciano* (August 15, 1882), 2. In Spanish.

Review of the concert at La Florida, which was well attended and well received.

312. *LCM* 2/85 (August 16, 1882), 6. In Spanish.

Albéniz was in Valencia for a concert on August 7 (reported in the local paper *La Nueva Alianza*), where his program of Boccherini, Liszt, and his own pieces was "frenetically applauded."

313.   *El Mercantil Valenciano* (August 17, 1882), 2. In Spanish.

Reports Albéniz's departure for Alicante, where he will give more concerts. In the event, he performed there only once, at the Teatro Circo.

314.   *El Mercantil Valenciano* (September 17, 1882), 2. In Spanish.

Confirms Albéniz's departure from the city on August 14 of that year, having arrived about 3 weeks earlier, on July 25.

315.   *LCM* 2/90 (September 20, 1882), 6. In Spanish.

Albéniz's concert in Alcoy (as reported in *El Serpis)* prompted "a very noisy tribute" to his artistry. After the recital, he was serenaded at his hotel by a local orchestra.

316.   *LCM* 2/97 (November 8, 1882), 6. In Spanish.

A report on Albéniz in Cartagena, where he is giving a series of successful concerts.

317.   *LCM* 2/98 (November 15, 1882), 6–7. In Spanish.

Review of a November 10 recital in Cartagena, featuring "very difficult pieces" rendered with "delicate taste."

318.   *LCM* 2/101 (December 6, 1882), 6. In Spanish.

Account of Albéniz's welcome participation in a program at the home of Señora Duquesa de Medinaceli in Madrid. [see no. 263, p. 200]

319.   *LCM* 2/103 (December 20, 1882), 5. In Spanish.

Review of his concert at the Círculo Vasco-Navarro in Madrid, which featured works by Scarlatti, Boccherini, Beethoven, Raff, and Mendelssohn and was warmly applauded. [see no. 263, p. 201]

320.   *La Ilustración Musical* 1/2 (April 14, 1883), 4. In Spanish.

Review of Albéniz's concert at the salon of the piano firm of Raynard y Maseras in Barcelona, declaring that he gave his audience "truly delicious moments."

321.   *La Ilustración Musical* 1/3 (April 21, 1883), 4. In Spanish.

Caricature of Albéniz as a slightly paunchy, mustached young fellow in a top hat and tails with the caption: "As a person, a boy; as a pianist, a giant."

322.   *LCM* 3/127 (June 7, 1883), 4. In Spanish.

Announces his engagement to a "beautiful and rich" señorita from Barcelona.

323.   *LCM* 3/130 (June 29, 1883), 5. In Spanish.

Reports his marriage to the "pretty and discreet" Rosina Jordana in Barcelona (on June 23).

324. *La Voz de Galicia* (September 15, 1883). In Spanish.

    Announcement of a concert by the Sexteto Fernández Arbós, with Albéniz as the ensemble's pianist, performing works by Mendelssohn, Weber, Rossini, Popper, Meyerbeer, Chopin, and Massenet.

325. *LCM* 3/143 (September 27, 1883), 6. In Spanish.

    Favorable report on Albéniz's participation in three concerts by Enrique Fernández Arbós's sextet in La Coruña (on the 20th).

326. *LCM* 3/144 (October 4, 1883), 7. In Spanish.

    Albéniz and Arbós's sextet makes a successful appearance in Santiago de Compostela.

327. *LCM* 3/147 (October 25, 1883), 6. In Spanish.

    Albéniz is passing through Madrid on his way back to Barcelona (where he is now living with his new bride), after a successful tour of the northwest provinces with Arbós's sextet (in truth, the tour was not a success).

328. *LCM* 5/249 (October 8, 1885), 5. In Spanish.

    States that Albéniz has played for the royal family in Madrid (where he is now living), giving two concerts at the royal palace. Describes him, without explanation, as the "spoiled child" of Madrid society. [see no. 263, p. 202]

329. *Archivo Diplomático y Consular de España* (Madrid) 3/114 (October 15, 1885), 684–85. In Spanish.

    Announces that Albéniz performed for the royal family and praises his "merit and talent." [see no. 263, p. 202]

330. *LCM* 5/253 (November 5, 1885), 5. In Spanish.

    Albéniz has played again (November 4) at the royal palace at the invitation of the Infanta Doña Isabel. He served up his latest compositions, which she enjoyed. [see no. 263, p. 202]

331. *LCM* 5/259 (December 17, 1885), 6. In Spanish.

    Announces that Albéniz is giving private piano instruction at his home at "Plaza de Antón Martín 52, 54 y 56." [see no. 263, p. 202]

332. *LCM* 6/262 (January 7, 1886), 4. In Spanish.

    Announcement of his upcoming program at the Salón Romero, listing the ambitious repertoire planned for the evening. [see no. 263, p. 202]

333. *El Liberal* (Madrid) (January 25, 1886), 2, by Miguel Moya. In Spanish.

    Fulsome review of his concert at the Salón Romero, praising his "extraordinary facility" and commenting on the public's enthusiastic reception of his program.

Contains biographical information extracted from Guerra y Alarcón's contemporary account (no. 151). [see no. 263, p. 203]

334.   *La Época* (Madrid) (January 27, 1886), 2. In Spanish.

Hail Albéniz's "complete mastery" of the piano and marvels at his recital of 34 works over 3 hours "without exhibiting the slightest fatigue." The audience heartily applauded his interpretations of works from the eighteenth and nineteenth centuries, from Scarlatti to Chopin to Rubinstein—as well as his own compositions. [see no. 263, p. 203]

335.   *La América* (Madrid) 27/2 (January 28, 1886), 10, 13–14, by Antonio Guerra y Alarcón. In Spanish.

Penned by Albéniz's first biographer, this lengthy review of his Romero appearance lauds him as nothing short of "exceptional" and one of the "greatest masters of the piano." Attributes his success to his systematic study and hard work. [see no. 263, pp. 206–07]

336.   *LCM* 6/265 (January 28, 1886), 1–3. In Spanish.

Front-page review of his highly successful recital at the Salón Romero on the 22nd of January. "Albéniz dominates the piano with surpassing ease, and in his hands, the keys reproduce in a marvelous manner the thoughts of the musician and of the poet." [see no. 263, p. 204]

337.   *LCM* 6/266 (February 4, 1886), 6. In Spanish.

Albéniz is receiving numerous invitations to perform from various cities in Spain as a result of his Romero appearance.

338.   *La Ilustración Española y Americana* 30/5 (February 8, 1886), 79, by J. M. Esperanza y Sola. (Reprinted in no. 139, Franco, ed. *Albéniz y su tiempo*, pp. 69–72.) In Spanish.

Review of the Romero performance, stating that his rendition of a Mayer etude "set off an explosion of thunderous applause." Albéniz is a "passionate and ardent interpreter, who sometimes poeticizes and at others nearly mistreats the piano, and who, in short, carries away and moves his listener." [see no. 263, p. 208]

339.   *La Iberia* (Madrid) (February 21, 1886), 2. In Spanish.

High praise for his concert at El Círculo de la Unión Mercantil on February 20, in collaboration with fellow pianist Manuel Guervós. [see no. 263, p. 208]

340.   *LCM* 6/269 (February 25, 1886), 4. In Spanish.

Played the piano in a "marvelous and exceptional manner" at El Círculo de la Unión Mercantil on February 20. His "prodigious abilities" wore out the piano provided by Benito Zozaya for the occasion! [see no. 263, p. 208]

341.   *La América* (Madrid) 27/4 (February 28, 1886), 16, by Antonio Guerra y Alarcón. In Spanish.

High praise for his performance at El Círculo de la Unión Mercantil on February 20. Marvels at the "refinement of his ear, the intensity of his emotions, and the lucidity of his imagination." [see no. 263, p. 208]

342.   *LCM* 6/271 (March 11, 1886), 3. In Spanish.

Announcement of his performance with the renowned soprano Adelina Patti at the Teatro de la Zarzuela in Madrid. [see no. 263, p. 210]

343.   *El Imparcial* (March 26, 1886), 3. In Spanish.

Finds this second Romero concert, on March 25, even better than the first, on this occasion accompanied by Manuel Guervós in works for two pianos. [see no. 263, p. 212]

344.   *La Época* (March 27, 1886), 2. In Spanish.

Marvels at Albéniz's chromatic scales, executed at "incredible speed and so perfectly that one can count the notes without much work." Also possesses a delicacy well suited to works by Scarlatti. [see no. 263, p. 212]

345.   *LCM* 6/274 (April 1, 1886), 5. In Spanish.

Favorable review of another performance at the Salón Romero the previous Thursday, featuring Albéniz and Manuel Guervós in two-piano arrangements. [see no. 263, p. 212]

346.   *LCM* 6/275 (April 8, 1886), 6. In Spanish.

Offers condolences to the Albéniz family on the loss of their 20-month-old daughter, Blanca.

347.   *LCM* 6/280 (May 13, 1886), 5. In Spanish.

Reports his return from Málaga, where he garnered applause and money, having had to repeat five or six numbers from a program of no less than 26 selections.

348.   *LCM* 6/290 (July 22, 1886), 5. In Spanish.

Conveys a review from *El Eco de San Sebastián* of his successful concerts in that city on the 17th and 19th of July.

349.   *LCM* 7/314 (March 10, 1887), 7. In Spanish.

Announcement of upcoming concert at the Salón Romero, on March 25, providing a program comprised exclusively of his own works, performed by himself as well as Manuel Guervós and Luisa Chevallier. [see no. 263, p. 213]

350.   *El Imparcial* (Madrid) (March 23, 1887), 3. In Spanish.

Reports that the audience at the Salón Romero included such luminaries as members of the royal family as well as Cánovas del Castillo, Count Morphy, and Francisco Barbieri. Albéniz's compositions and executions earned much applause. [see no. 263, p. 213]

351.   *LCM* 7/316 (March 24, 1887), 3. In Spanish.

Extols Albéniz's performance and music, saying that "it is a secret to nobody that he is one of our most applauded pianists." [see no. 263, p. 213]

352.   *La Iberia* (Madrid) (February 20, 1888), 4. In Spanish.

Encomiastic review of Albéniz's appearance on the third in a series of programs by the orchestra of the Sociedad de Conciertos, directed by Tomás Bretón, at the Teatro del Príncipe Alfonso. In addition to solo numbers, Albéniz performed the Schumann concerto. As always, the critics and public found nothing to criticize. [see no. 263, p. 214]

353.   *La Ilustración Musical Española* (Madrid) 1/14 (August 15, 1888), by Felipe Pedrell. (Reprinted in no. 139, Enrique Franco, ed., *Albéniz y su tiempo*, pp. 63–67.) In Spanish.

In the summer and fall of 1888, Albéniz performed no fewer than 20 recitals at the Exposición Universal in Barcelona. Pedrell hailed Albéniz's Piano Concerto No. 1 (*Concierto fantástico*) as "without precedent" in Spanish music history, lavished praise on the "poetic calm and inspiration" of his sonatas, and applauded his use of folkloric references in the *Rapsodia española* for piano and orchestra. In conclusion, Pedrell accurately predicted that "the name of Albéniz is destined to represent a grand personality in the European musical world."

354.   *El Liberal* (March 8, 1889), 3. In Spanish.

Favorable review of Albéniz's appearance with the orchestra of the Sociedad de Conciertos, conducted by Tomás Bretón, at the Teatro de la Comedia on March 7. This featured orchestral works by Albéniz, including the *Serenata española* and *Escenas sinfónicas*, the third movement of which, "La serenata," had to be repeated at the audience's insistence. The program also featured his *Concierto fantástico* and *Rapsodia española*, both well received. Albéniz also threw in some solo numbers by Liszt and Wagner (arrangements from the *Ring* cycle). [see no. 263, p. 216]

355.   *La Correspondencia de España* (March 9, 1889), 2. In Spanish.

Glowing review of the concert reviewed above. In attendance was the Infanta Doña Isabel, a noted fan of Albéniz. [see no. 263, p. 216]

356.   *La Ilustración Española y Americana* (Madrid) 33/13 (April 8, 1889), 206. In Spanish.

Hails his appearance at the Teatro de la Comedia with Bretón's orchestra, describing him as a composer "endowed with genius and inspiration" and predicting a brilliant future for him as a serious composer. [see no. 263, p. 216]

357. *La Ménéstrel* (Paris) (April 28, 1889), 136. In French.

Review of his appearance with the Orchestre Colonne on April 25. Praises Albéniz's energetic virtuosity, especially in staccato passages, but laments a lack of flexibility in his phrasing.

358. *Yorkshire Post* (May 13, 1889). In English.

Announces some of Albéniz's most recent compositions, including *Berceuse, On the Water, Mallorca,* and *Angoisse,* all published by Stanley Lucas, Weber & Co. in London.

359. *Trade & Finance* (June 19, 1889). In English.

Describes his playing as characterized by "delicate taste, refined reading, dainty execution" and states that his "strength lies in the rendering of light, graceful compositions."

360. *Pall Mall Gazette* (June 25, 1889). In English.

"He reminds one of [Anton] Rubinstein in his refined and delicate passages, and of Hans von Bülow in his vigor."

361. *Vanity Fair* (June 25, 1889). In English.

Praises his pianism and comments in particular on his "velvety touch."

362. *The Musical World* 69/36 (September 7, 1889), 617. In English.

Reports publication by C. Ducci and Co. of "Pavane espagnole," "Sevillanas," "Barcarolle Catalane," and "Cotillon Valse."

363. *Vanity Fair* (September 7, 1889). In English.

Recommends *Deux Morceaux caractéristiques,* recently published in London by Stanley Lucas, Weber & Co.

364. *The Musical World* 69/37 (September 14, 1889), 630. In English.

Favorable report on Albéniz's performance at Her Majesty's Theatre, as part of the Promenade Concerts. Also appearing was Hungarian violinist Tivadar Nachez.

365. *The Musical World* 69/39 (September 28, 1889), 675. In English.

Encomiastic review of Albéniz's performance of the Schumann piano concerto at Her Majesty's Theatre, as part of the Promenade Concerts.

366. *La Música Ilustrada Hispano-Americana* 2/20 (October 10, 1899), 10. In Spanish.

Reports that Albéniz conducted rehearsals of Wagner's *Tristan und Isolde* at the Gran Teatre del Liceu in Barcelona.

367. *Daily Telegraph* (October 24, 1889). In English.

Reports on his performance of works by Handel, Bach, Scarlatti, and Chopin at St. James's Hall, noting the "charming fashion in which he executes works by . . . masters of refinement."

368. *Daily Telegraph* (October 25, 1889). In English.

Announces that Albéniz has "received permission from the Spanish government to copy, for the purpose of [the upcoming] concert, several important manuscripts in the library of the Escorial." This was no doubt a fabrication for publicity's sake.

369. *The Musical Times* 30/562 (December 1, 1889), 724–25. In English.

Supportive assessment of Albeniz's performance of the Schumann piano concerto at the Crystal Palace.

370. *Star* (December 6, 1889), by George Bernard Shaw. In English.

Review of his concert at a *conversazione* of the Wagner Society, where he played excerpts from Wagner's *Ring* arranged by Louis Brassin. "The dead silence produced by his playing, particularly during the second piece ["Ride of the Valkyries"], was the highest compliment he could have desired."

371. *Huddersfield Daily Examiner* (January 10, 1890). In English.

"His pieces are light but remarkably beautiful, thoroughly distinctive, yet all full of the colour of the composer's nationality, and of that graceful individuality which is so strongly characteristic of his playing."

372. *Rochdale Observer* (January 22, 1890). In English.

"The velvety softness of touch—the cadences dying to almost a whisper, yet audible all over the room—must have been the wonder and the admiration—and also the despair—of the amateur pianists present."

373. *The Musical Times* 31/564 (February 1, 1890), 106. In English.

Favorable review of *Deux Morceaux caractéristiques* (*Spanish National Songs*) recently published in London by Stanley Lucas, Weber & Co.

374. *Bristol Times* & *Mirror* (February 6, 1890). In English.

Review of a recent concert, declaring that "his scales are perfect, and his tone shading is remarkable."

375. *Strand Journal* (February 14, 1890). In English.

"He performed lightning-like feats, varied by interludes of sweet, dreamy melody, which none but a past master of his art could hope to rival."

376. *The Times* (June 10, 1890). In English.

    Reports on his concert at Steinway Hall, remarking on his "rare power of producing the full tone of his instrument without having recourse to violence of any kind, or ever exceeding the limits of acoustic beauty."

377. *Musical Standard* (June 14, 1890). In English.

    Favorable review of his concert at Steinway Hall. Admires his "soft and sympathetic touch."

378. *Country Gentleman* (June 28, 1890). In English.

    Favorable review of Albéniz's concert at Steinway Hall on June 24. Mentions the presentation of several songs with Italian texts, which were clearly selections from the *Seis baladas* (T. 36A–F).

379. *Dramatic Review* (June 28, 1890). In English.

    Glowing review of his concert at Steinway Hall, where he moved "his audience not by astonishing them but by charming them." Compared his "dazzling brightness" and "exquisite delicacy" to the violin playing of his friend Pablo de Sarasate, also active in London at this time.

380. *Piccadilly* (July 3, 1890). In English.

    Commenting on Albéniz's Steinway Hall concert on June 24, it states that Marie Groebl "gave an effective rendering of four charming songs by Señor Albéniz that are likely soon to become very popular." These were from the *Seis baladas* (T. 36A–F).

381. *Musical Standard* (July 5, 1890). In English.

    Review of the June 24 concert, which further confirms that "four well-written Italian songs were sung by Miss Marie Groebl."

382. *The Musical World* 70/35 (August 30, 1890), 694. In English.

    Announces recent publication of *Two Mazurkas* by Stanley Lucas, Weber & Co. (taken from the earlier *Seis mazurkas de salón*, T. 68).

383. *The Musical Times*, 31/571 (September 1, 1890), 556. In English.

    Favorable review of *Two Mazurkas* published by Stanley Lucas, Weber & Co. (taken from the earlier *Seis mazurkas de salón*, T. 68).

384. *The Manchester Guardian* (September 9, 1890). In English.

    Announces recent publication of *Two Mazurkas* by Stanley Lucas, Weber & Co. (taken from the earlier *Seis mazurkas de salón*, T. 68.).

385. *St. James's Gazette* (September 15, 1890). In English.

    Review of his concert at Steinway Hall. "Señor Albéniz made as powerful an impression by his composition as by his playing."

386.   *The Yorkshire Post* (September 19, 1890). In English.

Announces recent publication of *Two Mazurkas* by Stanley Lucas, Weber & Co. (taken from the earlier *Seis mazurkas de salón*, T. 68.).

387.   *Lady* (October 30, 1890). In English.

Biographical account that is loaded with misinformation and outright fabrications. Provides a classic example of Albéniz's penchant for reinventing his past to impress the public, though his career was sufficiently impressive without embellishment.

388.   *The Musical World* 70/44 (November 1, 1890): 870. In English.

Biographical sketch of Albéniz, with the usual blend of reality and fantasy.

389.   *The Pictorial World* (November 2, 1890). In English.

Misinformed review expressing the belief that "there is no distinctive school of musical art belonging to [Spain], and . . . its music is but a pale reflection of French or German thought. It has gone out of use—if it ever was to the fore—with Cordovan leather and liquorice, or Baracco juice."

390.   *Figaro* (November 8, 1890). In English.

Negative review of the first orchestral concert he organized at St. James's Hall (November 7, 1890), featuring the Spanish conductor and composer Tomás Bretón, whose conducting passes muster but whose E-flat symphony is deemed nothing but a "bold imitation of Beethoven."

391.   *Pall Mall Gazette* (November 8, 1890). In English.

Unflattering report of the first orchestral concert he organized at St. James's Hall, which featured his own works as well as some by his compatriots Ruperto Chapí and Tomás Bretón. Chapí's offerings are rated as "cheap, trashy noise." Albéniz's rendition of the Schumann concerto demonstrated his lack "especially in the left hand of wrist power. There is too little contrast and he would be a much greater pianist if he would consent to let himself go."

392.   *Topical Times* (November 8, 1890). In English.

Biographical account that is only slightly less inaccurate than the others that appeared in the London press during his tenure in that city.

393.   *Referee* (November 9, 1890). In English.

Negative review of the first of Albéniz's orchestral concerts at St. James's Hall. Harshly dismisses the Chapí offerings as "circus music."

394.   *Daily Graphic* (November 10, 1890). In English.

Uncomplimentary assessment of the first of the orchestral concerts at St. James's Hall. Chapí's work was "sheer tea-garden blatancy," while Bretón's conducting lacked "the animation and impetuosity one associates with a Southerner." Albéniz's negotiation of the Schumann concerto displayed insufficient "romance and intellectuality."

395.   *Morning Post* (London) (November 10, 1890). In English.

Reports on the performance at St. James's Hall on November 7, of "some pieces from the hand of Señor Albéniz, namely, the 'Scherzo' from the First Symphony, and a 'Rhapsodie Cubaine', first performance."

396.   *World* (November 12, 1890), by George Bernard Shaw. In English.

Pans the recent orchestral concert at St. James's Hall, decrying the "procrustean torturings" of Bretón's symphony, "an ingeniously horrible work."

397.   *Footlights* (November 15, 1890). In English.

Negative review of the first orchestral concert at St. James's Hall, complaining that its length "savours of wanton cruelty to tax long suffering [*sic*] humanity so heavily."

398.   *Land* & *Water* (November 15, 1890). In English.

"Nothing can exceed the delicacy and charm of his touch, which seems to show to special advantage when he is giving us one of his own little Spanish dissertations." Hopes for a repetition of "these pleasing trifles" at his next concert.

399.   *Modern Society* (November 15, 1890). In English.

Claims that "it is said the clever pianist [Albéniz] is being exploited by an enthusiastic capitalist [probably Henry Lowenfeld, his manager], and the statement is credible."

400.   *Queen* (November 15, 1890). In English.

Contrary to all other reviews of the first orchestral concert at St. James's Hall, reports that Chapí's work (a "Moorish Fantasy") "met with a favourable reception, the third movement—the serenade—having to be repeated."

401.   *Star* (November 18, 1890). In English.

Biographical portrait of Albéniz. Dispenses claims contradictory to those that appeared in other periodicals of this time in London, including that he is an "opera conductor at Granada, Seville, et al.," and that he has written 12 piano sonatas (he wrote at most seven). The following observation suggests that the information was gained during an interview with him: "Personally, he is very agreeable, overflowing with a cheerful and inspiring humour."

402.   *The Musical World*, supplement (November 15, 1890): 916. In English.

Review of the first orchestral concert he organized at St. James's Hall, which featured his own works as well as some by his compatriots Ruperto Chapí and Tomás Bretón, who conducted.

403.   *Daily Chronicle* (November 22, 1890). In English.

Glowing review of the second orchestral program at St. James's Hall (November 21, 1890), which led the critic to speculate that Spain enjoyed greater importance in the realm of "high-class music" than commonly supposed, and that it was "quite possible that other nations have been wilfully blind as well as deaf to the labours of Spanish musicians."

404.   *New York Herald* (November 22, 1890). In English.

Enthusiastic review of the second orchestral concert at St. James's Hall. Albéniz's pieces demonstrated an "originality colored by national feeling which should . . . be shown by composers born and bred in countries with a musical history."

405.   *Pall Mall Gazette* (November 22, 1890). In English.

Favorable review of the second orchestral concert at St. James's Hall, in which Albéniz performed some solos: "Señor Albéniz is an undemonstrative pianist, with but few mannerisms, but much technical ability."

406.   *Standard* (November 22, 1890). In English.

Generally favorable review of the second orchestral concert at St. James's Hall. Albéniz's Piano Concerto No. 1 was "clearly written and easy to follow," though the first movement was "monotonous" and the finale "not very dignified." Albéniz's orchestral works on the program were reminiscent of French ballet music rather than Spain. His solo-piano works "were the greatest success of the evening" and "so much applauded that the pianist-composer had to throw in another piece."

407.   *Country Gentleman* (November 29, 1890). In English.

Favorable review of the second orchestral concert at St. James's Hall. States that Bretón "has all the proverbial solemnity of his race [and] may now be considered an established favorite, both as a conductor and composer."

408.   *Musical Standard* (November 29, 1890). In English.

Reports that Albéniz's "Cuban Rhapsody in G" at the second orchestral concert at St. James's Hall "failed to satisfy strict connoisseurs."

409.   *The Musical World*, supplement (November 29, 1890), 957. In English.

Supportive review of the second orchestral program at St. James's Hall (November 21, 1890), which featured Arthur Hervey's *Dramatic Overture* and Albéniz's "Concerto fantastique" and "Rapsodie cubaine," as well as the Prelude to Bretón's *Los amantes de Teruel.*

410.   *Vanity Fair* (November 29, 1890). In English.

States that Albéniz has won over the public in a remarkably short time: "Señor Albéniz may well inscribe upon his escutcheon the words, 'veni, vidi, vici'; and

I am sure that everyone will be glad to hear that he has elected to make London his home."

411. *The Musical Times* 31/574 (December 1, 1890), 724–25. In English.

Generally favorable assessment of the orchestral concerts organized by Albéniz in November at St. James's Hall, featuring works by himself as well as compatriots Bretón and Chapí.

412. *Leeds Mercury* (January 14, 1891). In English.

Concerning his Leeds concert, states that he possesses a "full, singing touch, facile command of the keyboard, and a masterly adaptation and management of the pedals. He also attaches due importance to . . . the thorough assimilation of what he has to expound, so that . . . he appears to be virtually improvising."

413. *Yorkshire Post* (January 14, 1891). In English.

Review of a concert Albéniz gave in Leeds, assessing his own compositions as "drawing-room music of the daintiest, most polished, and artistic description . . . brilliant and effective, as well as charmingly melodious."

414. *Pall Mall Gazette* (January 30, 1891), "Señor Albéniz at Home: An Interview with the Spanish Pianist." In English.

In this interview, Albéniz gives a brief account of his life in which he declares that he first ran away from home at age eight and a half. Later, after spending 3 years touring in South America, he received a stipend from the Spanish king with which to study in Leipzig, beginning in 1874. After studying for 3 years in that city, he spent a year in Italy with Liszt. Here is an account of his life that conforms neither to the historical record nor to the version he provided to Guerra y Alarcón (no. 151).

415. *Queen* (January 31, 1891). In English.

Review of a chamber-music concert organized by Albéniz at St. James's Hall, featuring the composer at the piano accompanying Enrique Fernández Arbós, violin.

416. *England* (February 4, 1891). In English.

Albéniz possesses an "exquisitely delicate and tender style of playing [that] is peculiar to himself."

417. *Dramatic Review* (February 14, 1891). In English.

States that Albéniz is writing a light patriotic opera set in Spain at the beginning of the War of Independence (1808); the hero is a reformed brigand converted into a guerilla chief. Nothing ever came of this plan.

418. *Bazaar* (February 16, 1891). In English.

Of his performance at St. James's Hall, this reviewer perceives that "his great excellence lies in the power to play softly. . . . He can preserve a special shade of tone for a very long period without the slightest fluctuation or variety." He "produces tones which resemble the ripple of water, and which charm the ear by their delicate softness."

419.   *Daily Telegraph* (February 27, 1891). In English.

A qualified assessment of his playing that states, "The Spanish artist is far happier in his moments of subdued neatness and delicacy when all the finest qualities of a peculiarly feathery touch become evident." Applauds the innovations Albéniz has made in his concert series at St. James's Hall, beginning on January 17, 1891. These include moderate length, free cloak room and programs, inexpensive tickets, and the opportunity to begin a subscription with any concert in the series.

420.   *Pall Mall Gazette* (February 27, 1891). In English.

Favorable review of his concert at St. James's Hall. "Albéniz represents . . . a reaction against the slap-bang-and-hack school which the genius of Liszt invented. . . . Albéniz possesses the rare Thalbergian art of making the piano sing." Describes Spaniards as a "people implacable alike in love and war, and ready to languish at one moment and stab the next."

421.   *Queen* (February 28, 1891). In English.

Reports that the libretto of his new opera will be written by H. Sutherland Edwards. No such work was written, however.

422.   *Mistress & Maid* (March 4, 1891). In English.

A mildly critical assessment of his pianism, stating that he "lacks strength . . . not delicacy."

423.   *World* (March 4, 1891). In English.

Review of an Albéniz piano recital pronouncing him "one of the pleasantest, most musical, and most original of pianists" and "a man of superior character."

424.   *Woman* (March 5, 1891). In English.

Declares that he is "more charming . . . in delicate and fanciful music than in the more severe school."

425.   *Gentlewoman* (March 28, 1891). In English.

Reports that Albéniz's new opera (which was never written) is set in Salamanca in 1808.

426.   *The Queen* (April 11, 1891). In English.

Interview with Albéniz in which he states that he has composed two symphonies, two piano concertos, and eight piano sonatas. Also claims 8 months of study with Liszt in Italy and subsequent directorship of an Italian opera company in Spain. The truth was somewhat less impressive.

427.   *Bazaar* (May 13, 1891). In English.

Review of Albéniz's piano recital at St. James's Hall, in which he played his own *Rêves, On the Water (Barcarole)*, and *Angustia: Romanza sin palabras*.

428.   *Bazaar* (May 13, 1891). In English.

Favorable commentary on his recent performance at St. James's Hall, particularly of his own compositions.

429.   *Deutschen Reiches Anzeiger* (March 2, 1892). In German.

Encomiastic report of his concert at the Singakademie in Berlin on March 1, 1892. Praises his rendering of Beethoven's "Moonlight" Sonata, with the exception of the last movement, in which he used the pedal too much. Chopin was the highlight of the evening, and Albéniz's own pieces exhibited "grace and lively expression."

430.   *Vossischen Zeitung* (March 2, 1892). In German.

Praises his "marvelous technical feats," refinement, and taste. The public reacted to his interpretations with "lively and well-deserved applause."

431.   *Berliner Tageblatt* (March 3, 1892). In German.

States that he made a favorable impression at the Singakademie but that he should leave aside Beethoven and Bach, because his rapid tempos reveal much practice but a superficial rapport with the music. His rendering of Chopin, however, was excellent, especially in the clarity of his technique and tone control.

432.   *National Zeitung* (March 3, 1892). In German.

Praises both the sensitivity and strength in his playing, stating that his Beethoven interpretation revealed both a profound understanding of the music and a well-developed technique.

433.   *Berliner Börsen-Zeitung* (March 4, 1892). In German.

Finds his Beethoven (the "Moonlight" Sonata) lacking in sensitivity, a necessary "dream-like character," and altogether too "conventional and coldly correct." States that his own pieces make a pleasant impression but are basically bagatelles in salon clothing and rather superficial.

434.   *Berliner Zeitung* (March 4, 1892). In German.

"A pianist of the first order . . . technically and musically well trained and elegant."

435.   *Nordeutschen Allgemeinen Zeitung* (March 4, 1892). In German.

Praises his tone and general facility but faults his lack of dynamic contrast, "rhythmic sharpness," and clarity in his runs and arpeggios.

436.   *Die Post* (March 4, 1892). In German.

Lauds his well-developed, clean technique and pure (though small) tone.

437.   *Stadtburger Zeitung* (March 4, 1892). In German.

Applauds his "artful phrasing," beautiful tone, and clean technique. Describes the Bach as "lacking energy" and states that "he did not capture the spirit of Beethoven." But he praises Albéniz's handling of pieces by Chopin and Liszt.

438.   *Volks-Zeitung* (March 4, 1892). In German.

Equivocal review of his concert at the Singakademie. Finds Albéniz's compositions polished and flowing but remarkable in their lack of any "trace of the fiery blood that one really ought to expect from a Southerner."

439.   *L'Art Moderne* (March 20 1892), 91–92, by Octave Maus(?). In French.

Review of Albéniz's Brussels concert, in which he played a Steinway piano "as if it were an orchestra," with "surprising strength, precision, security, and delicacy of touch."

440.   *L'Eventail* (March 20, 1892), 3–4. In French.

Review of a concert given by Albéniz in Brussels, praising him as "a virtuoso of the first order," one possessing a broad repertoire and a technique of "rare strength and agility."

441.   *Le Mouvement Littéraire* (March 23, 1892), 33, by Raymond Nyst(?). In French

Albéniz and Arbós appeared in concert together and garnered justifiable encomiums. "Under Albéniz's fingers, the piano becomes an instrument of seduction."

442.   *The Stage* (London) (July 21, 1892). In English.

Announces that Albéniz is composing a second piano concerto, a work he never completed.

443.   *Heraldo de Madrid* (August 26, 1894), by Louis Bonafoux. In Spanish.

Summary of an interview with Albéniz that offers the following explanation for his choosing to live outside Spain: "Albéniz is more Spanish than [Spanish author Marcelino Menéndez] Pelayo, but for Albéniz Spanishness does not consist in writing pages of music at five francs a page, nor in resigning himself, as a consequence, to eating cold food in a garret. Albéniz lives in Paris and in London because there he can eat and sleep. He is not a bullfighter, and therefore he cannot live well in Spain."

444.   *La Correspondencia de España* (September 17, 1894). In Spanish.

Report on his concert in San Sebastián for the family of the Grand Duke of Wladimiro and other notables at the Miramar Palace on September 13. Describes him as the "emulator of [Anton] Rubinstein" and states that the Steinway piano "responded in docile fashion to his mastery" in "moments of great inspiration."

II. REVIEWS OF THE STAGE WORKS. COMPOSITIONS ARE IN CHRONOLOGICAL ORDER, REVIEWS IN ALPHABETICAL ORDER BY PERIODICAL TITLE. SEE THE CATALOG OF WORKS IN CHAPTER TWO FOR PREMIERE DATES AND LOCATIONS. (Note: "The" is not alphabetized, though definite articles in foreign languages are.)

Cuanto más viejo, T. 1

445.   *LCM* 2/58 (February 8, 1882), 8. In Spanish.

States that Albéniz is completing a zarzuela that will be premiered that week in Bilbao.

446.   *Noticiero Bilbaino* (Bilbao) (February 13 and 15, 1882). In Spanish.

Announces premiere of the work on Wednesday, February 15, along with *Amor que empieza* and *Ya somos tres.*

447.   LCM 2/60 (February 21, 1882), 6. In Spanish.

Review of the premiere at the Coliseo. States that the "performance has been good and the success gratifying for its authors, especially for the composer Sr. Albéniz."

Catalanes de Gracia, T. 2

448.   *Crónica de la Música* (Madrid), no. 184 (March 29, 1882): 5. In Spanish.

Announces premiere of the work. [see no. 263, p. 201]

449.   *El Liberal* (Madrid) (March 29, 1882), 4. In Spanish.

Describes the zarzuela as a comic-lyric "skit" and reports a favorable public reaction to the characters' high jinks. [see no. 263, p. 201]

450.   LCM 2/64 (March 22, 1882), 7. In Spanish.

Announces the premiere of the zarzuela the following Saturday at the Teatro Salón Eslava, with music by the "distinguished" concert artist Don Isaac Albéniz. [see no. 263, p. 201]

451.   LCM 2/65 (March 29, 1882), 7. In Spanish.

States that the "little work" has accomplished its objective, describing the music as "pleasant" and the drama as "amusing." The performance of the singers was warmly applauded, as were the authors themselves. [see no. 263, p. 201]

452.   LCM 2/67 (April 12, 1882), 7. In Spanish.

States that the zarzuela is continuing to draw large audiences at the Eslava. [see no. 263, p. 201]

The Magic Opal, T. 5

453.   *Anglo-American Times* (February 25, 1893). In English.

Reports that the work is still going strong at the Lyric Theatre, because "frolic and laughter, sparkling wit and melodious tunes abound in this charming *pot pouri* [sic]. It is variegated, fascinating, a combination of music and dance, of bright lively dialogue, and brilliant quaint scenery."

454.   *Athenaeum* (January 28, 1893), 131. In English.

"The melodies are for the most part fresh and piquant, and there is no sense of incongruity in the Spanish rhythms which are conspicuous at times. . . . The part-writing for the voices is excellent, and the orchestration is at once refined and picturesque." The writer further characterized it as "the most artistic of the many pieces of the same nature upon which theatrical managers have pinned their faith—unwisely, as it would seem, for the most part—during the current season."

455.   *Bazaar* (January 25, 1893). In English.

". . . it is meant to amuse, and amuse it certainly does; everything throughout it is bright, light, and gay. The music from Señor Albéniz's pen is of an essentially superior style. Replete with pure and graceful melody, it does not leave any frothy impression on the mind, but satisfies the musical sense almost as completely as the light works of the Italian lyric stage."

456.   *Bradford Daily Argus* (February 7, 1893). In English.

States that Horace Sedger has made "several alterations and improvements" to the operetta at the Lyric, including a new solo for Miss May Yohe and a reduction in the second-act quartet's length.

457.   *Bristol Times* (January 21, 1893). In English.

"From beginning to end there is a continuous flow of graceful and refined melody."

458.   *City Press* (April 15, 1893). In English.

A short review states that Albéniz's "charming musical setting of the work is too well known now to require any detailed notice."

459.   *Clarion* (January 28, 1893). In English.

Though this reviewer takes a dim view of the production overall, he reserves highest praise for the overture, which is "very promising. [Albéniz] uses all (especially the brass) gently, and the introductory movement ripples along with reedy murmur."

460.   *Court Circular* (January 21, 1893). In English.

"Albéniz has been chiefly known here for his pianoforte work, but he now shows that he can write very pleasant operatic music. . . . The opera was received with every manifestation of approval."

461.   *Daily Graphic* (January 20, 1893). In English.

States that Albéniz, a composer of "graceful trifles" for piano, has scored a "decided success" as a composer of comic opera.

462.   *The Daily News* (February 7, 1893). In English.

Favorable report of the operetta, which makes clear that changes were still being made to the score just before and even after the premiere.

463.   *The Daily Telegraph* (January 20, 1893). In English.

"It is, perhaps, hardly necessary to say that Mr. Albéniz's nationality shines through much of his music. Indeed he is never happier than when he relies upon passages which, in their progressions and harmonies, are fully Spanish."

464.   *The Daily Telegraph* (February 6, 1893). In English.

Favorable report of the operetta, which makes clear that changes were still being made to the score just before and even after the premiere.

465.   *Dramatic Review* (January 28, 1893). In English.

"The composer has imparted to his work a higher standard than one is accustomed to expect in modern comic opera from a foreign pen, and his melodies are flowing and graceful, while the orchestration is skilful and musicianly." The critic remarks that there is nothing of Greece in the score but rather of Spain, which was to be expected, given the composer's nationality.

466.   *Eastern Morning News* (Hull) (May 3, 1893). In English.

A somewhat lukewarm review nonetheless states that "there is occasionally pleasant relief in some of the lighter melody with which the opera is interspersed, some of the duets and trios are sufficiently original, whilst the concerted music was more ambitious than is usually to be found in work of this description. Taken as a whole, the music is too refined to even raise popular enthusiasm."

467.   *Encore* (February 3, 1893). In English.

Declares that "there has rarely been seen on the London boards a more brilliant spectacle of colour than there is at the Lyric Theatre just now." Goes on to describe the various costumes in considerable detail.

468.   *Era* (January 21, 1893), 9. In English.

In addition to praising the libretto (a minority view, to be sure), it declares that "those who can appreciate anything better than the thinly-orchestrated jingle of the ordinary comic opera composer will revel in the refinement and grace of

Señor Albéniz's work. The music . . . is sure to improve upon acquaintance, and is decidedly of the sort which will bear to be heard again and again."

469.   *Evening Post* (York) (April 22, 1893). In English.

Brief review that nonetheless reports that the work has been a success in Newcastle at the Tyne Theatre and at the Royal.

470.   *The Evening Times* (February 18, 1893). In English.

Announces changes in the times of the performances as well as additions to the second act, including a new solo for Miss May Yohe.

471.   *Figaro* (January 26, 1893). In English.

A very affirmative review of the new work. "It is, however, in the music that the strength of 'The Magic Opal' chiefly lies. It may be that his melodies are often reminiscent of Sullivan on the one hand and Offenbach on the other; but it is even more satisfactory to notice that Mr. Albéniz in many numbers shows an individuality of his own, based no doubt upon the national Spanish style."

472.   *Figaro* (February 23, 1893). In English.

Ascribes the failure of *The Magic Opal* to the "popular leaning towards the 'Ta-ra-ra' and 'The Man who Broke the Bank at Monte Carlo' style of melodies."

473.   *Financial World* (January 20, 1893). In English.

It is pleasant to be able to record the success of M. Albéniz. . . . Originality, melody, and brightness in music are desirable qualities, and these . . . he has in abundance. From beginning to end the opera sparkles with musical gems, some of which are bound to achieve popularity."

474.   *Gentlewoman* (February 11, 1893). In English.

Favorable report of the operetta, which makes clear that changes were still being made to the score just before and even after the premiere.

475.   *Glasgow Evening Citizen* (February 14, 1893). In English.

Albéniz "appears to be a composer who is in search of a style. While the story is supposed to be Greek, the short overture, and the first two or three vocal numbers have a distinctly Iberian flavour. There is thus nothing of what is commonly called "local colour" in the music, but this circumstance in no wise detracts from the quality of the work, and it is readily enough accounted for by reason of the composer's nationality. Anon he drops into a completely opposite channel, which assimilates closely with the French style of comic opera, and, indeed, with the most extreme opera bouffe. A scene in the first act, and more particularly a concerted piece and chorus in the second, show the composer at his best as a writer for the stage. Here he rises above the ordinary level, and in the latter number he has produced a scene which would not do discredit to some of the best specimens of the lyric drama."

476. *Glasgow Evening Times* (February 14, 1893). In English.

Though expressing some reservations about the drama itself, Albéniz's music "is decidedly above the average. It not of the jingling, ear-tickling order, but refined, artistic, some of it almost classical. As an example of the clever orchestration, may be mentioned the weird accompaniment to the legend song of the bandit chief. There are highly effective choruses, and the accompaniment is the work of a thorough musician."

477. *Glasgow Herald* (February 14, 1893). In English.

States that it is a "the work of a young composer of great promise." Despite stormy weather, the house was sold out. Several numbers in act two were repeated at the audience's insistence.

478. *Globe* (January 20, 1893). In English.

"Señor Albéniz has proved himself a consummate master of his art, and last night commanded the admiration of musicians, who could not fail to appreciate his mastery of orchestration, his fertility of melodic invention, and his faculty of varying melodies and accompaniments in accordance with all kinds of sentiment. . . . To name those portions of "The Magic Opal" score which merit hearty praise would involve a list of nearly all the solos and concerted pieces included in the score. For such a list we cannot find sufficient space, and must be content with assuring our readers that they will find a large number of musical gems in this new opera."

479. *Graphic* (January 28, 1893). In English.

A laudatory review that nonetheless faults the obvious traces of French *opéra comique* in the score.

480. *Hawk* (January 24, 1893). In English.

Though the reviewer expresses the usual qualms about the book, he praises Albéniz, "who has shown himself equal to the demands made on him. In his choruses and concerted pieces he is most often successful, showing a mastery over an orchestra which seems quite extraordinary in one who has been noted only for the prettiness of his songs. Yet, in the solos there is a certain distinction always, and a sweetness of melody which augur future great things."

481. *Illustrated & Dramatic News* (January 28, 1893). In English.

Hails Albéniz's stature as a pianist and piano composer, and favorably notes that he is "gifted with inventive power of more than ordinary excellence," in addition to being an excellent orchestrator.

482. *La Ilustración Musical Hispano-Americana*, no. 107 (June 30, 1892). In Spanish.

Announces that Albéniz and Arbós have finished work on a musical entitled "The Opal Ring." In fact, Arbós did not see the work through to completion and left that task for Albéniz to perform.

483.   *Lady* (February 9, 1893). In English.

Expresses skepticism about Albéniz's eclectic approach: "It is called, with equal justness, either light opera or comic opera. As a matter of fact, the composer has chosen to attempt a compromise between both styles, and, moreover, has made several departures into the field of grand opera. Whether such a course is exactly a wise one is doubtful. The plain and simple methods of Offenbach, Lecocq, and other composers of the palmy days of comic opera, have been discarded of late by most composers."

484.   *Lady's Pictorial* (January 28, 1893). In English.

As was usually the case in reviews of this work, the music won greater plaudits than the libretto: "Señor Albéniz's melodies are as a rule singularly graceful, and tinged with a warmth of colouring suggestive of the author's native land."

485.   *Leeds Evening Express* (April 26, 1893). In English.

"Señor Albéniz is a Spaniard, which accounts, perhaps, for the Spanish colouring and rhythm that are frequently noticeable."

486.   *Liverpool Post* (April 11, 1893). In English.

Provides a plot summary and concludes with this encomium: "Lovers of light opera may be confidently recommended not to miss this agreeable and pleasant example of that class of entertainment."

487.   *Man of the World* (January 25, 1893). In English.

Parts with the majority of reviewers in finding something good to say about the libretto: ". . . although the music by Señor Albéniz is the better part of the new piece at the Lyric, *The Opal Ring* [sic] has a more coherent and entertaining story, simple as it is, than nine out of ten works of its class."

488.   *Manchester City News* (March 18, 1893). In English.

A short review reporting on the *The Magic Opal*'s lackluster reception in London and hopes for improved prospects with the revision: "Señor Albéniz writes pretty music, original too beyond the usual scheme for this class of work, and characterized by many quaint and dainty effects and attempts at local colour."

489.   *Manchester Courier* (March 14, 1893). In English.

Hails the work as "pleasing from a musical point of view, the scenery is picturesque and realistic, the costumes bright and effective, and as a whole the production may be described as fairly up to the average of such works."

490.   *Manchester Evening Mail* (April 12, 1893). In English.

"This opera has the advantage of musicianly and tuneful music composed by Señor Albéniz, but when first produced a short while back it was allied to a poor libretto. . . . The story is not, however, worth the trouble bestowed upon it, and the attempt to strengthen it is not entirely successful."

491. *Manchester Examiner* (March 14, 1893). In English.

Remarks on the early demise of the operetta, noting its auspicious opening but failure to continue to hold the public's interest. Along with many other critics, he considers this "a pity."

492. *Manchester Weekly Times* (March 17, 1893). In English.

Provides a complete inventory of the operetta's various numbers, as well as a generally favorable estimation of the music.

493. *Morning Post* (February 20, 1893). In English.

This very supportive review reports that "Señor Albéniz has once more proved that it is possible for a musician to write music of a light description without abdicating all artistic feeling." Goes on to compare the score to works by Délibes and Bizet.

494. *Music Trades Review* (February 20, 1893). In English.

Favorable review that cites as "gems" in Act I the serenade of the bandit chief Trabucos, "a pretty song for the heroine in waltz time," and Candida's Spanish-style dance in Act II. Expresses some doubts about Albéniz's eclectic approach, however, finding that many songs were reminiscent of the style of Sir Arthur Sullivan.

495. *The Musical Times* 34/600 (February 3, 1893), 91. In English.

Observes that the score exhibits "pleasant Spanish colouring."

496. *Pelican* (January 28, 1893). In English.

A generally favorable estimation of the work: ". . . it contains all the elements of a prosperous Comic Opera. Its music is charming; it is splendidly staged and dressed; it is capably sung and acted, and it is moreover at times a trifle dull."

497. *People* (January 22, 1893). In English.

"[Albéniz] has furnished a remarkably charming and masterly score. . . . His orchestration is specially worthy of admiration; far surpassing that of nearly all the comic operatic works produced within the last dozen years."

498. *Piccadilly* (January 25, 1893). In English.

"Señor Albéniz has done the musical part of the work in the style one has a right to expect from such a thorough master of his art, and the score is graceful, spirited, and melodious."

499. *Pick Me Up* (February 18, 1893). In English.

A favorable review that offers a detailed plot summary and drawings of the costumes. Hails the music as "an extra special inspiration of Señor Albéniz."

500. *Pioneer Allahabad* (February 16, 1893). In English.

Heralds the work as a "pretty opera of the light and comic order. . . . Tuneful choruses and bright music make the opera a distinct success."

501. *Princess* (February 4, 1893). In English.

Heralds the work as "one of the most brilliant, if not one of the best, of the operas produced lately at the Lyric Theatre." Albéniz's score is "throughout delicate, charmingly orchestrated, and worthy of praise."

502. *Queen* (January 28, 1893). In English.

"Albéniz has written some very charming and agreeable music, much of which is Spanish in character, but all of which is fresh, graceful, and refined." As did many reviewers, notes an indebtedness to Sullivan and Offenbach.

503. *Saturday Review* (January 28, 1893), 97–98. In English.

"The cardinal point about it is the extremely bright and pretty music . . . [though the book] is not very robust." Has high praise for the costumes and sets and especially for Candida's dance in Act II.

504. *Scotsman* (Edinburgh) (February 14, 1893). In English.

Hails the work's favorable reception by local audiences, due in large measure to its "tuneful airs" and "pleasing" orchestration.

505. *Scotsman* (Edinburgh) (February 21, 1893). In English.

"The music has attractive features. It is fresh, and has associated with it a considerable amount of local colour. The opening balcony duet is an exceedingly pleasing piece of work."

506. *Scottish Leader* (Glasgow) (February 14, 1893). In English.

An enthusiastic appraisal that remarks, "The songs and choruses are bright and tripping, and are admirably wedded to the delightful music of Señor Albéniz. The composer, by many ever-present, but seldom obtrusive touches, has given a half Spanish tone to the whole score, which lends to the opera an added piquancy and originality."

507. *Sheffield Telegraph* (March 21, 1893). In English.

"Albéniz proves himself capable of good work, excelling in his instrumentation, which is often novel, and always effective."

508. *Sketch* (February 8, 1893), 95. In English.

Positive critique that nonetheless faults Albéniz for not having "chosen to write music that shows off the voice." Provides a detailed description of Candida's dance in Act II, which has a "strange flavour of mystery." Ascribes to the production the power to "do something to raise the tone of comic opera, which been sinking a good deal of late years."

509. *Smart Society* (January 25, 1893). In English.

A fictitious dialogue that spoofs English tastes and critical reaction to works like *The Magic Opal*. Concludes by praising the music Albéniz has conferred on a rather weak libretto.

510. *Society* (January 28, 1893). In English.

Albéniz is deemed "equal to the obligations of grand opera, and if he descends a step to opera, after he has acquired more experience, will certainly be the gainer. He exhibits great powers in the composition of his concerted creations. . . . There are times when he shows the most delicate conceits—conceits which touch the fancy as greatly as some of his airs arouse the emotions."

511. *Society* (February 18, 1893). In English.

Announces changes in the times of the performances as well as additions to the second act, including a new solo for Miss May Yohe.

512. *Sporting Dramatic News* (January 28, 1893). In English.

Summarizes Albéniz's stature as a pianist and piano composer, then goes on to laud him as demonstrating that he is a composer "gifted with inventive power of more than ordinary excellence, coupled with consummate skill in orchestration."

513. *Sporting Mirror* (January 23, 1893). In English.

"This opera is simply delightful and is certainly the best production of its class that has appeared during the past year. It is full of melody. The opera is undoubtedly the best of its kind that I have witnessed for a long time."

514. *Sportsman* (January 20, 1893). In English.

Despite serious reservations about the "thin" plot, the reviewer finds the music to be "above the average of light opera. The orchestration is masterly, and musicianly qualities are to be found throughout the score. The music, vocal and instrumental, should suffice to make the reputation of the opera."

515. *Sportsman* (March 3, 1893). In English.

After the failure of *The Magic Opal*, the critic worries about "what a strange, inexplicable, incomprehensible people [Albéniz] must by now think that we English are." Asserts that Albéniz "has the capacity to do something which must win him fame far exceeding any that even the phenomenal success of 'The Magic Opal' would have brought in its train."

516. *Stage* (January 26, 1893), 12. In English.

"There will be no necessity to bemoan the fate of comic opera while Señor Albéniz continues to write for the stage. . . . There is much originality in [his] music, and a freshness of treatment that is very acceptable is apparent throughout the score."

517. *Sunday Chronicle* (Manchester) (March 13, 1893). In English.

Reports that the number "Lovey Dovey Rosey Posey" was "rapturously encored." Otherwise mocks the production's director, Horace Sedger, with the following little poem: "Dear O-pal, costly O-pal / Dear O-pal, costly O-pal / Making for Sedger / a hole in the ledger / Give us one better than dear Opal."

518. *Sussex Daily News* (April 4, 1893), 159. In English.

Very favorable review: "Señor Albéniz's music is artistically scored, and the melodies are graceful and refined, several of the numbers being very dramatic and a distinct advance upon those associated with ordinary comic operas."

519. *Theatre* (March 1, 1893), 154–55. In English.

Praises Albéniz's music as "distinguished by a melody, a force, and an eloquence rare indeed in compositions for the comic opera stage." He even had praise for the libretto (a rare occurrence with Albéniz's operas), which he describes as "full of happy humour, dramatic vigour, and pretty sentiment."

520. *The Times* (January 20, 1893), 6. In English.

Lauds the music as "bright, tuneful, and original," and goes on to say: "No inexperience is to be traced . . . in the construction of the many effective numbers, or in the vocal and instrumental writing. The orchestral scoring is, indeed, remarkably interesting and refined, and the ideas throughout original and most characteristic."

521. *The Topical Times* (January 21, 1893). In English.

"Señor Albéniz may rest assured that his charming work will penetrate every ballroom and his vocal numbers be heard in every household."

522. *The Topical Times* (February 4, 1893). In English.

Favorable report of the operetta, which makes clear that changes were still being made to the score just before and even after the premiere.

523. *The Topical Times* (February 18, 1893). In English.

Announces changes in the times of the performances as well as additions to the second act, including a new solo for Miss May Yohe.

524. *The Topical Times* (April 15, 1893). In English.

"[I]t is undoubtedly one of the prettiest and most attractive musical works that I have seen for some time on the comic opera stage."

525. *Truth* (January 26, 1893). In English.

Perceives the influence of Sullivan and Offenbach in Albéniz's style, which nonetheless exhibits an originality grounded in his Spanish nationality. Thus, "no light opera for many years has been received with a more unanimous outburst of commendation."

526.   *Truth* (February 23, 1893), "The Decline of Comic Opera." In English.

An article dealing with the early demise of Albéniz's operetta, which received generally excellent notices but nonetheless ran less than 2 months. The popularity of music halls had cut into the operetta market; ticket prices were too high, along with production costs. The expenses of *The Magic Opal* exceeded £720 a week. The Lyric Theatre could hold enough to bring in £1,800 if only half full every night, but the production still lost money and closed after 7 weeks.

527.   *Weekly Scotsman* (Edinburgh) (February 25, 1893). In English.

Lukewarm reaction to its production at the Lyceum, stating that "neither the composer nor the librettist strikes a vein that is altogether free from conventionality, but the work of each is clever enough in its way."

528.   *Weekly Sun* (March 12, 1893). In English.

Positive review that states that Miss May Yohe (an American) received an ovation for her singing in the second act.

529.   *Westminster Gazette* (April 12, 1893). In English.

"Few modern comic operas can show anything equal to the overture."

530.   *World* (January 25, 1893), George Bernard Shaw. In English.

"The Magic Opal, at the Lyric, is a copious example of that excessive fluency in composition of which Señor Albéniz has already given us sufficient proofs. His music is pretty, shapely, unstinted, lively, goodnatured, and far too romantic and refined for the stuff which Mr Arthur Law has given him to set. But Albéniz has the faults as well as the qualities of his happy and uncritical disposition; and the grace and spirit of his strains are of rather too obvious a kind to make a very deep impression. And he does not write well for the singers. It is not that the phrases are unvocal, or that the notes lie badly for the voice, but that he does not set the words from the comedian's point of view, his double disability as a pianist and a foreigner handicapping him in this department."

531.   *Yorkshire Post* (January 20, 1893). In English.

"[T]here are some delightful incidental dances, including one by a Spanish 'danseuse', which is reminiscent of the best type of Indian Nautch dancing."

Madrid Revival (concert version, Auditorio Nacional, February 27, 2010)

532.   http://www.zarzuela.net/ref/reviews/magic-opal10_eng.htm, by Enrique Mejías García. In English and Spanish.

An insightful review of the revival of this operetta in a concert version at the Auditorio Nacional in Madrid on February 27, 2010, with Silvia Sanz Torres conducting the Orquesta Sinfónica Charmartín. Places *The Magic Opal* in the context of a transitional phase in English operetta during the 1890s, citing not only its traditional and forward-looking qualities but also possible influence from zarzuela. Still, the work sounds "purely British." Finds it to be more "theatrically effective" than any of his other stage works, with the exception of *Pepita Jiménez.*

The Magic Ring (Revision of *The Magic Opal*)

533.   *Chronicle* (May 10, 1893). In English.

Notes that "a new topical song introduced by Mr. Monkhouse—'It never happens here'—is cordially received."

534.   *Court Journal* (April 15, 1893). In English.

Despite continuing problems with the actual libretto, "the composer's music is, however, as delightful as ever, and the opera, with its charming Grecian scenery and background, is lively and interesting."

535.   *Dramatic Review* (May 6, 1893). In English.

Notes that Mr. Monkhouse sings a song, "Oh, never, never," which was not sung in the premiere at the Prince of Wales's Theatre.

536.   *Era* (April 15, 1893), 11. In English.

Compliments the changes made to the libretto and states that "unreserved praise may be given" to the score. He finds not only the influence of *opéra comique* but ascribes its charm to its "Spanish character, which harmonizes perfectly with the subject. The melodies, always full of grace, sometimes combine a fascinating vein of sentiment with sparkling effects."

537.   *Fashions of Today* (May 1893). In English.

Derides the libretto as "weak" but hails Albéniz as possessing "the gift of melody which flows on from number to number with unfailingly pleasant effect. His music is deeply tinged with a sunny hue reflected from the Iberian peninsula, and is none the worse for that," despite the action's setting in Greece.

538.   *Globe* (April 13, 1893). In English.

Comments on the excision of certain numbers, "those allotted to the sister of the bandit," from the original operetta.

539.   *Morning Leader* (April 13, 1893), "Stave." In English.

"The music of Señor Albéniz was always prepared to stand the test of criticism, and under the present conditions may yet receive the success it undoubtedly deserves and ensure a run in its new habitation."

540.   *Royal Court Theatre* (April 11, 1893). In English.

Praises the operetta, in particular Lolika's "Love sprang from his couch 'mid the roses," sung by Miss Annie Schuberth, which was "an exacting song and brightly scored."

541. *Stage* (April 15, 1893), 11. In English.

   Considers that Albéniz's music for *The Magic Opal* was of "too high an order of merit to be finally shelved after a few performances only." Expresses doubts, however, about the merits of the libretto, even in its revision.

542. *Telegraph* (April 15, 1893). In English.

   Refers to Albéniz's music as "graceful and musicianly" but finds that the mediocre libretto remains a liability, despite the improvements made to it.

543. *Theatre* (May 1, 1893), 294, by Percy Notcutt. In English.

   Does not view the new version as an improvement over the old. States that, in spite of revisions in the text and restructuring of the cast, the libretto remains "lamentably weak." Albéniz's score, however, is "really excellent throughout . . . being musicianly and artistic in the extreme."

544. *The Times* (April 13, 1893), 13. In English.

   States unequivocally that the revision is "far superior, musically speaking, to the average comic opera of the day." Though it describes the comic interest of the first version as "meagre," it extols the "distinct improvements" that have been made in the second, especially the addition of an "extremely effective duet for Lolika and Trabucos."

545. *Umpire* (April 16, 1893). In English.

   "The most attractive feature of 'The Magic Ring' remains to be mentioned. It is the music of Señor Albéniz. I proclaimed this young Spaniard a valuable recruit to the ranks of light composers, and I adhere to my opinion."

546. *The Westminster Gazette* (April 4, 1893). In English.

   Remarks that "Miss Susie Vaughan has Miss Yohe's part tacked on to her own," but without the number that "made the hit of the original production."

547. *The Westminster Gazette* (April 12,1893). In English.

   "The work is rather more lively than before, but still the delightful music of Señor Albéniz is hampered by a heavy book. . . . Few modern comic operas can show anything equal to the overture, or the fascinating serenade of Trabucos, whilst several other numbers might be named for admiration." Singles out orchestration, melodic grace, and thematic novelty for praise.

548. *World* (April 19, 1893), George Bernard Shaw. In English.

   Describes the new production as an "attempt . . . to rescue Señor Albéniz's score of *The Magic Opal* from sinking under the weight of its libretto." He concedes, however, that "the revised version of the opera leaves [Albéniz] easily ahead of the best of his rivals."

La sortija (Spanish revision of *The Magic Opal*)

549.   *El Correo Español* (November 24, 1894), 2, by "Pipí." In Spanish.

Declares that neither the book nor the music is suited to Spanish taste, despite its success in London, and that the performance was not good. His conclusion is that "Albéniz and Sierra are too *foreignized*."

550.   *El Heraldo de Madrid* (November 24, 1894), 3. In Spanish.

"Those scenes of bandits, those falsified Andalusians, that amulet ring, and those mishandled love interests could not interest anybody or inspire a musician [of Albéniz's stature]." [see no. 263, p. 221]

551.   *El Imparcial* (November 24, 1894), 2–3, by "J. de L." In Spanish.

Albéniz "has nothing to learn; on the contrary, he has much to forget." [see no. 263, p. 221]

552.   *El Liberal* (November 24, 1894), 3, by "J. A." In Spanish.

States that the music was too good for the simple and uninteresting story. "The audience was cold and reserved and did not accord *La sortija* . . . the general applause that decides the success of a premiere in favor of the author." [see no. 263, p. 221]

553.   *El Nacional* (November 24, 1894), 3. In Spanish.

Criticizes the libretto's lack of dramatic interest and the superabundance of musical numbers, more than many three-act zarzuelas contain. Does, however, praise Albéniz's instrumentation.

554.   *El Resumen* (November 24, 1894), 2, by E. Contreras y Camargo. In Spanish.

"The numbers follow one another without interruption, without allowing time for the ear to rest. Moreover, the numbers are so long that they constitute an invasion of oppressive notes. Twenty-some numbers in two acts! . . . Choruses and more choruses, romances, duets, trios." [see no. 263, p. 222]

555.   *La Correspondencia de España* (November 24, 1894), 1, "Telones y Bambalinas," by "El Abate de Pirracas." In Spanish.

"Albéniz, as a composer, is one of those eternal talkers . . . who spout words and words and words without pause and without saying anything." He further avers that "the music of *La Sortija does not sound*. And I will add that it is *hollow* and lacks color, sonority, grace, freshness, and the *stamp* of that which is inspired and spontaneous. . . . Therefore, the music of Sr. Albéniz is opaque and cold. The notes fall on the ear and remain in the ear, accumulating to form an offensive noise." [see no. 263, p. 223]

556.   *La Época* (November 24, 1894), 3, by "Z." In Spanish.

"Intelligent people say that the music is very *learned*. But logarithmic tables are also learned, and I do not believe there is a spectator capable of enduring a recital of them for two and a half hours. The public, despite giving evidence of the patience of Job, manifested, at various times, its disgust. [see no. 263, p. 221]

557.   *La Iberia* (Madrid) (November 24, 1894), 2. In Spanish.

"The book is deplorable" and the score "contains enough music for three zarzuelas." Though the music also exhibits "inspiration and freshness," the libretto did not deserve so much as "a single bad note." The audience, which included the Infanta Doña Isabel, quickly wearied of the work. [see no. 263, p. 222]

558.   *La Justicia* (November 24, 1894), 2, by "Don Cualquiera." In Spanish.

"Perhaps, within the melodic mania that obsesses him, the cognoscenti will find no musical defect in the whole score. But the public, the anonymous masses, are extremely bored." [see no. 263, p. 222]

Poor Jonathan, T. 6

559.   *Black & White* (July 1, 1893). In English.

Expresses the conviction that "the music of Señor Albéniz is far superior to that contributed by Herr Millöcker."

560.   *Daily Graphic* (June 19, 1893). In English.

"The additions to the score for which the Spanish composer is responsible are in nearly every instance superior in construction, charm, and elegance to the work of the original composer [Karl Millöcker]."

561.   *Era* (June 17, 1893). In English.

Positive critique describing Albéniz's numbers as "charming in style and admirably scored for the orchestra."

562.   *Morning Leader* (May 16, 1893). In English.

Complimentary assessment of Albéniz's contributions as composer, describing his music as "nearly always delightfully charming and graceful, and more than once he gives us some real comedy in his orchestration."

563.   *Standard* (May 16, 1893). In English.

Generally favorable review of the several numbers composed by Albéniz for the production of Millöcker's operetta. Albéniz capably conducted the performance at the Prince of Wales's Theatre.

564.   *Telegraphe* (May 15, 1893). In English.

"Albéniz, skilled and graceful composer that he is, flounders hopelessly in his struggles to write the light and lilting tunes which alone could make such a piece acceptable."

565.   *The Times* (June 17, 1893). In English.

Declares it "a decided success," calling it a "variety entertainment" on an "elevated level."

566.   *Topical Times* (June 17, 1893). In English.

"Speeches are too long, the songs are too long, and the action is too slow."

567.   *World* (June 21, 1893), by George Bernard Shaw. In English.

Complains that Albéniz's numbers (and those by others) "have made the work more pretentious; but they have also . . . weakened it by making it far too long." In a more sympathetic vein, however, he states that Albéniz's "management is an example to London in point of artistic aim and liberal spirit" (Albéniz also conducted the production).

San Antonio de la Florida, T. 7

Madrid Production (1894):

568.   *Crónica del sport* (September 1894), by "Krieg." In Spanish.

An inside look at the upcoming premiere. "The music that he is writing, on a book by Eusebio Sierra, is prodigious in its freshness, exuberance, and anima-tion. There are numbers that must garner infinite applause and demands for repetition when it is premiered in Madrid. May it be so!"

569.   *El Correo Español* (October 27, 1894), 3, by "Pipí." In Spanish.

Rare positive estimation of the work ("a lot of good music") that gives insight into the audience's reaction: "The hall was completely full, the intelligent ele-ment predominating, who applauded all the numbers with enthusiasm, espe-cially the prelude, the serenade, and some of the choruses."

570.   *El Heraldo de Madrid* (October 27, 1894), 3. In Spanish.

Reports that Albéniz "forcefully aroused the interest and curiosity" of the public with his new zarzuela. Concurs with the other critics, however, that the music was too good, too sophisticated for the type of work it was (light zarzuela) and for the audience and venue. [see no. 263, p. 218]

571.   *El Imparcial* (October 27, 1894), 3, by "A." In Spanish.

Acerbic denunciation that accuses Albéniz of having "taken the work as a pretext for demonstrating that he is a musician of great talents. Has he demonstrated that? To excess, in my judgment, insofar as the enormous quantity of music, though of the highest quality, is too great for so diminutive a book. The public received Albéniz with genuine affection . . . and requested the repetition of three or four truly beautiful numbers, at the end calling Isaac Albéniz and the author of the text, D. Eusebio Sierra, to the stage." [see no. 263, p. 218]

572. *El Liberal* (October 27, 1894), 3, by "J. A." In Spanish.

Expresses reservations about the zarzuela, for though "it abounds in melody, and the instrumental parts are handled admirably," Albéniz "sometimes ascends in flight to altitudes in which the exigencies of the genre are lost from view, lacking the sobriety necessary in order to contain himself in the limits the poet has set for him in the poem he has placed at his service." [see no. 263, p. 219]

573. *El Nacional* (October 27, 1894), 3, by "Blas." In Spanish.

Generally favorable review but faults the music as "too learned" for such a light work. Describes the premiere as "un succès d'estime an plus haut degré."

574. *El Resumen* (October 27, 1894), 2. In Spanish.

With lighter, more appropriate music, the work might have been effective, but Albéniz's score was too operatic and unsuited to the performers, theater, and audience. [see no. 263, p. 220]

575. *La Correspondencia de España* (October 27, 1894), 3. In Spanish.

Reports that "the public of the Apolo, despite being accustomed to popular music—inspired and playful—applauded extraordinarily last night the [music] of Sr. Albéniz, demanding a repetition of the introductory chorus, the duet in the first scene, and the prelude of the second [Intermedio]." [see no. 263, p. 220]

576. *La Correspondencia de España* (December 30, 1894), 1, "Porvenir de los compositores españoles," by Conde Guillermo Morphy. In Spanish.

Declares that though the critics accused it of breaking established molds and of being "dangerously innovative," the public reacted well enough to the freshness of his stage works. In response to a critic who had accused Albéniz of "using a frigate to cross a river," he replied that a "simple raft" could only appear like a frigate to someone accustomed to crossing rivers, like the Africans, "on an inflated hide." He let fly another shaft in the direction of the notorious "Zeda" (no. 577), who had accused Albéniz of abusing truffles by putting them in everything: "Could it not be closer to the truth to affirm that in the *género chico* the garlic and the onion have been so abused that the tired palate does not know how to distinguish the potato from the truffle?" He lamented the lack of national musical theater on a grand scale (that is, with several acts, serious, elevated subjects and style) and encouraged the public and critics to support young composers like Albéniz (only 34 years old at this time) who were attempting to do something new and out of the ordinary. [see no. 263, p. 224]

577. *La Época* (October 27, 1894), 2, by "Zeda." In Spanish.

"The lyrical comedy premiered last night at the Teatro de Apolo belongs to the *boring* genre. . . . The text is made up of a series of drab scenes, without interest, without grace, without types, with neither customs, nor comic situations, nor jokes, nor originality, nor anything." Though he offers praise for the introduction and the finale of the first scene, his conclusion is that "Sr. Albéniz has incurred the defect of the character in *Los pavos reales*, who wanted to put truffles in everything. . . . He has abused the truffles." [see no. 263, p. 219]

578.   *La Iberia* (October 27, 1894), 3. In Spanish.

Rare positive review of the work, singling out the prelude to scene two as a "concert piece" with a "delicious melody and magisterial orchestration." States that the audience received the work with enthusiasm and only regrets that he expended his considerable talents on such a lightweight type of entertainment as the "género chico" (light genre of zarzuela). [see no. 263, p. 219]

579.   *La Ilustración Musical Hispano-Americana*, no. 157 (July 30, 1894). In Spanish.

Reports that Albéniz is writing a stage work that will premiere at the Teatro de la Zarzuela in Madrid. [see no. 263, p. 221]

580.   *La Justicia* (October 27, 1894), 4, by "Don Cualquiera." In Spanish.

States that "from the first note to the last there dominates a taste and an elegance in the composition, and [in] the intermedio between the first and second scenes a brilliant melody is developed with enchanting simplicity." But "when the public goes to see a little piece of a popular kind, it does not request excellence of composition or lofty harmonic effects; it is content with something light that the ear can enjoy." Finds that the "text of *San Antonio de la Florida* is poor, and what is more than poor, insubstantial and lacking in verisimilitude." [see no. 263, p. 220]

Barcelona Production (1895):

581.   *El Correo Catalán* (November 7, 1895), 2. In Spanish.

Declares that the work was well received and that the duet had to be repeated. However, "the libretto has no literary value" and possesses "many scenic deficiencies."

582.   *La Dinastía* (November 7, 1895), 3. In Spanish.

Favorable estimation of the work, whose music "conforms to the diverse situations of the argument, which has a lot of movement." The orchestra was well directed by Albéniz.

583.   *La Renaixensa: Diari de Catalunya* (November 8, 1895), 6267. In Catalan.

"Sr. Albéniz has attempted to perform the miracle of imparting interest with his inspired music to a libretto that possesses absolutely nothing to recommend it . . . but as it is impossible to raise the dead, so here all the charming melody the music breathes is lost in futility. It is a genuine pity that the composer finds himself in a labor that under other circumstances would reward him with glory and profit."

584. *La Vanguardia* (November 7, 1895), 3, by "V." In Spanish.

    Praises the music, particularly the Preludio, but finds that the libretto produced fatigue and heaviness, the result of "repetition of situations," "lack of popular atmosphere," "dimensions disproportionate to a few scenes," and "lack of novelty and interest in the plot and the text." However, he credits it with "initiating a new current in this genre of works."

585. *La Vanguardia* (November 10, 1895), 5, "S. Antonio de la Florida," by Amadeo Vives. In Spanish.

    Vives states his conviction that the only kind of uniquely and distinctively Spanish music is the zarzuela. He goes on to declare that Albéniz has produced a "masterpiece" of the genre by "balancing the expectations of the public with the needs of the artists. The melodies are fresh, spontaneous, vital, and animated, simple without being sterile, clear without a loss of flavor, and full of inspiration and local color. The instrumentation is rich and brilliant." However, he cites a "disequilibration" between the beautiful music and the utterly inadequate libretto, which Vives dismisses in scathing terms.

586. *Lo Teatro Català (El Teatro Catalán)* 6/252 (November 9, 1895), 2, by Armando de la Florida. In Catalan.

    "The work of Sr. Sierra is a disgrace.... The music is ... a calamity."

    Brussels Production (in French, retitled *L'Hermitage fleuri*) (1905):

587. *La Chronique* (January 4, 1905), 3, by "J. D'A." In French.

    Praises the score's "joyous and vibrant sonorities, rhythmic exuberance, and melodic character, inspired as they are by Spanish folklore." In fact, Albéniz serves as a "brilliant example of the conservation of the character of national music," an example younger composers should follow.

588. *La Chronique* (May 1, 1905). In French.

    Reports that Albéniz received three enthusiastic curtain calls from the audience. In attendance was Juan Pérez Caballero, the Spanish ambassador, and his wife.

589. *La Chronique* (June 1, 1905). In French.

    Lauds its "joyous and vibrant sonorities, exuberant rhythm, and melodic accents of a special character," all of which are "essential elements" in Spanish music.

590. *La Fédération Artistique* (August 1, 1905), 14, by "Robert M." In French.

    Describes it a "youthful work" that is not lacking in inspiration but in which the orchestration is very simple, if not exactly boring.

591. *La Gazette* (January 4, 1905), 2, "Edm. C." [Edmond Cattier]. In French.

    Praises the zarzuela's "shine, sparkle, and movement," finding it "amusing, young, gay, and nicely written."

592.   *La Réforme* (July 1, 1905), 1, by "TABARIN." In French.

Hails the "gracious allure" of the work though finding it somewhat insubstantial.

593.   *L'Art Moderne* (August 1, 1905), 11–12, by Octave Maus. In French.

Praises the work's many pages of music "spiritually written and of very delicious humor." [Same article in *Le Courrier Musical* 8–3 (February 1, 1905), 76–78.]

594.   *Le Courrier Musical* 8–3 (February 1, 1905), 76–78, by Octave Maus. In French.

Lauds the "delicious humor" and local color of the zarzuela, though he overstates the case for its popularity in Spain, where it never found a regular place on the stage. [Same article in *L'Art Moderne* (August 1, 1905), 11–12.]

595.   *L'Etoile Belge* (January 1, 1905), 1–2. In French.

Review of a premiere of *L'hermitage fleuri* at the Théâtre Royal de la Monnaie for a select group of invitees. Praises the work's "finesse" and "distinction."

596.   *L'Etoile Belge* (May 1, 1905), 4. In French.

Finds that this "youthful peccadillo " reveals many of the "native qualities" that would later characterize *Pepita Jiménez*, which also appeared on the Brussels stage at this time.

597.   *L'Eventail* (January 1, 1905). In French.

Reviews this same private preview at the Monnaie, finding satisfaction in its "direct inspiration from national rhythms and melodies."

598.   *L'Eventail* (August 1, 1905), 1, by Georges Eekhoud. In French.

Welcomes this repetition of a very amusing work, with especially high praise for the performers.

599.   *Le Messager de Bruxelles* (June 1, 1905) 2, by "Ch. G." In French.

A youthful work where the "many rare gifts of the brilliant composer" are present in germinal form.

600.   *Le Patriote* (January 5, 1905), 4. In French.

Describes it as a "gay satire" and lauds its rhythmic vitality, "at once studied and natural." As with all the other reviews, claims it was received with affectionate enthusiasm by the public.

601.   *Le Peuple* (January 5, 1905), 2, by F. [Ferdinand] Labarre. In French.

Contrasts the zarzuela to *Pepita Jiménez,* praising the former's elegant comedy and popular melody. It was no less a success than the opera, which was a triumph.

602.   *Le Soir* (January 5, 1905), 2, by "L. S." [Lucien Solvay]. In French.

Finds it reminiscent of Italian *commedia dell'arte, opera buffa,* and French *opéra comique.* Its "piquant form and abundant melody" reflect Spanish "gaiety and spirit." Despite its apparent simplicity, it is not easy to sing, but the performers acquitted themselves admirably.

603. *Le XXe Siècle* (June 1, 1905), by "G. S." [Georges Systermans]. In French.

   The score presents a "succession of pretty pages, sparkling and frolicsome."

604. *L'Indépendance Belge* (Brussels) (January 6, 1905), by "XX." In French.

   Hails Albéniz as a composer "of the future." Finds that the expressive accents and rhythmic movements of the score give evidence of its origins below the Pyrenees.

605. *Signale für die Musikalische Welt* (January 11, 1905), 37–39, by Ernest Closson. In German.

   "The entire score breathes a fresh inspiration, youthfulness, and gaiety." Believes that the genre of zarzuela is perfectly suited to Albéniz's temperament, a finding with which the Madrid critics could not have disagreed more.

606. *Vlaamsche Gazet* (June 1, 1905). In Dutch.

   Lauds its "pleasant melodies" of a very Spanish character.

   Madrid Production (1954):

607. *ABC* (November 20, 1954), 51, by Antonio Fernández-Cid. In Spanish.

   Though the score was lost during the Civil War, Pablo Sorozábal rendered a new orchestration and directed the production at the Teatro Fuencarral. Fernández-Cid finds the music worthy of the composer but faults the weakness of Sierra's libretto.

608. *El Pueblo* (November 1954), by "L. A." In Spanish.

   Albéniz's score "exhibits talent but not genius." Praises Sorozábal's revision and direction of the work at the Fuencarral.

609. *Informaciones* (November 20, 1954), 9, by "A. P." In Spanish.

   The audience responded warmly to Albéniz's score, but the drama failed to match the quality of the music.

610. *Ya* (November 20, 1954), by "N. G. R." In Spanish.

   Praises the production and the freshness and verve of the music but finds that the story does not possess dramatic merit or interest.

Henry Clifford, T. 8

611. *Diario de Barcelona* (May 10, 1895), 5561–63, by F. Suárez Bravo. In Spanish.

   Admires the "mastery demonstrated in the instrumentation—full, picturesque, and of an extreme fineness. Albéniz does not subject himself to the rigorous theory of the *Leitmotiv* . . . but neither does he absolutely scorn it. There are a few characteristic themes that, handled with skill, underline situations and characters."

612.   *El Correo Catalán* (May 9, 1895), 3. In Spanish.

Praises the opera because "*Henry Clifford*, in reality, does not belong to any school: it bears the stamp of originality of all the works of its author."

613.   *El Diluvio* (May 12, 1895), 11–12, "Una oleada de música," by "Fray Veritas." In Spanish.

Credits Albéniz with helping initiate a "regeneration of Spanish lyric art." Heaps special praise on the second act, but has the usual reservations about the text: "The day that Albéniz works with a libretto that is fashioned to his manner of being and feeling, Albéniz the composer will rival Albéniz the pianist."

614.   *La Dinastía* (May 10, 1895), 2, by Joaquín Horns y Parellada. In Spanish.

Offers warm praise for Albéniz's opera, citing the public's enjoyment of several numbers in the first two acts and enthusiastic reception of the authors on stage.

615.   *La Ilustración Artística* 14/698 (May 13, 1895), 346. In Spanish.

Reports that Albéniz's work was received by the public with "genuine enthusiasm." The first two acts contained many fine numbers, though "deficiencies in the execution" of the third act prevented this critic from appreciating its "beauties."

616.   *La Publicidad* (May 9, 1895), 2. In Spanish.

The opera was an "incomparable success," and the audience "listened in religious silence, manifesting great interest in the work," which now establishes Albéniz among the "foremost modern composers."

617.   *La Renaixensa. Diari de Catalunya* (May 16, 1895), 2763–65, "Carta Oberta a Don Isaac Albéniz," by Enrich Morera. In Catalan.

An open letter from the composer Enric Morera to his friend Albéniz praising the "musical conception, melodic richness, and correct orchestration" of the work. Finds in it the "sincerity, exuberance, richness, and genial originality" characteristic of the composer. Expresses support for the development of national theater, particularly with a Catalan orientation.

618.   *La Vanguardia* (May 9, 1895), 5–6. In Spanish.

"Applause, acclamations, and shouts of enthusiasm still sound in our ears, mixed and confused with the capital themes [of the opera]." In particular, he cites the funeral chorale in the first act (sung for Lord Clifford), saying that it was received amidst bravos and clapping and had to be repeated. The second act, which all critics agreed was the best, received a "genuine ovation" from the public at its conclusion, with Albéniz, Money-Coutts (in Barcelona for the premiere), and the singers appearing on stage to receive the applause. The third act was a disappointment, a fact ascribed to an inferior performance.

619. *La Vanguardia* (May 12, 1895), 4, "La Semana en Barcelona," by J. Roca y Roca. In Spanish.

Describes the difficult genesis of the production. Declares that "Albéniz triumphed over everything: over the distrust of certain unimaginative spirits ill-disposed to recognize the superior merits of a composer who has excelled as an outstanding concert pianist; he has triumphed over the suspicions and fears of a theater management that gives every aid to works like *L'amico Fritz* and *I pagliacci*, for no other reason than the nationality of a powerful Italian publisher, and then sits back when the work of a compatriot is tried; Albéniz, finally, has succeeded in becoming a prophet in his own country."

620. *La Vanguardia* (January 1, 1896), 8, "El año musical," by J. Puig-Samper. In Catalan.

"The popular and beloved Albéniz" was not content merely to be a piano composer but sought to establish himself on the stage. In *Henry Clifford*, the reviewer detects two main defects: first, the libretto is "very ordinary and without interest"; second, like many first-time opera composers, Albéniz sought to demonstrate his "knowledge and ability by writing a very grand work." Next time, he should find a book that will not "torture his aptitudes or corrupt his inspiration." The result should be a work of "simple love, elegant and genuinely Spanish." This is what the critic hopes for *Pepita Jiménez*.

621. *Lo Teatro Català (El Teatro Catalán)* 6/226 (May 11, 1895), 4, by Armando de la Florida. In Catalan.

Ascribes "the exuberant sonority of the new work" to the high tessitura of the voice parts. Criticizes Albéniz as an "enthusiast of the modem school who prefers the orchestra and relegates the voices to a secondary role.... His characters within the musical drama possess complete uniformity in their manner of being, feeling, and thinking."

622. *Lo Teatro Català (El Teatro Catalán)* 6/230 (June 8, 1895). In Catalan.

Reports on the performance of the dances from *Henry Clifford* at the Tívoli. States that they were warmly received by the public and that they were "the best numbers of the opera."

Pepita Jiménez, T. 9

Barcelona Production (1896):

623. *Diario de Barcelona* (January 7, 1896), 247–48, by F. Suárez Bravo. In Spanish.

States that Spanish "audiences ... are in the worst position to appreciate works of this kind, because it deals with a drama in which there is no development of important events, and external movement is practically nonexistent; therefore, everything depends on that which is said ... the beauties [of the music] can be grasped only after two or three hearings." He observes that Money-Coutts had to pull out what action there was in order to "weave the fabric of the libretto," and concludes that "the drama, such as has remained, is sufficiently complete." It required "a few more days of study and rehearsals."

624.   *El Correo Catalán* (January 8, 1896), 5–6. In Spanish.

Praises the orchestration as possessing "originality and great richness," though this may have worked against the voices in the soprano–tenor duet, causing them to appear "languid and much less expressive." The libretto itself is deemed to make little more than a "general allusion" to Valera's work, but it did possess the virtue of not presenting any scene or expression that was "objectionable from a moral point of view." The duet between Pepita and Don Luis had to be repeated at the audience's insistence. Albéniz was subsequently called to the stage to receive the accolades of the public, something that occurred after other "fragments" of the work as well as at its conclusion.

625.   *La Renaixensa. Diari de Catalunya* (January 6, 1896), 134–35. In Catalán.

"As a result of the libretto, the characters have roles of little substance, which is a real problem for the composer to solve. Only an imagination like Albéniz's could succeed, and this he has done. For, in the few musical situations provided him, he has conquered the applause of the intelligentsia."

626.   *La Vanguardia* (January 6, 1896), 5, by Amadeo Vives. In Spanish.

"In truth and justice we can proclaim that our art is coming to life and that already blood is flowing in its veins, blood regenerated and vivified, whose power and force all feel and experience." Regarding the use of leitmotiv, Vives declares it was "applied in a magisterial fashion."

627.   *Lo Teatro Català (El Teatro Catalán)* 7/263 (January 25, 1896), 1, by Armando de la Florida. In Catalan.

Deals more with critics and criticism than with the opera itself, finding that most critics do not have the musical training necessary to judge such a work. The general current of praise for the new opera reflects this, and he states that the work lacked sufficient rehearsal and was not a success.

628.   *Lo Teatro Regional* 5/205 (January 11, 1896), 15. In Catalan.

The opera has obtained an "extraordinary success," and its score's "many beauties" are proof of the young maestro's talent.

629.   *The Musical Times* 59 (March 1, 1918), 116–17, by Herman Klein. In English.

Regarding the libretto, the most controversial aspect, he avers that "an undercurrent of deep passion compensates for lack of dramatic climax ... its rare poetic feeling and truth to life, made it exactly *en rapport* with the temperament and imaginative qualities of the musician." Compares it favorably to Mascagni's *L'amico Fritz* and further deems Albéniz to have been as "up-to-date" as Verdi in *Falstaff,* and his use of leading motives "more ingenious, more skilful than the rather obvious method affected by Puccini, and consequently more interesting."

630.   *The Sunday Times* (January 5, 1896), 6, by Herman Klein. In English.

Praises Albéniz's handling of the thematic material and his treatment of the voices, saying he writes with great "consideration and melodic freedom." Lauds Albéniz's avoidance of direct quotation of folk melodies, and compares his work favorably to other operas of the 1890s, including those by Verdi, Puccini, and Bretón. Klein also has kind words for the librettist, citing "the infinite tact and skill with which he has evolved from [the novel] a lyric comedy full of deep human interest, and combining pathos and passion with abundant contrast in the shape of characteristic humour and strong local colour." Praises the libretto's condensing of the scant dramatic material in the novel to maintain the "three unities."

Prague Production (1897):

631.   *Beilage zu Bohemia* (June 24, 1897), 3, by "K." In German.

"The libretto does not contain any exciting event and exercises no arousing effect. . . . A deliberate and thought-out method of composition prevails in the work, so that not infrequently profundity has as a consequence heaviness and lack of melodic grace in the voice." Expresses the opinion that the outcome of Don Luis's "spiritual struggle" was too much delayed in the opera as opposed to the novel.

632.   *Deutsches Abendblatt* (June 23, 1897), 2. In German.

Praises Albéniz's training and ability. The reviewer especially appreciates Albéniz's handling of the orchestra, though he concedes that it often over-whelmed the singers. He also comments on the predominance of triple meter and complains about Albéniz's predilection for double accidentals and the dif-ficulties they posed to reading. But he concludes by declaring that "through its rich polyphony and wealth of ideas it will arouse the interest of the musician, though it may otherwise be caviar for the public."

633.   *Neuefreie Presse Abendblatt* (June 24, 1897). In German.

Lauds Albéniz's opera for its color and rhythm and reports that the audience received it with enthusiasm. Expresses reservations about the dramatic merits of the libretto and finds Albéniz's vocal writing lacking in impact.

634.   *Prager Tageblatt* (June 23, 1897), 10, by "Dr. A. G." In German.

Favorable assessment of the opera that reports it "engaged the lively interest of the audience. The premiere of the interesting work was a success. The composer was repeatedly called [to the stage] and received more laurels."

635.   *Prager Tageblatt* (June 24, 1897), 7, by "Dr. A. G." In German.

Provides a relatively detailed plot summary and praises Albéniz's originality and avoidance of "banal eclecticism." Finds the "subdued tone" that dominates most of the opera and its "sweet and dreamlike" lyricism appropriate to the drama. Though the rhythm verges on the monotonous at times, it is rescued by "energetic accents" that preserve its effect. Praises Albéniz's masterful orchestration and "passages of rich polyphony."

636.   *Prager Zeitung* (June 24, 1897), 2. In German.

"The plot offers no event with which the music can direct itself toward external effect. . . . He composes what only he, the great virtuoso, can play at the piano [and it is] altogether music out of which the bloom of piano virtuosity opens to the full. In the theater, however, before the orchestra and the stage, many a musical Moravian might shake his clever head with great circumspection."

637.   *Prager Zeitung* (June 24, 1897), 3, by Julius Steinberg. In German.

"The composer demands of his public that they follow him through labyrinthine ways of musical speculation, and to listen more with reason than with the ear. . . . All kinds of baroque figurations emerge and disturb the organic relationship of the individual parts to the overall structure and break up the plasticity of the architecture through the tangle of details."

Madrid Audition (1902):

638.   *El Evangelio* 2/118 (August 7, 1902), 2, by López Muguiro. In Spanish.

"When we heard the presentation of *Pepita Jiménez*, we felt pleasure and pain, pride and discouragement. We knew that here was a purely Spanish opera, replete with beautiful ideas, fresh, inspired, with an irreproachable form." [see no. 263, p. 225]

639.   *El Imparcial* (August 6, 1902), 3. In Spanish.

The audition of the "pretty score" was "extremely pleasant and interesting." In particular, the melodic character of the work was "simple and elegant, always fresh and characteristic." Singles out Pepita's "Romanza," the Prelude to Act II, the children's *villancico*, and the "passionate and ardent" finale for praise. [see no. 263, p. 226]

640.   *La Correspondencia de España* (August 7, 1902), 1. In Spanish.

Praises the melodious character of the work and cites several numbers as highlights, especially Pepita's famous "Romance" and the closing duet. Views it as the composer's "major triumph."

641.   *La Época* (August 6, 1902), 3. In Spanish.

Reports that Albéniz was the "object of sincere and enthusiastic congratulations on the part of those who were fortunate to hear the music of *Pepita Jiménez*." [see no. 263, p. 226]

Brussels Production (1905):

642. *Bruxelles Mondaine* (August 1, 1905), by "Montmoris." In French.

Accuses Albéniz of exhibiting "pretentious aspirations," particularly in the over-wrought orchestral writing. His melodic style is indebted to the "modern school," while Italian influence is also perceptible. Despite all this and the "monotonous" libretto, Albéniz's score preserves a "very personal character."

643. *La Chronique* (January 4, 1905), 3, by "J. D'A." In French.

Provides some background on Valera and his novel, then praises several aspects of the opera, in particular the choral and dance numbers.

644. *La Chronique* (May 1, 1905), 1. In French.

Reports that Albéniz was received three enthusiastic curtain calls from the audience. In attendance was Juan Pérez Caballero, the Spanish ambassador, and his wife.

645. *La Chronique* (June 1, 1905). In French.

Despite a mediocre libretto, Albéniz imparts to his music a "powerful and original charm," through the presentation of "graceful melodic themes" over a "deliciously worked orchestral fabric."

646. *La Fédération Artistique* (August 1, 1905), 14, by "Robert M." In French.

Finds much to applaud in Albéniz's use of local color and very personal style as a composer. Detects the influence of Bizet's *Carmen* and use of Wagnerian leitmotiv throughout the work.

647. *La Gazette* (January 4, 1905), 2, "Edm. C." [Edmond Cattier]. In French.

Has high praise for Albéniz's distinctive style, which is nonetheless rooted in his national identity and revealed in his skillful evocation of Spanish folklore. The score exhibits many modern refinements in harmony and orchestration, and overall the opera offers "very lively and sincere . . . and interesting music."

648. *La Réforme* (July 1, 1905), 1, by "TABARIN." In French.

It contains many "interesting passages," but the critic complains that the orchestral part is "excessively symphonic" and "covers the voices."

649. *L'Art Moderne* (August 1, 1905), 11–12, by Octave Maus. In French.

In assessing the opera, the critic concludes that there are "three characteristics of his sympathetic and delicate talent: melodic abundance, local color [especially that imparted by the influence of flamenco], and harmonic refinement." [Same article in *Le Courrier Musical* (February 1, 1905), 76–78.]

650. *Le Courrier Musical* 8/3 (February 1, 1905), 76–78, by Octave Maus. In French.

"In the place of banal and artificial exoticism, conventional picturesqueness, he has substituted a color more discreet but more truthful, which marvelously evokes the places, customs, and distinctive characters of Spain. The music becomes impetuous, vehemently oppressed. It possesses spirit and warmth." [Same article in *L'Art Moderne* (August 1, 1905), 11–12.]

651.   *L'Etoile Belge* (January 1, 1905). In French.

Review of a private premiere of *Pepita Jiménez* at the Théâtre Royal de la Monnaie for a select group of invitees. Praises the work's "finesse" and "distinction."

652.   *L'Eventail* (January 1, 1905), 1–2. In French.

Praises this same private preview at the Monnaie, citing the orchestral accompaniment for its finely crafted presentation of many themes based on Spanish folklore.

653.   *L'Eventail* (August 1, 1905), 1, by Georges Eekhoud. In French.

"The entire score is a jewel adorably set." Finds much to praise in the performance as well.

654.   *Le Guide Musical* (August 1, 1905), "J. Br." [Jules Brunet]. In French.

Despite the opera's "learned and very modernistic form and its constant logic," the score exhibits a rare abundance of melody revealing a noticeably Spanish character.

655.   *Le Ménéstrel* (Paris) (January 8, 1905). In French.

Lauds Albéniz's originality in extravagant terms: "At last, a young composer who brings us a new, personal note that is not a pastiche and who does not want to do again what others have done before him."

656.   *Le Messager de Bruxelles* (June 1, 1905), 2, by "Ch. G." In French.

Finds the work "perfectly charming" as well as "fascinating, moving, and exquisite." It is a "work of art in the strictest sense of the word."

657.   *Le Patriote* (January 5, 1905), 4. In French.

Places Albéniz "among the colorists, possessing innate melody and musical thought." Unfortunately, "there prevails in the dialogue of Pepita a vague scorn for religious matters, an atmosphere of Voltaire-style libertinism, which accentuates the intervention of a vicar, a moralist in the manner of Count Des Grieux in *Manon*. But with an attitude less noble, less sympathetic, so that he does not deliver the appropriate discourse." Still, he regards the work as a "revelation," and "there reigns from one end to the other a discreet emotion and an inimitable something called sincerity, [and the second] act is delicious to listen to."

658.   *Le Petit Bleu du Matin* (January 4, 1905), 2, by "R. V." In French.

Albéniz's music demonstrates a useful "reciprocal penetration" of various "schools of music," though this opera eschews the "brutality" of Italian verismo.

Finds the score's instrumental color, orchestral balance, rhythm, and harmony very commendable.

659. *Le Peuple* (January 5, 1905), 2, by F. [Ferdinand] Labarre. In French.

"Two roles dominate the entire work, that of Pepita and that of Don Luis, and the rest remain in the shade. Fatally, the situations are repeated without providing much variety. This fault is common in all works inspired by short stories or novels, and very exceptional are those that conserve in their adaptation to the stage all their interest and that which creates their charm." Nonetheless, he judges *Pepita Jiménez* "a very expressive, coherent work, of an absolute sincerity and beautiful lyric flight, which is worthy of gaining and retaining attention."

660. *Le Soir* (January 5, 1905), 2, by "L. S." [Lucien Solvay]. In French.

Describes the opera as "the revelation of a composer at last original, bringing with him the color, the movement, the warmth of his nationality, of which he wants to convey the atmosphere and express the feelings."

661. *Le Temps* (Paris) (April 11, 1905), by Pierre Lalo. In French.

Views the libretto as the major weakness of the work but attributes "charming qualities" to the music, praising its handling of leitmotiv, transformation of themes, and symphonic development. Nonetheless, he regards the work as redolent not of Bayreuth but rather of Spain and its "fragrance, flavor, and color." He declares that Albéniz is "one of the greatest inventors of rhythms in the entire universe" and describes the music as "sensual and melancholy, sad and passionate, ardent and fine." "And to add to his subtle eloquence, M. Albéniz has the most lively, the most supple, the most brilliant orchestra, an orchestra in ceaseless movement, changing, glistening, an orchestra that flows . . . like a stream."

662. *Le XXe Siècle* (June 1, 1905), by G. S. [Georges Systermans]. In French.

The score reveals a "musician of taste, tact, and restraint; his writing is elegant, his invention . . . distinguished; his 'espagnolisme' never strident; his musical tableaux neither brutal nor rushed."

663. *L'Indépendance Belge* (January 6, 1905), by "XX." In French.

Finds the choral and dance numbers especially effective and convincingly evocative of the opera's Spanish setting. The composer was not only inspired but also well versed in technical procedures.

664. *Signale für die Musikalische Welt* (January 11, 1905), 37–39, by Ernest Closson. In German.

Finds Albéniz's music to be charming, national in character, and very impressively orchestrated. Makes special note of his handling of leitmotiv and the

counterpoint between the orchestral commentary and the vocal lines. The introduction to Act II is "especially precious."

665.   *Vlaamsche Gazet* (June 1, 1905). In Dutch.

Describes the opera as "charming" and finds it reminiscent of Massenet's early
works.

Paris Production (1923):

666.   *Comoedia* (June 18, 1923), 1–2, by Raymond Charpentier and Georges Linor. In
French.

Finds a "regrettable" Italian influence in the opera and labels it a kind of
"Cavalleria Iberica." Describes it as a "flagrant mélange of French romanticism—viewed through Schumann—of Italian verismo, and of hispanism." The
overture to the second act, which was repeated, demonstrated a resemblance to
the "exaggerated flights" of Puccini. Derides the music as "composed principally
of locutions borrowed from the decadence of romanticism."

667.   *La France* (June 25, 1923), 1–2, by André Fijan. In French.

"This music of Albéniz, so seductive on the piano, loses, like that of Granados,
a great many of its qualities in the orchestra . . . the instrumentation is implacable and heavy [and] consists of always doubling the strings with woodwinds
or with brass. One can possess the most beautiful qualities as a musician and
compromise the career of a dramatic work by neglecting to submit to that law
that is the supremacy of the human voice over the symphony or, if you prefer,
over the hundred voices of the orchestra. . . . Nevertheless, the lyric comedy of
Albéniz pleases [and] envelops us, despite all, in a perfectly warm and intoxicat-
ing atmosphere."

668.   *L'Écho de Paris* (June 18, 1923), 5, by "Le Capitaine Fracasse." In French.

Compares Albéniz's style of writing to that of Chopin, particularly the latter's
sonatas. He also invokes Liszt, Wagner, and Chabrier as prototypes. Albéniz's
ideas are "gushing, spontaneous, fresh, abundant, lyrical." These and other elements of his style are "unified, vivified, transfigured by an interior happiness, a
joy in inventing melodies."

669.   *Le Figaro* (June 19, 1923), 6, by André Messager. In French.

Reveals Messager's unfavorable feelings, perhaps explaining why the opera never
made it to Covent Garden, where he was director: "The style is rather hybrid and
inclines too often towards Italianism of the verist school. The heavy orchestration does not allow a large enough part to the declamation."

670.   *Le Quotidien* (July 5, 1923), 6, by Paul Dukas. In French.

"[The music] is animated by all the life lacking in the play. It breaks the bonds
of the little story and sings by itself the most evocative song of Spain, the most

sparkling [song] of popular verve, or the most poetical languor of delicate melancholy one can hear. Without pause, without any trifle entering to break its flight, it is elevated in the orchestra, quivering on wings of rhythm, and spreads in charming caprices across each scene ... so alive, so spontaneous, so delicious."

671.   *Le Siècle* (June 18, 1923), 1. In French.

"The local color is less marked in his *Pepita Jiménez*, but one finds in this score a vaporous poetry, of ideas happily created and developed with a ... delicate art. One listened to it with lively pleasure."

672.   *Le Temps* (June 20, 1923), 3, by Henry Malherbe. In French.

Expresses reservations about the work: "But, decidedly, despite the engrossing music of Albéniz, the plot appeared too simple and too naïve. It is the music that, alone, is vital and of an agile animalism, hardy and inflamed. It shudders like a beast of prey, it shimmers like a fleece. Languid and ardent, chaste and passionate, it blends mysticism and voluptuousness, the sacred scents of incense and candles with the odors of wet and whirling dancers. The rhythmic frenzy of the composer suffices to our pleasure."

673.   *L'Événement* (June 19, 1923), 1, by Maurice Bouisson. In French.

Praises the music's picturesque use of folk rhythms and local color, particularly in the instrumental writing, as well as its suggestion of "divine aspiration."

674.   *Lyrica* 2/17 (July 1923), 102–04, by "Mercutio." In French.

Derides it as a "banal love story that oscillates between Joscelyn and Desgrieux without the charm of the former and the passion of the latter." Finds Pepita's character unconvincing both dramatically and musically, and the work as a whole exhibits a cloying sentimentality. The opera's lack of dramatic impact is unrelieved by the richness of the instrumentation and Albéniz's lyric fecundity.

675.   *Revue des Deux Mondes* (July 1, 1923), 226–27, by Camille Bellaigue. In French.

Introduces the work as a collaboration between the "exquisite" musician Albéniz and the "mediocre" poet Money-Coutts. Describes the music as "charming, lively, melodic, and also symphonic." Though it is of a decidedly Spanish character, it does not conform so strictly to national forms that it lacks a wider appeal.

Barcelona Production (1926):

676.   *Diario de Barcelona* (January 15, 1926), 32, by "A. M." In Spanish.

Recalls the "exquisite grace" of Albéniz's personality. He was, above all else, a great melodist, but he also enveloped his melodies in beautiful harmonies that revealed the influence of modern French music. The entire work is "impregnated with poetry."

677.   *El Día Gráfico* (January 16, 1926), by "J. N." In Spanish.

Although the reviewer does not believe that Albéniz reached his zenith as a composer of stage works, still, *Pepita Jiménez* is an inspired work, especially in the choral and dance numbers. He also singles out the "orchestral commentary" for praise.

678.   *El Diluvio* (January 15, 1926), 29, by "Alard." In Spanish.

Finds that the score is distinguished by "Andalusian themes and rhythms of frank and elegant inspiration." Singles out the choral and dance numbers of the second act for special praise, as well as the "very rich harmonies of the orchestral commentary."

679.   *El Noticiero Universal* (January 15, 1926), 456, by Alfredo Romea. In Spanish.

Finds the tribute to Albéniz altogether fitting and appropriate and approves the choice of this opera for production, a work too seldom seen and heard on the stage. Praises the work's lyricism and grounding in Spanish folklore, in addition to the composer's evident technical acumen evident in the various dance, instrumental, and choral numbers, as well as his handling of harmony and orchestration.

680.   *La Noche* (January 15, 1926), 1. In Spanish.

"*Pepita Jiménez* exhibits all the characteristics of the music of Albéniz. The spontaneity, the melodic flight, the winged rhythm of the *Iberia* suite, all are there with the identical freshness and melodic grace. The parallel inspiration and technique proceed in so sympathetic a manner that the melodic line never decays, maintained without deformations, in a vivid expression of the Andalusian soul. In the Romance, the second-act duet, and in the dances the orchestra achieves "a supreme brilliance and grace."

681.   *La Publicidad* (January 19, 1926). In Catalan.

Though the libretto offers little of interest, it is the music that sets the scene, establishes the atmosphere, and propels the drama, particularly in the skillfully written dialogues, the orchestral numbers, and the dances.

682.   *La Vanguardia* (January 12, 1896), 4, "La Semana en Barcelona," by J. Roca y Roca. In Spanish.

The score bears the "stamp of Albéniz's personality . . . his personal grace and rich orchestration." The libretto comes nowhere near matching the literary quality of the novel, but the score shines very brightly in the instrumental passages, which exhibit "brilliant coloration." These the public received with great enthusiasm.

683.   *La Vanguardia* (January 15, 1926), 14, "Música y teatros," by "Romea." In Spanish.

A brief review that comments mostly on the libretto, "which adequately conserves the flavor of human interest provided by the novelist." The public received the work with great enthusiasm.

684. *La Vanguardia* (February 7, 1926), by Vicente M. de Gibert. In Spanish.

   Laments the fact that Albéniz's opera lives in obscurity and appears only sporadically on the stage. Recalls its premiere in 1896 and finds much to praise in the "freshness of its motives and rhythms . . . its expressive and evocative character." Compares it very favorably to *Cavalleria rusticana.*

685. *La Veu de Catalunya* (January 15, 1926), 6, by "J. U." In Catalan.

   Despite a variety of influences at work in the opera, it has a decidedly Spanish flavor and bears the stamp of the composer's style. The dialogues and duets in the first act receive special praise, as do the prelude to the second act and other orchestral numbers. This critic hears echoes of Albéniz's earlier piano works, especially *Cantos de España,* in the score.

686. *Las Noticias* (January 16, 1926), 2, by "Salvatore." In Spanish.

   A favorable estimation of Albéniz's only Spanish-themed opera. Praises the composer's lyric gift, rhythmic animation, and skillful handling of the orchestra. Although the libretto is merely adequate, the inspired score carries the drama forward.

   Madrid Production (revision by Pablo Sorozábal) (1964):

687. *ABC* (June 7, 1964), 109, by Federico Sopeña. In Spanish.

   Objects to the plot change, describing it as "irritating" in view of the wide currency of the novel. He calls for a new arrangement of the opera with a restoration of the original ending.

688. *ABC* (July 5, 1964), "Unas cartas de Albéniz sobre el estreno de 'Pepita Jiménez' in Prague," by A. Laborda. In Spanish.

   Includes excerpts from Albéniz's letters to his wife during the spring of 1897 as he fretted over the rehearsals of the opera and exulted in its eventual, though short-lived, triumph.

689. *Arriba* (June 6, 1964), 23, by Pablo Sorozábal. In Spanish.

   Explains the rationale and method of his revision of the opera. The changes included (1) alteration of the declamatory style of the vocal writing to make it more lyrical; (2) adaptation of the libretto from French to Spanish; (3) reinstrumentation where appropriate; and (4) alteration of the drama itself, giving it a tragic character. Sorozábal was a successful zarzuela composer whose motives were correct but whose procedures were questionable and final product regrettable.

690. *El Alcázar* (June 9, 1964), "Ópera: 'Pepita Jiménez' de Albéniz-Sorozábal, en estreno mundial," by Fernando Ruiz Coca. In Spanish.

   Declares that Sorozábal has restructured both the text and the music while respecting the "original materials and conserving the stylistic air of the epoch."

Finds the local color particularly attractive, especially the *villancico* in the second act. Does express doubts about the advisability of altering the ending not only of the original opera but also the novel itself. It may be more theatrical, but the dramatic context does not really conduce to a suicide.

691.   *El Pueblo* (June 1964), by Ángel del Campo. In Spanish.

The score exhibits the distinctive musical voice of Albéniz, with its rhythmic vitality and melodic charm. But the transformation of the drama into a tragedy conflicts with the literary original from which the libretto is derived. This is a difficult hurdle to overcome for listeners who grew up reading Valera's novel.

692.   *Informaciones* (June 8, 1964), 7, by Antonio Fernández-Cid. In Spanish.

Ventures to say, as someone familiar with all of Sorozábal's work, that he (Sorozábal) "has placed at the service of his work love, care, mastery, and noble renunciation of all personal ambition. If in other cases—*San Antonio de la Florida* above all—it was fitting to point out many moments where the adapter intruded in the line of the creation itself, here, no. That is the foremost virtue."

693.   *La Hoja Oficial* (June 9, 1964), by "T. M." In Spanish.

Enthusiastic praise for Sorozábal's revision and direction of the opera, declaring a triumph for both the composer and the director/reviser.

694.   *La Prensa* (Barcelona) (June 22, 1964), "La semana teatral en Madrid," by M. Díez Crespo. In Spanish.

Hails the great success of the opera's revival in Madrid. Though some numbers from the opera, such as the Intermedio, were already known, much of the work had lain in total obscurity. Praises Sorozábal's work in reviving *Pepita Jiménez*.

695.   *Madrid* (June 8, 1964), 2, "Estreno Triunfal de 'Pepeita Jiménez,' de Albéniz, en la capital de España," by J. Espinos Orlando. In Spanish.

States that Sorozábal's revision is "truly admirable" in the improvements it makes to the original libretto. Finds particular inspiration in the various choral and dance numbers.

696.   *YA* (June 7, 1964), "'Pepita Jiménez,' de Albéniz, se estrena triunfalmente en Madrid," by José María Franco. In Spanish.

Hails Albéniz as a "100% Spanish composer" and praises Sorozábal's "careful revision" of the score. States that the prelude to the second act has been used at the conclusion of the opera, when Pepita takes her own life. Finds this new ending moving.

Barcelona Concert Version (1994):

697.   *La Vanguardia* (Barcelona) (December 11, 1994), 50, "La Orquestra del Teatre Lliure recupera la ópera *Pepita Jiménez*," by Albert Mallofré. In Spanish.

Concert rendition of the edition by Josep Soler (see nos. 5 and 33). Praises the work and quotes Albéniz's grandson Alfonso Alzamora on the composer's close relationship with Catalonia, its language and culture. "Though he was a tireless traveller, within his nomadic spirit there was always a love for Barcelona and Catalonia, which for him was his home, where he had his roots and the bonds of friendship."

Buenos Aires Production (2012):

698.   *Clarín* (October 30, 2012), 67, by Sandra de la Fuente. In Spanish.

Generally favorable review of this revival of Albéniz's opera at the Teatro Argentino de la Plata on October 28, 2012, conducted by Manuel Coves and utilizing the two-act version premiered in Prague in 1897 (see no. 4). The staging by Calixto Bieito represented a radical departure from the composer and librettist's (not to mention the novelist's) original conception of the work, emphasizing the conflict between human and profane love through explicit sexuality and a sharp-edged critique of the Catholic Church's abuse of power.

699.   *Efe* (October 30, 2012), by Mar Marín. In Spanish.

Reveals that the staging by Bieito is "very personal and contains many of my memories from my childhood and stories I have been told."

700.   *La Nación* (October 28, 2012), by Jorge Aráoz Badí. In Spanish.

An interview with Calixto Bieito, in which he states that he views himself as a "messenger whose job it is to be an aesthetic provocateur."

701.   *Página/12* (October 28, 2012), by Diego Fischerman. In Spanish.

Contains interview material with scenic director Calixto Bieito, who sheds important light on his conception of the opera and the relevance this story has to contemporary social and political issues, especially in Spain.

Madrid Production (2013):

702.   *ABC* (May 14, 2013), 50, by Susana Gaviña. In Spanish.

Interview with Calixto Bieito in which the scenic director disclaims any intention to present a "radical modernization" of the 1897 opera. "I want to create a poem between eroticism and religion, with the latter understood as an oppressive element."

703.   *ABC* (May 23, 2013), 50, by Alberto González Lapuente. In Spanish.

Favorable review of the revival of this opera at Los Teatros del Canal, on May 19, 2013, with José Ramón Encinar conducting the Orquesta de la Comunidad de Madrid in a production by scenic director Calixto Bieito.

704.   *El País* (May 20, 2013), Juan Ángel Vela del Campo. In Spanish.

Praises the "tragic reading of enormous structural precision and dramatic energy" by the conductor, Encinar. Also approves Bieito's allegorical interpretation of the work, in which "every scene is a play of light and shade, desires and repressions, longings for liberty and oppressive atmospheres."

Merlin, T. 12A

Brussels Private Audition (1905):

705.   *Le Guide Musical* (February 19, 1905). In French.

Very favorable review of a private audition of Albéniz's *Merlin*, sponsored by Emile Tassel and his wife, with the composer accompanying at the piano. Apart from the large choral numbers, the entire score was performed, and it exhibited "a noble and magnificent attractiveness, always original and of a rare musicality."

706.   *L'Eventail* (February 19, 1905), 4. In French.

Reviewing this same performance, reserves highest praise for the final act, which is in an "original form and very personal," a "sort of grand sung ballet," interspersed with dramatic episodes.

Barcelona Concert Version (1950):

707.   *Diario de Barcelona* (December 20, 1950), 23, by A. Catalá. In Spanish.

Gives a brief background of the work and of Albéniz as an opera composer. Praises the performance (listing the cast) and reports that the audience received it warmly. No discussion of the music itself.

708.   *El Noticiero Universal* (December 19, 1950), 8, by Alfredo Romea. In Spanish.

Notes the influence of Wagner, particularly in "the robustness with which the orchestral commentary is handled." Though the first and third acts offered "much that was spectacular," the second was "frankly boring."

709.   *La Vanguardia Española* (December 20, 1950), 14, by V. F. Zanni. In Spanish.

Heaps praise on the opera, stating that "the writing is noble, frank, and intelligently adapted to the inspiring themes. The orchestration reveals a firm and skilled hand in the conception of instrumental combinations . . . it is a very worthy opera."

710.   *La Vie Musicale* (December–January, 1951–52), 8–9, by M. Casamada. In French.

A favorable though not enthusiastic review. Presents a useful summary of the dramatic and musical development of the opera, illustrated with various leading motives.

Madrid Production (2003):

711.   *ABC* (May 17, 2003), 65. In Spanish.

Overview of forthcoming production at the Teatro Real on May 28, 2003, conducted by José de Eusebio, who edited, revived, and recorded it (see nos. 1 and 30). Includes drawings of costumes and interview material with scenic director John Dew, who cites the opera's chief liability: "it is a prologue to an incomplete trilogy. Its conclusion is open." A sidebar presents a brief essay by Alberto Ruiz-Gallardón, celebrating *Merlin*'s emergence from obscurity, thanks to José de Eusebio.

712.   *ABC* (May 29, 2003), 54–55, by Antonio Iglesias. In Spanish.

Iglesias hails the production as a historic night for Albéniz. The opera reveals the composer's mastery of leitmotiv and orchestration and successfully refutes the opinion expressed by earlier commentators, such as Arbós, that Albéniz had wasted his time and energy on a Wagnerian trilogy.

713.   *ABC* (May 29, 2003), 55, by Susana Gaviña. In Spanish.

Lauds the production as a vindication of Albéniz's reputation as a composer for the stage. Has high praise for Eusebio, Dew, and the performers.

Appendix

Chronology of Albéniz's Life

1860   Albéniz born on May 29 in the town of Camprodón, near the French border in Catalonia. His father, Ángel, is Basque; his mother, Dolors, is Catalan.

1863   The Albéniz family moves to Barcelona in December.

1864–67   Albéniz studies piano with his sister Clementina and with Narciso Olivares, a local teacher. Gives his first public performance, at the Teatre Romea, possibly in 1864. Sister Enriqueta dies of typhoid in late 1867.

1868   Family relocates to Madrid around the time of the Revolution of 1868, in the fall. Albéniz begins study at the Escuela Nacional de Música y Declamación (now Real Conservatorio).

1869   Publication of Albéniz' s first composition, the *Marcha militar* for piano solo, which is dedicated to the Vizconde del Bruch (the 12-year-old son of General Prim) and presented to him in person.

1872–75   Albéniz's studies at the conservatory are desultory as he travels throughout Spain giving concerts. The young prodigy creates a sensation wherever he goes. Concertizing comes to a halt after his sister Blanca commits suicide on October 16, 1874. Touring resumes in 1875 and culminates in successful appearances in Puerto Rico and Cuba in the summer and fall of 1875, where he accompanies his father after the latter's appointment as Inspector General in the Revenue Department in Havana.

1876   Begins studies in May at the Hochschule fiir Musik "Felix Mendelssohn Bartholdy" in Leipzig, but leaves after less than 2 months. Upon gaining financial support from King Alfonso XII in Madrid, commences studies at the Conservatoire Royal in Brussels.

1879　Completes his studies at the Conservatoire and ties with Arthur de Greef for first prize, "with distinction," in the piano class of Louis Brassin.

1880　After a triumphal return to Spain, travels to Budapest, ostensibly to study with Liszt. But Liszt is not in Budapest at this time, and Albéniz returns to Spain and then Cuba to give more concerts.

1882　Successful premieres of his zarzuelas *Cuanto más viejo* (in Bilbao) and *Catalanes de gracia* (in Madrid). Concertizes throughout Spain.

1883　Moves to Barcelona from Madrid. Studies composition with Felipe Pedrell and marries Rosina Jordana Lagarriga, one of his students and the daughter of a wealthy businessman in Barcelona.

1884　Birth of his first child, Blanca, in Barcelona.

1885　Birth of his second child, Alfonso, during the summer in Tiana outside Barcelona. Moves with his growing family to Madrid, where he enjoys great celebrity as a performer and composer.

1886　Triumphant concert at the Salón Romero in January and the appearance of the first biography of Albéniz, by journalist Antonio Guerra y Alarcón. Death of his daughter Blanca in April. Gives numerous concerts throughout Spain.

1887–89　Continued residence in Madrid and increasing output of works, published by houses in Madrid and Barcelona. Death of daughter Cristina in January 1888. Series of 20 recitals at the Universal Exposition in Barcelona in the summer and fall of 1888. Birth of his daughter Enriqueta in 1889. Well-received performance at the Salle Erard in Paris in 1889 attracts many of that city's finest musicians. Begins touring in England that same year.

1890　Moves to London. Birth of his daughter Laura. Enters into a contractual agreement with the businessman Henry Lowenfeld, who becomes his manager. Numerous concerts in London are lauded by the critics, who appreciate his technical mastery, "velvety touch," and sensitive interpretations.

1892　Composes two numbers for the operetta *Incognita*, an English adaptation of *Le Coeur et la main* by Charles Lecocq. Composes his own operetta, *The Magic Opal*. Concerts in Berlin mark the apex of his concert career and the turning point after which he will devote himself mostly to serious composition.

1893　Premiere of *The Magic Opal* at the Lyric Theatre in January. Run ends soon thereafter, in late February. Though the critics praised the work, it did not draw large enough audiences. Touring company is formed to take it throughout Britain, and it is a success on the road. Revised and renamed *The Magic Ring*, it opens at the Prince of Wales's Theatre in April, but again it fails to achieve popularity. Writes several numbers for and conducts a production of

Millöcker's *Poor Jonathan* at the Prince of Wales's Theatre. The independently wealthy poet Francis Burdett Money-Coutts enters into the contract between Albéniz and Lowenfeld (who drops out of it the following year). Albéniz agrees to set Money-Coutts's librettos to music in exchange for a generous income. Albéniz then leaves London for Spain to give concerts.

1894   After giving several concerts in Barcelona, he settles permanently in Paris in mid-year. Completes work on the zarzuela *San Antonio de Ia Florida,* which premieres to negative notices in Madrid in October. The Madrid premiere of a Spanish version of *The Magic Opal (La sortija)* is a fiasco and closes after three nights in November. Begins work on the opera *Henry Clifford.*

1895   Premiere of *Henry Clifford* in May at the Liceu in Barcelona, to mixed reviews. Begins work on the opera *Pepita Jiménez.* November production of *San Antonio de la Florida* in Barcelona unsuccessful.

1896   Premiere of *Pepita Jiménez* in January at the Liceu. The most successful of all his operas, it nonetheless finds no permanent place on the stage in Spain.

1897   Production of *Pepita Jiménez* in Prague at the Neues Deutsches Theater in June. Meets with mixed reaction in the press and does not remain in the repertoire of that theater. Composes *La vega* for piano. Begins work on *Merlin.*

1898   Onset of Bright's disease and gradual decline in health. Premiere of the Prelude to Act I of *Merlin* in Barcelona, conducted by Vincent d'Indy.

1899   Premiere of *La vega* at the Société Nationale de Musique in January. Premiere of *Catalonia* at the Société Nationale de Musique in May. Commences reorchestration of *Pepita Jiménez.*

1901   Catalan Lyric Theatre project in Barcelona collapses when Enric Morera withdraws from the contract with Enrique Granados and Albéniz.

1902   Finishes *Merlin* and reorchestration of *Pepita Jiménez.* Leaves Barcelona for Madrid but fails to gain a production of either opera in Madrid. Returns to Paris.

1904   Publication in Leipzig of the new version of *Pepita Jiménez.*

1905   Production of *Pepita Jiménez* (new version) and *San Antonio de la Florida* (*L'Hermitage fleuri*) at the Monnaie in Brussels. Greatest stage triumph of his career. Begins work on *Iberia.*

1906–09 Publication of the vocal score of *Merlin* in 1906. Despite increasing illness, completes work on *Iberia* in 1908, whose four books are premiered by Blanche Selva in France. Several numbers premiered in Spain by Joaquim Malats. Leaves *Navarra* and *Azulejos* incomplete upon his death from kidney failure on May 18, 1909, in Cambo-les-Bains, in the French Pyrenees.

Index of Authors, Editors, and Performers

(Roman font indicates page numbers; boldface, entry numbers)

Works Index

(Roman font indicates page numbers; boldface, entry numbers)

To Nellie: Six Songs, T. 39, 13, 21, 31; "To
    Nellie," T. 39D, **178**
Tres mazurkas, T. 58, 33
Trio No. 1 in F, T. 28, 30

V

Vocal works, **9, 12, 38–39, 41–42, 251**

Y

Yvonne en visite!, T. 104A–B, 17, 38; **189**

Z

Zambra granadina (Danse orientale), T. 97,
    10, 37

Subject Index

(Roman font indicates page numbers; boldface, entry numbers)